BLACK AMERICA SERIES

ST. PETERSBURG FLORIDA

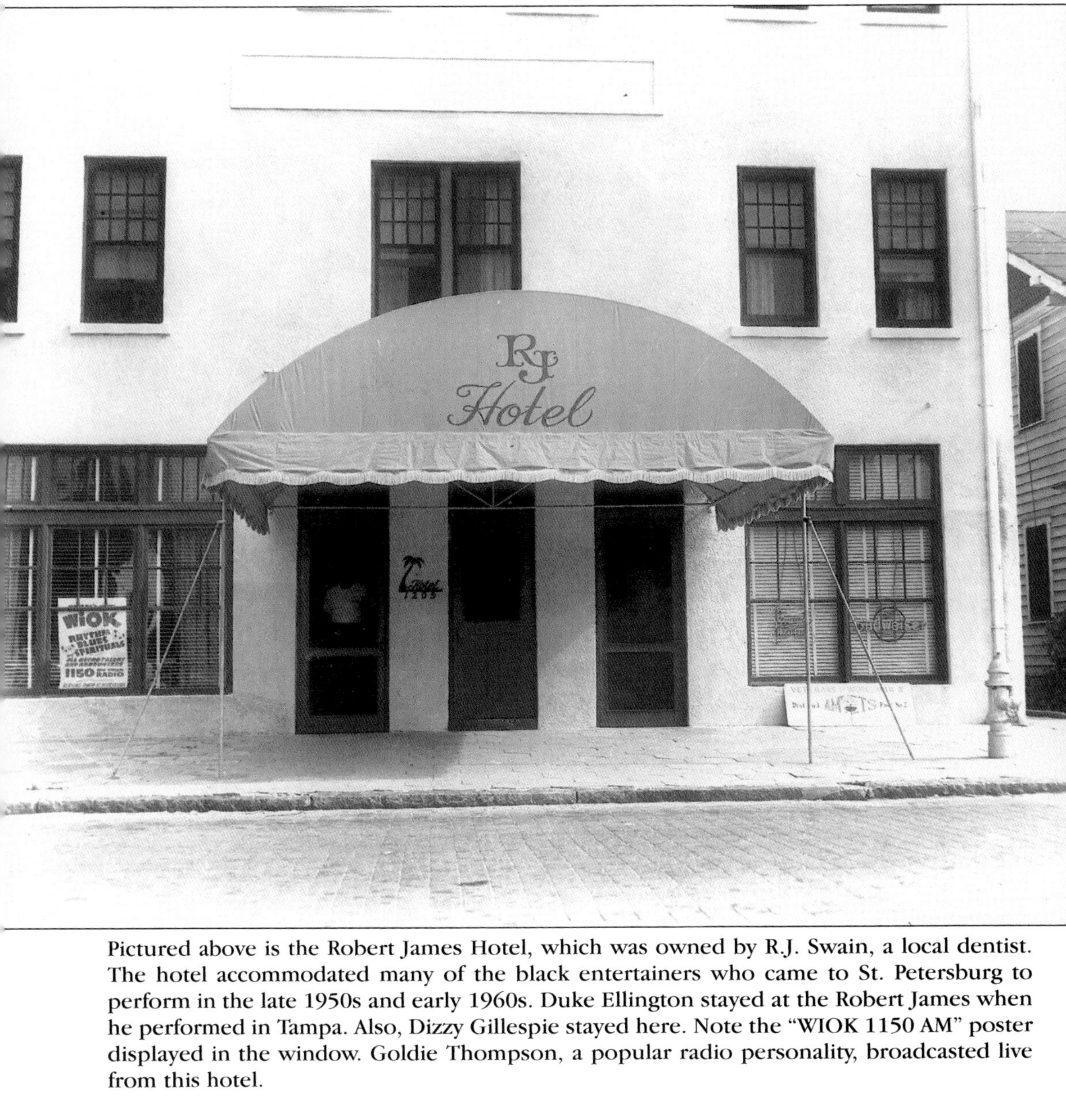

Pictured above is the Robert James Hotel, which was owned by R.J. Swain, a local dentist. The hotel accommodated many of the black entertainers who came to St. Petersburg to perform in the late 1950s and early 1960s. Duke Ellington stayed at the Robert James when he performed in Tampa. Also, Dizzy Gillespie stayed here. Note the "WIOK 1150 AM" poster displayed in the window. Goldie Thompson, a popular radio personality, broadcasted live from this hotel.

BLACK AMERICA SERIES

ST. PETERSBURG FLORIDA

Sandra W. Rooks

ARCADIA PUBLISHING

ISBN 978-0-7385-1517-5

Published by Arcadia Publishing
Charleston, South Carolina

Printed in the United States of America

Library of Congress Catalog Card Number: 2003101269

For all general information contact Arcadia Publishing at:
Telephone 843-853-2070
Fax 843-853-0044
E-mail sales@arcadiapublishing.com
For customer service and orders:
Toll-Free 1-888-313-2665

Visit us on the Internet at www.arcadiapublishing.com

I would like to dedicate this book to my parents, Madison Wilson Sr. and Leola Gant Wilson. As a child my parents supplied our home with books that piqued my interest and developed in me a desire to read as much as I could. In turn, I developed an interest in writing and sharing my thought with others. I thank them for being hard-working parents who persevered during difficult times and knew how to make a little last for ten children. In 1969, my father arranged for me to travel from Tallahassee, my hometown, to St. Petersburg to live near his brother Leroy and sister Bertha while I did my student teaching at John F. Kennedy Middle school in Clearwater. I was hired as a full time teacher before I completed my internship. My teaching career in Pinellas County began in August of 1969.

Contents

ACKNOWLEDGMENTS

An immense amount of gratitude is owed to my friends, relatives, and colleagues who contributed to *Black America Series: St. Petersburg*. First of all, thanks to Ellen Babb, whose passion for recording the history of women and African Americans in Pinellas County enabled her to share with me a wealth of information and material she had accumulated over the years.

There are many that deserve credit for the completion of this publication. Most notable is my cousin Doretha Faye Jones, whose interviews provided an abundance of information for the book. Thank you, Faye, for having a winning personality that allows others to freely open up and share their stories with you. Thank you, Cheryl Garnes, who moved to St. Petersburg about four years ago from Harlem, New York. In those four short years, she has grown to love the city and has developed a desire to find out as much as she possibly can about her new home. In turn, she has shared some of her findings with me. For sharing their stories, pictures, and church and civic programs, I would like to thank William "Buddy" West and his wife, Ruth; Mordecai Walker and his wife, Anna; Paul Barco Sr.; Joseph Albury Jr.; Emmanuel Stewart; the late Ira "Big H" Wilson; Emma Cavin; Alfred Williams; Buster Cooper; Norman Jones II; Vermell Johnson; Katrina Henderson McDonald; Jacqueline Small Ware-Moore; Velma Ross; Faye Lumpkin Hines; and Myron Mills. I thank Christine Wigfall Morris for sharing her home and allowing me to stretch out on the floor and organize information, and Loretta Hunter for coming over to my place, bringing food, sometimes cooking it, and assisting with sorting and organizing. Thanks also to Milton Rooks Jr. for words of encouragement when I got a little impatient.

The Pinellas County African American History Museum, Pinellas County Historical Museum, and the LiveArts Peninsula Foundation were also valuable sources of information. Historians Donald J. Ivey and Minson Rubin were also contributors and valuable sources of inspiration.

Please accept my apology if I have overlooked anyone. I am sincerely grateful to everybody who assisted me with this project.

INTRODUCTION

Every community, large and small, has its quiet heroes—men and women whose local accomplishments go largely unheralded by historians that focus on the so-called "bigger picture." As a result, many stories have been untold, ignored, or worse yet, completely forgotten. This is a great tragedy because the study of history in its purest form *begins* at the local level. Like the pieces of a giant jigsaw puzzle, history is a series of collective memories that tell the story of our neighborhoods, communities, and ultimately, of our nation itself. History is you and I, our families, our memories, *ourselves*.

In this, the St. Petersburg edition of the *Black America Series*, author Sandra W. Rooks captures this spirit brilliantly. As with her earlier work in the series on *Clearwater*, she has evoked the essential and compelling history of this important African-American community in Florida.

It is sadly true that the history of St. Petersburg has often been a tortured one, rife with lynchings, beatings, protests, riots, and other disturbances. Like many areas of the Deep South, forced segregation left an ugly scar on the area. But, as you will discover from these pages, beyond the pain and frustration lies another story, of a world full of dignity, courage, and hope—a world in which ordinary people achieved greatness despite the adversity that surrounded them. The early African-American community in St. Petersburg was in many ways a parallel but completely separate world to the one inhabited by white neighbors, who knew or cared little about it.

But this work is not merely the story of one people. Ultimately, it is the story of the struggle of all persons for progress and dignity. Through the stories that are revealed about the history and nature of the African-American community in St. Petersburg, much can be learned—not of dates and facts, but of far more valuable things: to have patience in the face of adversity; to hold tightly to hope in the midst of struggle and crisis; and above all, to have a sense of humor and a firm faith in God. All of these things—and more—we can learn from the story of the African-American community in St. Petersburg that Sandra has uncovered in the pages of this book.

"The past," a historian once wrote, "is prologue." If we can recognize that education is the key to enlightenment, and that in this and other works in the *Black America Series* we have that key, perhaps we can begin to unlock the doors of ignorance and prejudice so that finally—finally—the wounds of the past can begin to heal. To begin that journey, just open your mind, open your heart, and read on.

—Donald J. Ivey

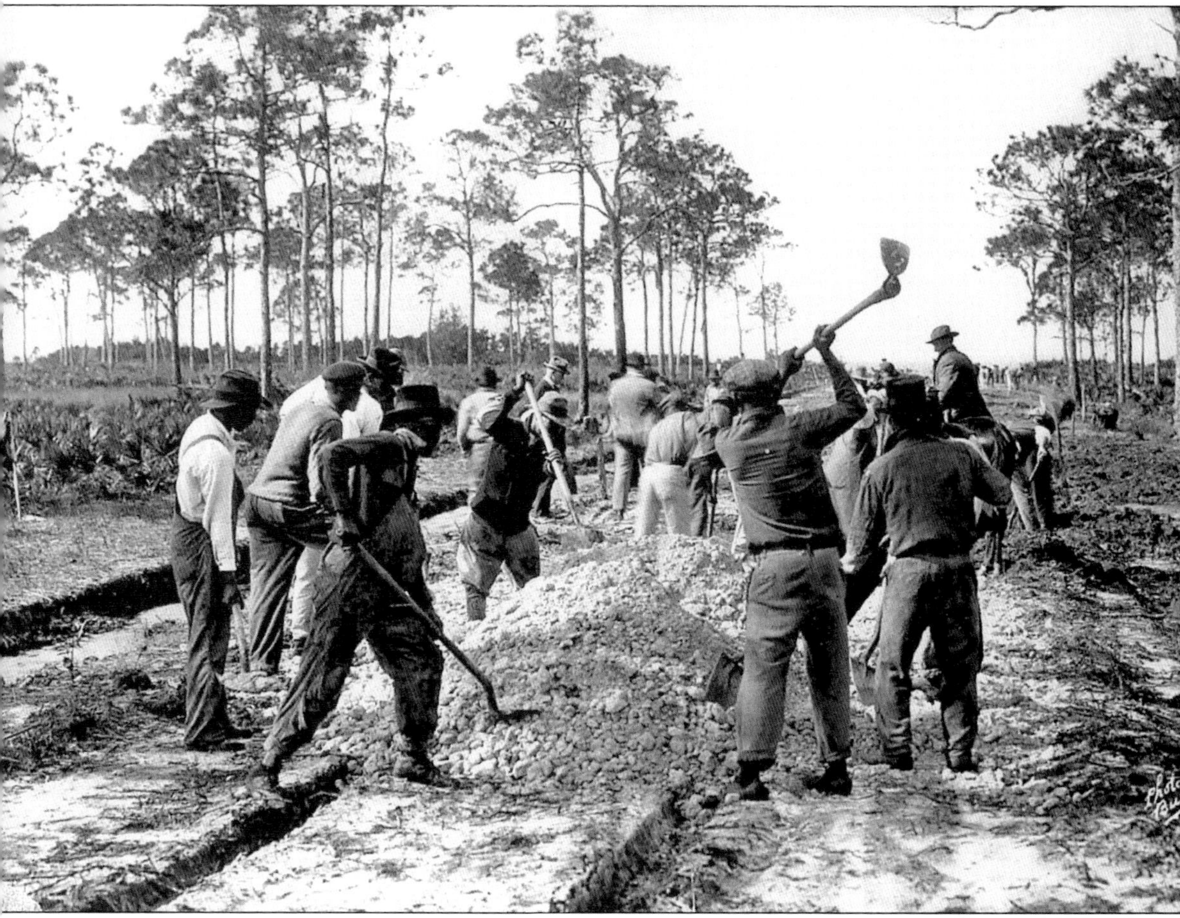

African Americans were instrumental in helping to build many of St. Petersburg's first roadways, as this 1922 photograph of road workers grading 4th Street North illustrates.

One

Early Settlers and Pioneers

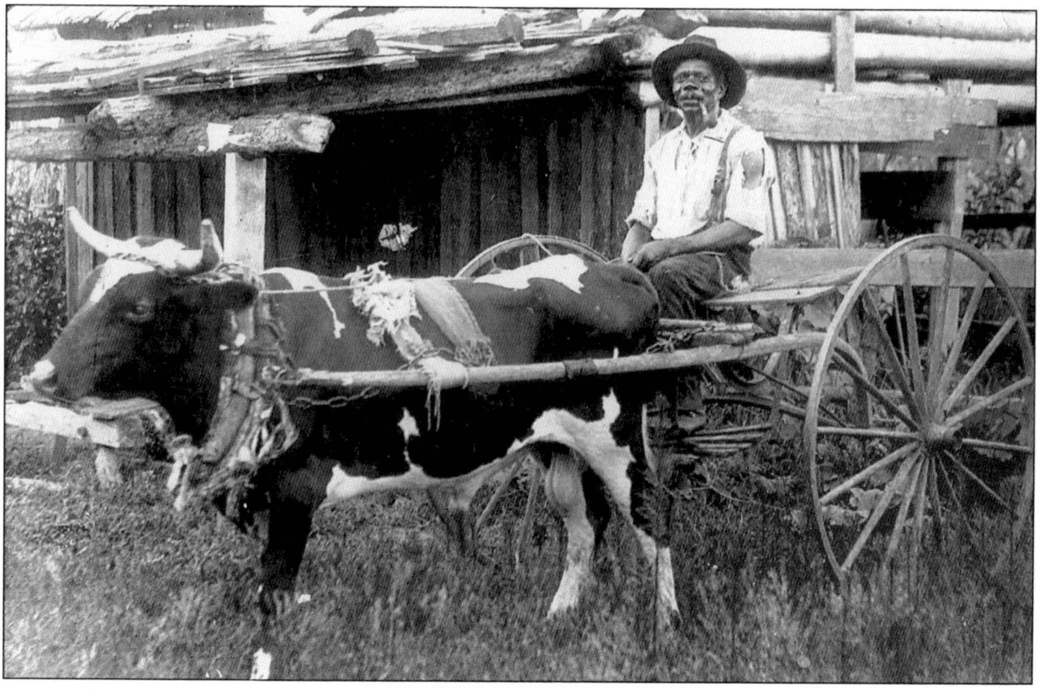

Pictured above is John Donaldson on board an ox cart in 1885. Donaldson was the first black man to settle on the lower Pinellas Peninsula after the Civil War. He was an ex-slave who came to St. Petersburg in 1868 as an employee of Louis Bell Jr. Donaldson married Anna Germain, a housekeeper of Louis Bell, and they had 11 children. The Donaldsons purchased a 40-acre farm located one mile northeast of Lake Maggiore (then known as Salt Lake). In 1887, John Donaldson signed a petition calling for a separation from Hillsborough County. The pioneer never saw the creation of Pinellas County because he died in 1901, and the creation of Pinellas County occurred in 1911.

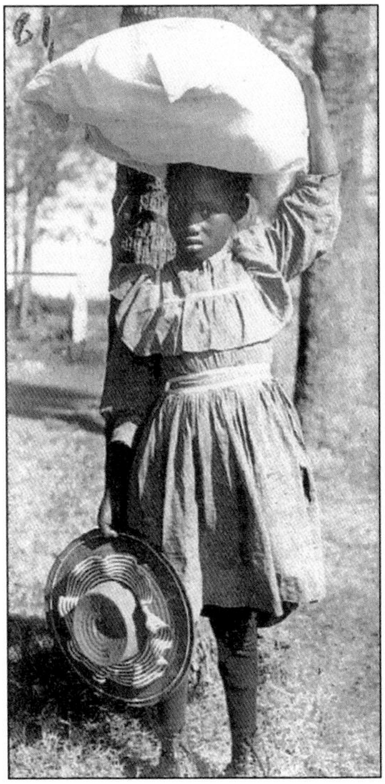

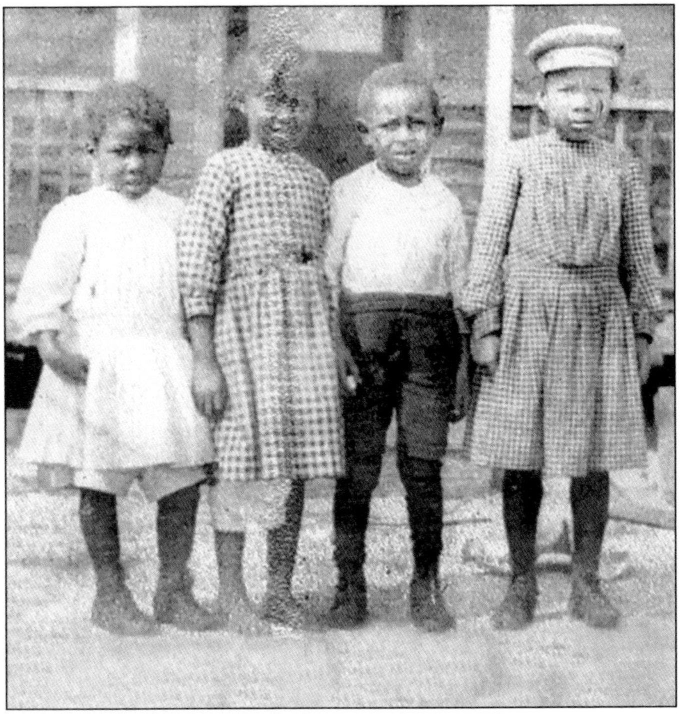

(above, left) A young girl stands by a tree with a pillow on her head and a hat in her hand in this late 1800s photograph. All of the pictures on this page are courtesy of the Pinellas County Historical Museum.
(above right) Four children pose in front of a house in this photograph taken in the late 1800s.

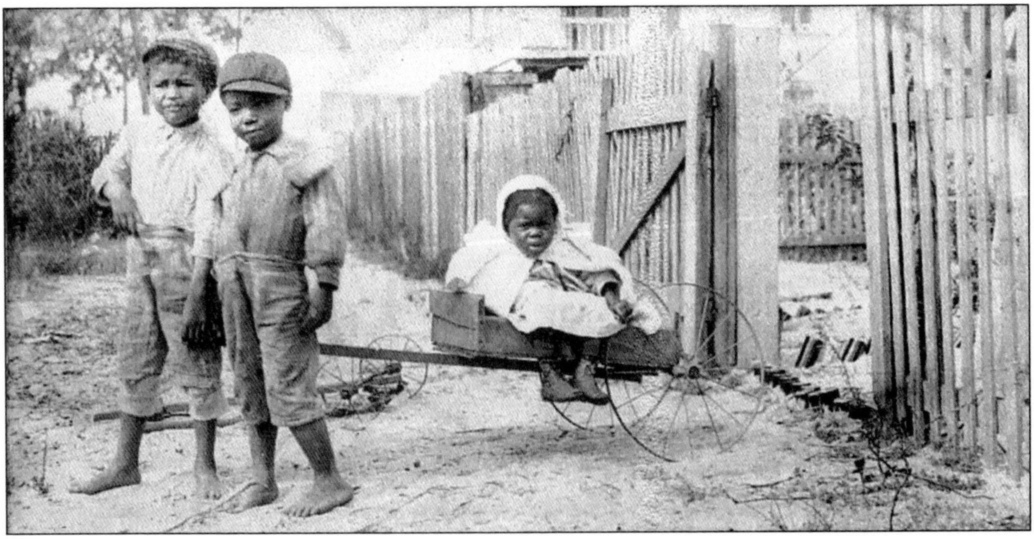

Two boys pull a baby on a sled in the late 1800s.

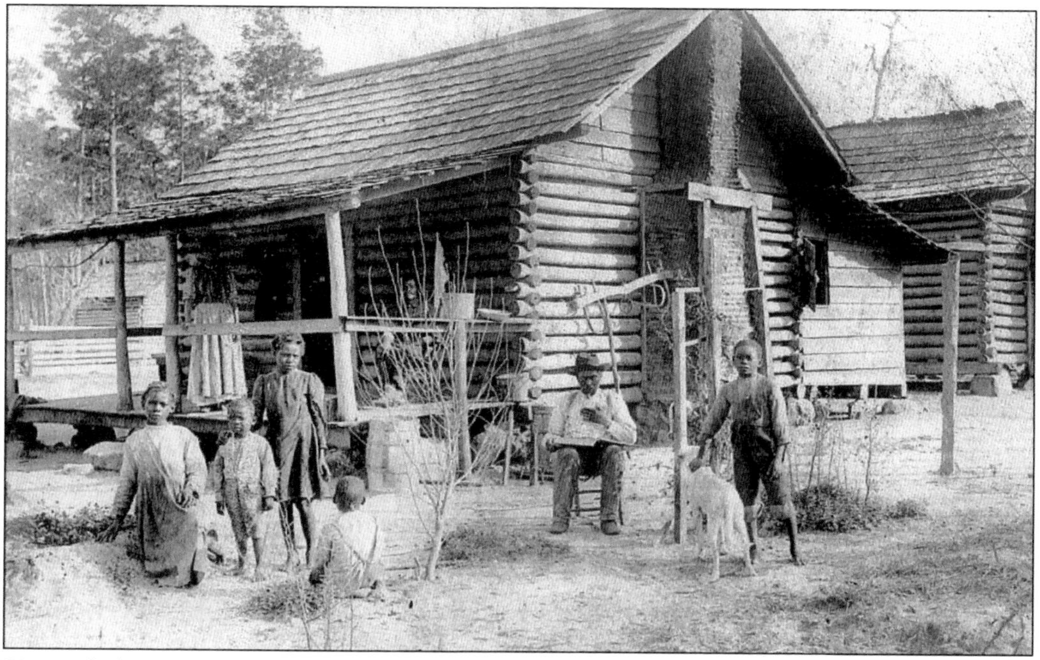

Pictured above is a St. Petersburg family about 1895. A gentleman is seated in the middle of children and family dog. A woman, possibly his wife, stands on the porch. The first black settlers were laborers who stayed on after helping build the first railroad into town in 1888.

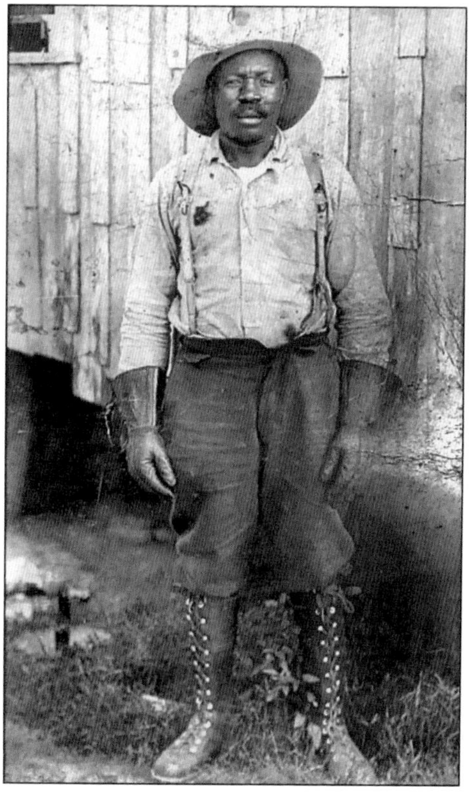

Pictured at right is Martin Rutledge in a photograph taken during the early 1900s. Rutledge was a butcher and is standing in front of a slaughterhouse. He is the grandfather of Jacqueline Small.

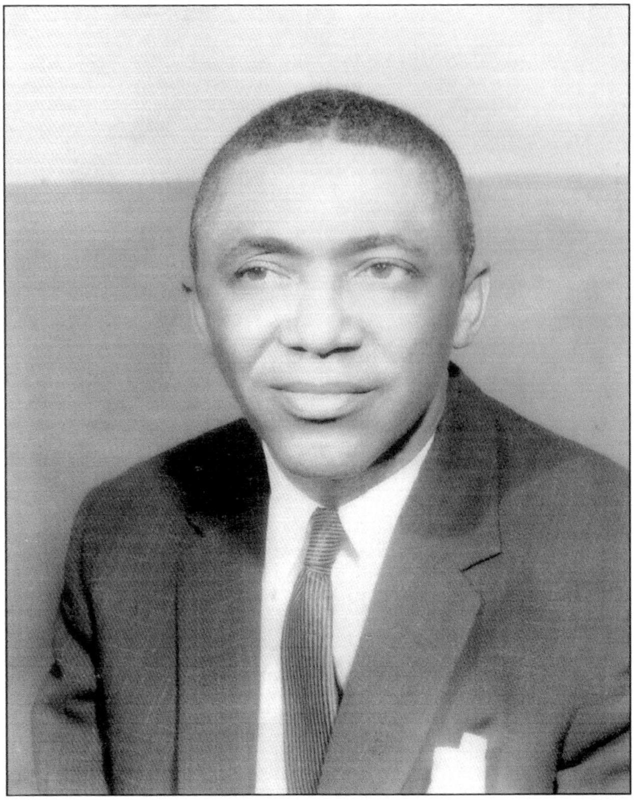

Goldie Thompson, portrayed in this early photo, first moved to St. Petersburg in 1916. He attended Fessenden Academy near Ocala and was ordained a minister in the Baptist church in 1940 in Council Bluffs, Iowa. As a radio host of WIOK, which later became WTMP AM radio, Goldie was so widely respected by his listening audience that when he urged them to "tell 'em Goldie sent you," they repeated Thomason's plea with the hope of receiving better treatment from area merchants.

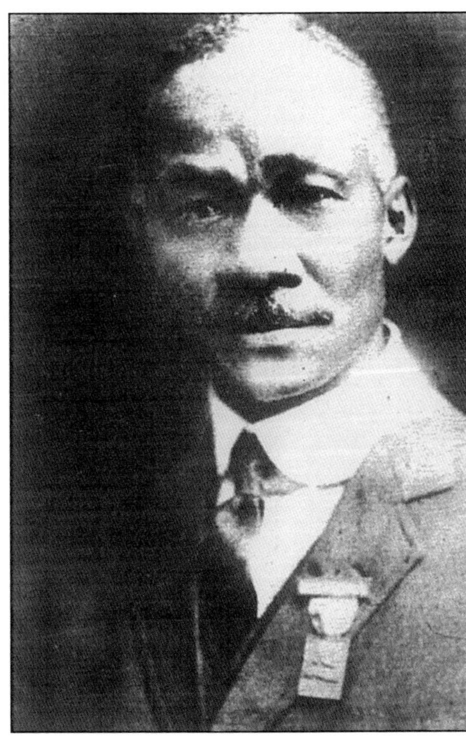

At right is Mr. Noah Griffin, who served as principal of Gibbs High School from 1933 to 1938.

This is a picture of Henry W. West and Daisy Pearl West taken in the early 1900s. They are the parents of William "Buddy" West, owner of Buddy's Barber Shop on 22nd Street South.

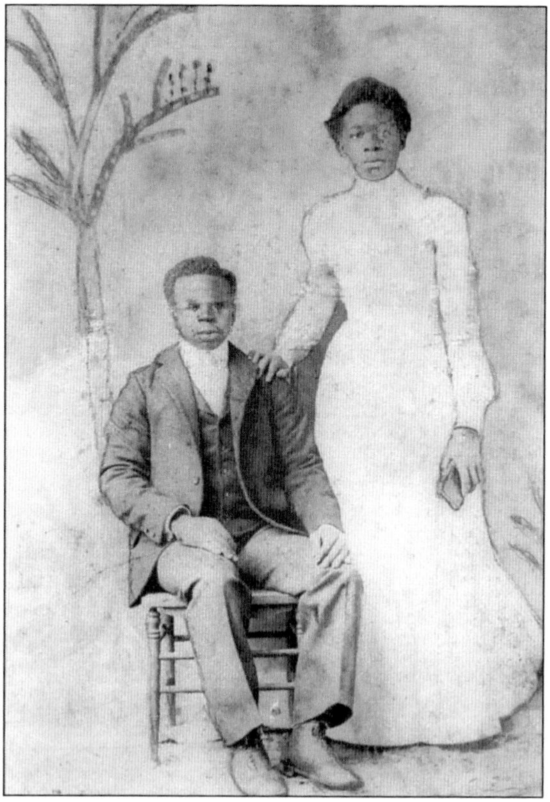

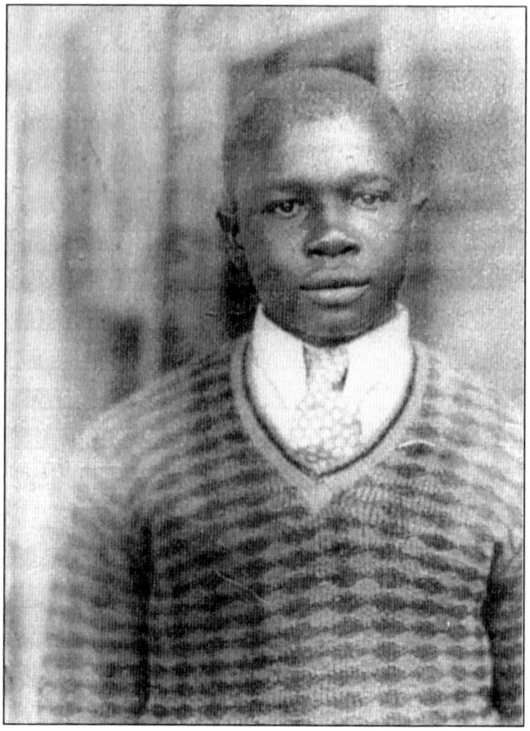

Buddy West, left, has resided in St. Petersburg most of his life. He booked famous people like Lena Horne, Duke Ellington, and Louis Armstrong for engagements at the Manhattan Casino on 22nd Street while working as a reporter for the casino.

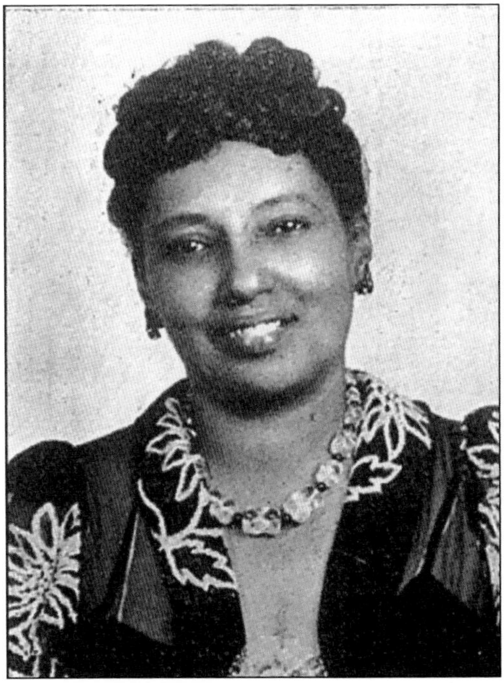

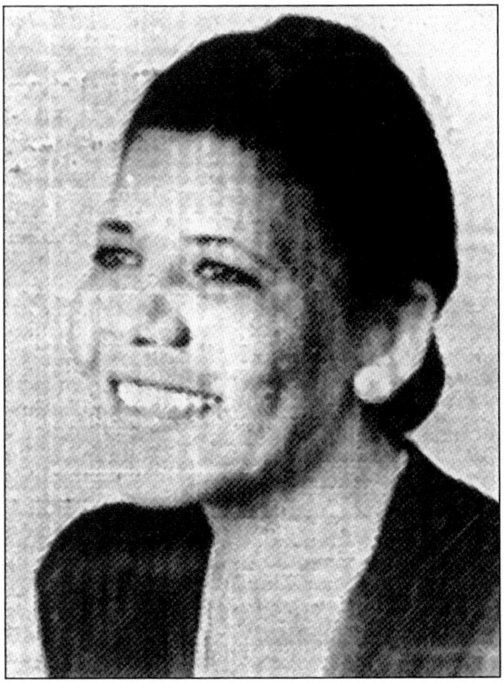

(above, left) Fannye Ponder organized and founded the local Colored Women's Federated Club, and later the St. Petersburg Metropolitan Council, an affiliate of the National Council of Negro Women.

(above right) Mary McRae was the second president of the City Federation of Colored Women's Clubs. Along with her husband, Edward, she established the McRae-Fulford Funeral Home in 1928.

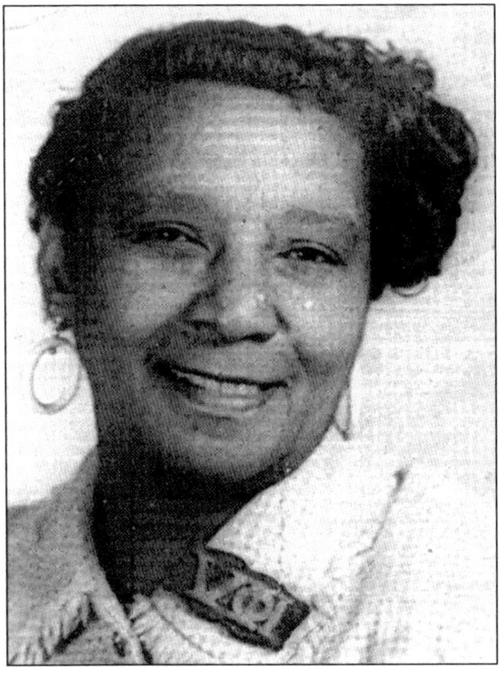

Amanda R. Howard was the third president of the City Federation of Colored Women's Clubs. She was also the first president of Quest Federated Club (pictured on the front of the book.) She was principal of Union Academy School in Tarpon Springs and Davis Elementary in St. Petersburg.

Chester Lucius James Sr. worked to improve the living conditions for people in Methodist Town, later renamed Jamestown in his honor. In 1963, he received the NAACP's Distinguished Service Award, and in 1967, he received the Council on Human Relations Brotherhood Award. Chester James arrived in St. Petersburg in 1911 and shortly afterwards married Rachel Ella Daniels. He and his wife raised four children.

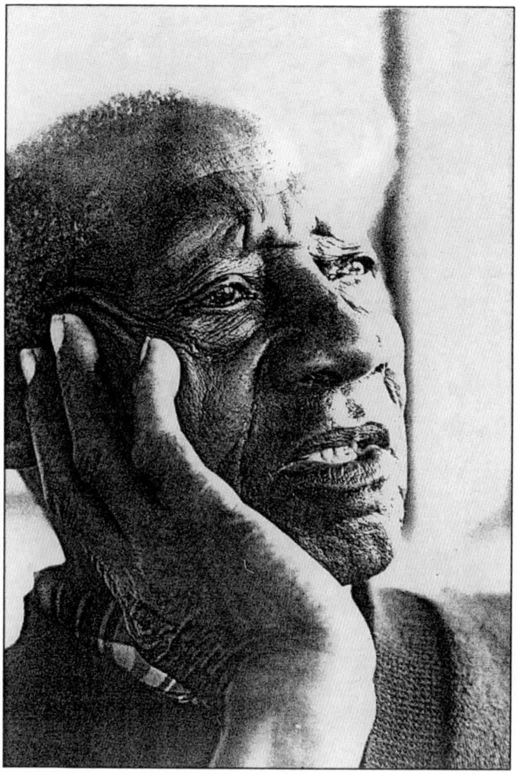

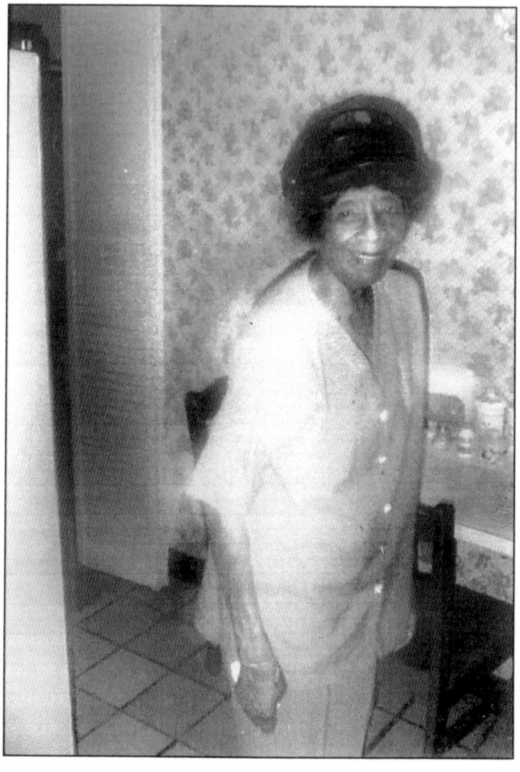

Ella Mary Holmes, left, was the daughter of Chester James Sr. She worked for many years as an area teacher and later served as principal of Union Academy in Tarpon Springs.This picture was taken after the Mad Hatter's Tea at St. Augustine Episcopal Church.

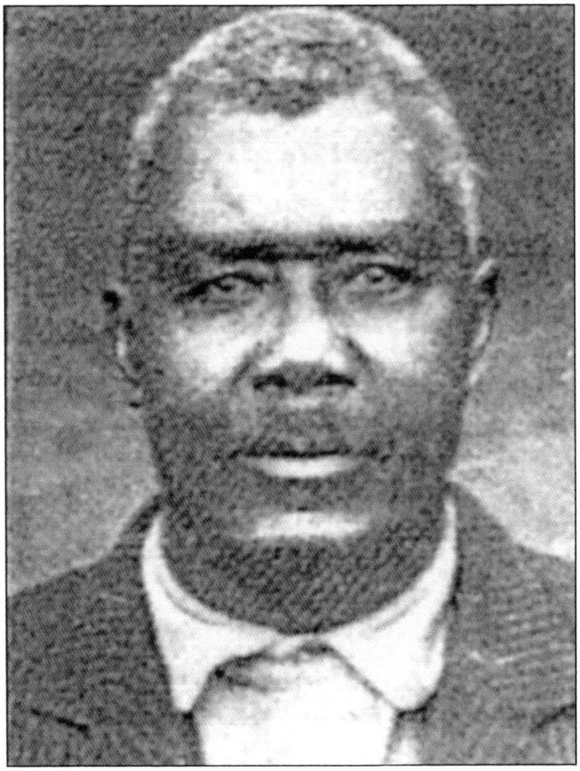

Pictured to the left is Elder Jordan Sr., who first settled in St. Petersburg in 1904. According to a September 27, 1987 article that appeared in the *St. Petersburg Times*, he owned acres of real estate, beaches, nightclubs, and even a bus line. Both Jordon Park and the former Jordan Elementary School were named after him. The Jordon family owned dozens of properties during the 1920s and 1930s, including portions of Campbell Park. Jordan Park spans the blocks between 22nd and 25th Streets from 9th Avenue to Melrose Avenue South. In a July 1924 issue of *The Business World Magazine*, Elder Jordan was eulogized with an original poem composed by Joseph Singleton, an editor of that magazine. He referred to Mr. Jordan as a "dear friend" who "fought the battle faithful and endured until the end."

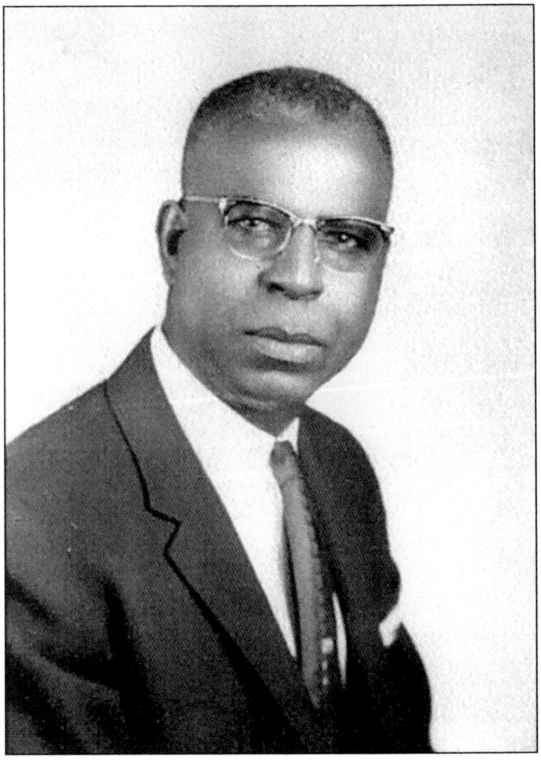

Rev. Enoch Davis, right, was a minister of Bethel Community Baptist Church. He fought for Civil Rights in St. Petersburg. Reverend Davis was born in Burke County, Georgia and moved to St. Petersburg in 1925. According to an article in Scott Hartzell's *Voices of America: St. Petersburg,* Enoch Davis delivered his first sermon at Second Baptist Church, now Bethel Community Baptist, at the age of 21. He received a bachelor of arts degree from Florida A&M University and a master's degree from Georgia's Interdenominational Theological Center. Reverend Davis championed registration drives to get African Americans to vote and forced city officials to open their green benches to African Americans. On September 13, 1981, Reverend Davis was honored with the opening of the Enoch Davis Center at 1111 18th Avenue South.

Standing in front of their home at 805 22nd Street South are John and Betsy Black, parents of John "Geech" Black Jr. of Geech's Barbecue. Next to them is their grandson, Hubie Black.

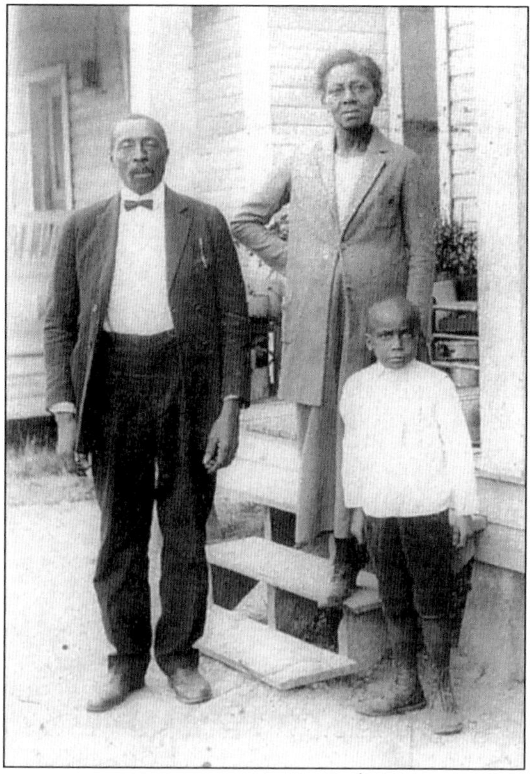

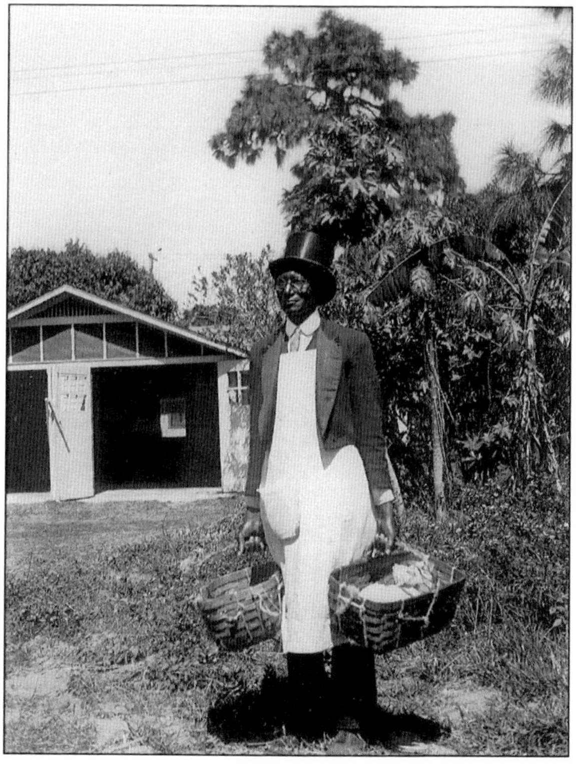

At left is Elijah Moore, a.k.a "I got 'em", from a 1920s photograph. He is sporting his trademark attire, a top hat, tail coat, and a long white apron. Moore would sell fresh fish and produce on the streets of St. Petersburg by shouting out "catch 'em alive and sell 'em dead." Moore came to St. Petersburg in 1912 and was ordained a minister at the Church of God in Methodist Town in 1955. He died on March 16, 1972 in a nursing home at the age of 92.

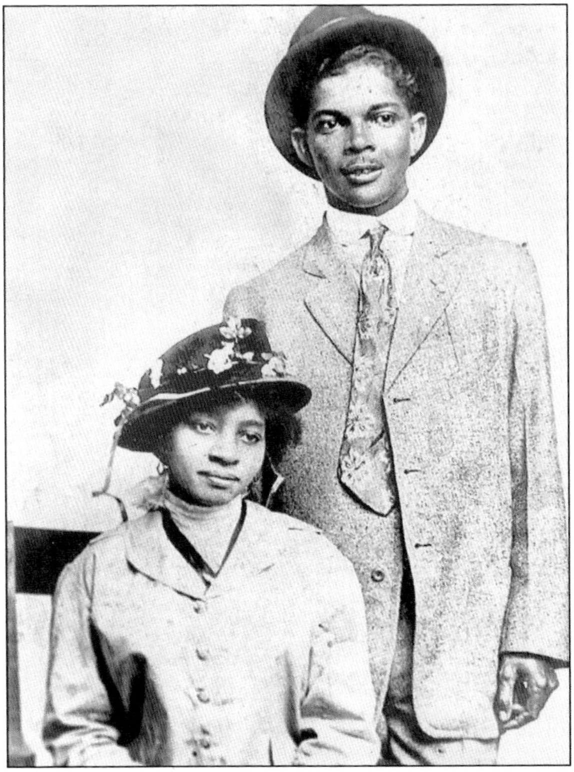

Pictured to the left is a photograph taken in 1914 of Mary Fields, a pioneer teacher at Davis Elementary School. Standing next to her is her husband, Irvin Fields.

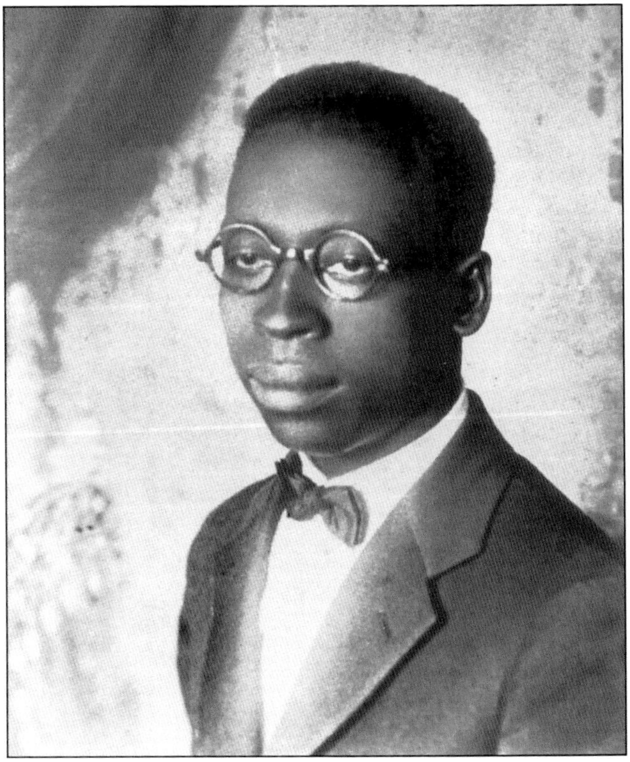

At right is Professor G.T. Wiggins in the 1920s. He served as principal of Davis Elementary, formerly Davis Academy, from 1924 to 1927, and later he was a teacher at Gibbs High School, the only high school in Pinellas County for African-American students at this time.

Two

Religion

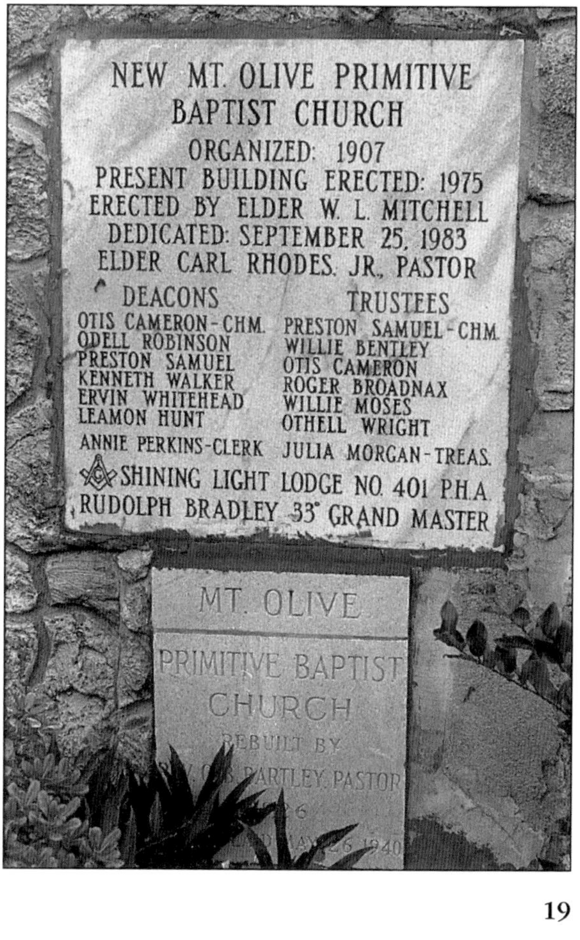

Black churches began as institutions of hope and places where slaves could escape. In St. Petersburg, the black church today represents one of the most influential institutions in the black community. Shown here is a cornerstone for New Mount Olive Primitive Baptist Church. Mt. Olive Baptist Church was organized in 1907. It was located at 308 10th Street North in St. Petersburg. It was organized by the late Elder Ford, who served until his death. Mount Olive has had several pastors following Elder Ford. They were the Elders Tillman, O.B. Bartley, J.E. White, A.L. Lewter, W.L. Mitchell, and Elder Carl Rhodes Jr. According to an article in *The Business World Magazine* in July 1924, the church held Sunday School at 9:45 a.m., preaching at 11 a.m. and 8 p.m. every Sunday, and Bible Institute on Friday night. Rev. O.B. Bartley was the minister at that time. In September 1975, Mt. Olive became New Mount Olive Primitive Baptist Church. It is presently located at 3012 18th Avenue South.

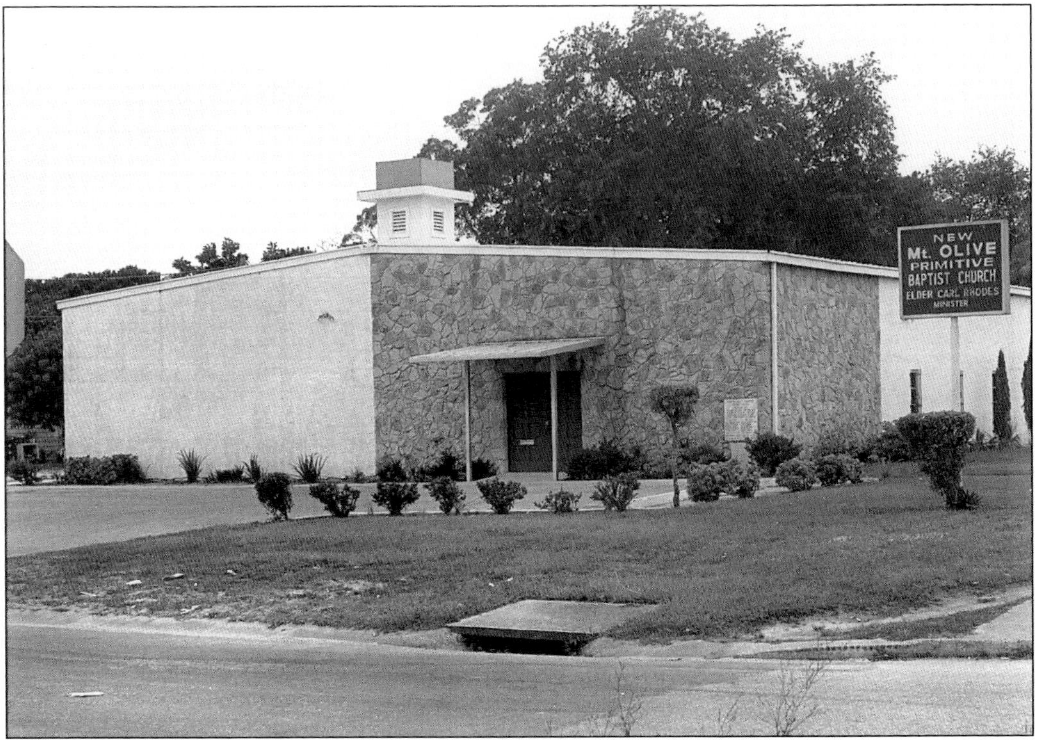

Pictured above is New Mt. Olive Baptist Church with Elder Carl Rhodes as pastor.

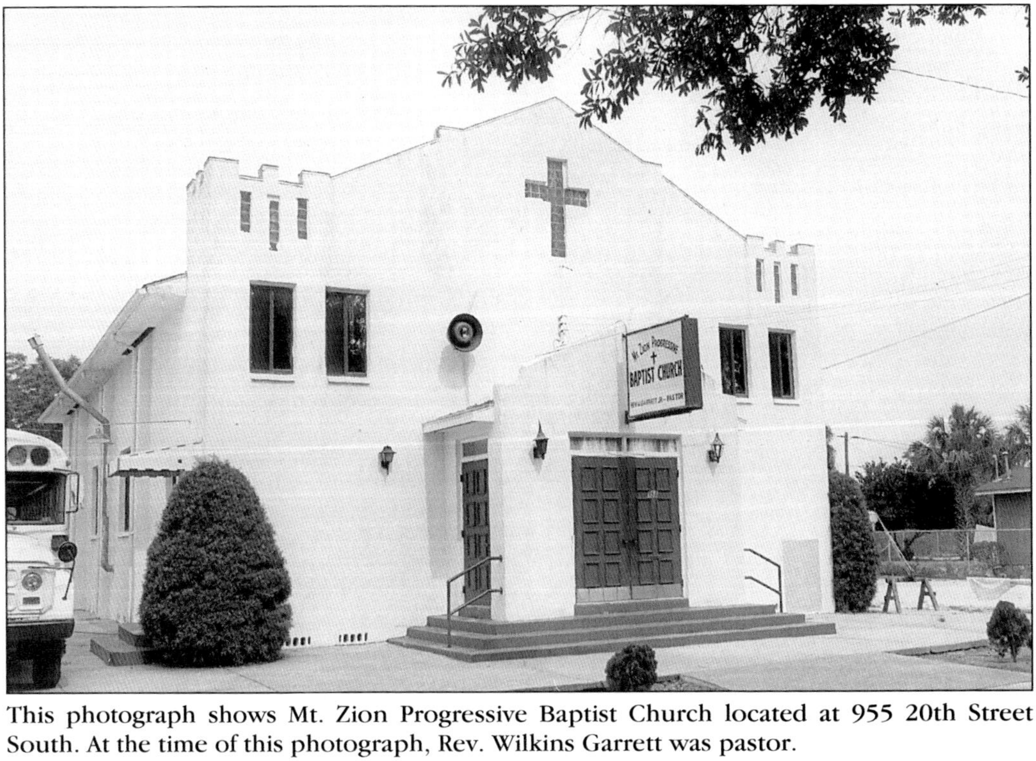

This photograph shows Mt. Zion Progressive Baptist Church located at 955 20th Street South. At the time of this photograph, Rev. Wilkins Garrett was pastor.

At right is the cover page of a souvenir booklet for Trinity Presbyterian Church. The program was celebrating the church's 20th anniversary.

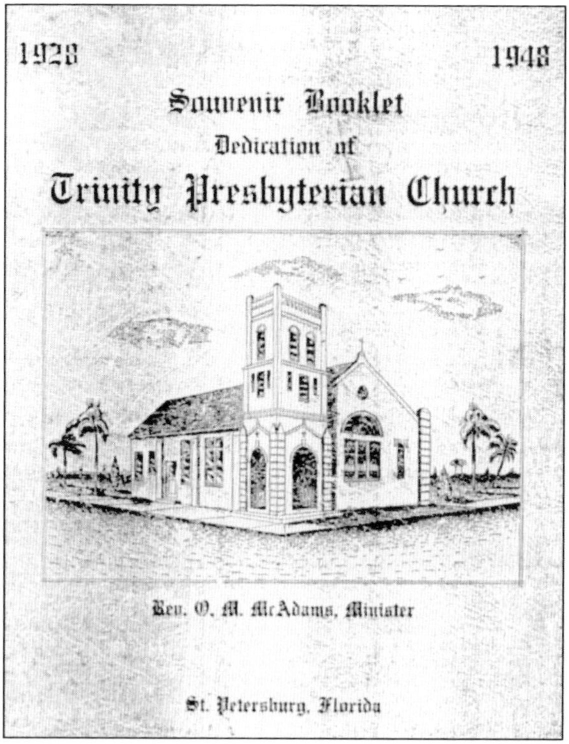

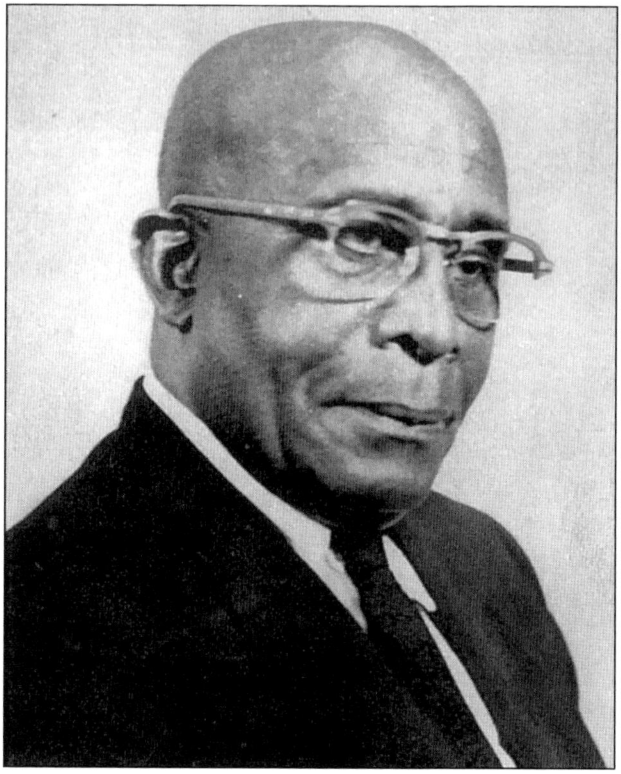

Trinity Presbyterian Church was organized by commission from Knox Presbyterian, Atlantic Synod. In 1929, Rev. Oscar M. McAdams, left, was contacted as the church searched for a minister. He and his wife Willie Lee arrived in St. Petersburg on August 14, 1929. Reverend McAdams also served as president of the Interdenominational Ministerial Alliance and as president of the St. Petersburg Branch of the NAACP.

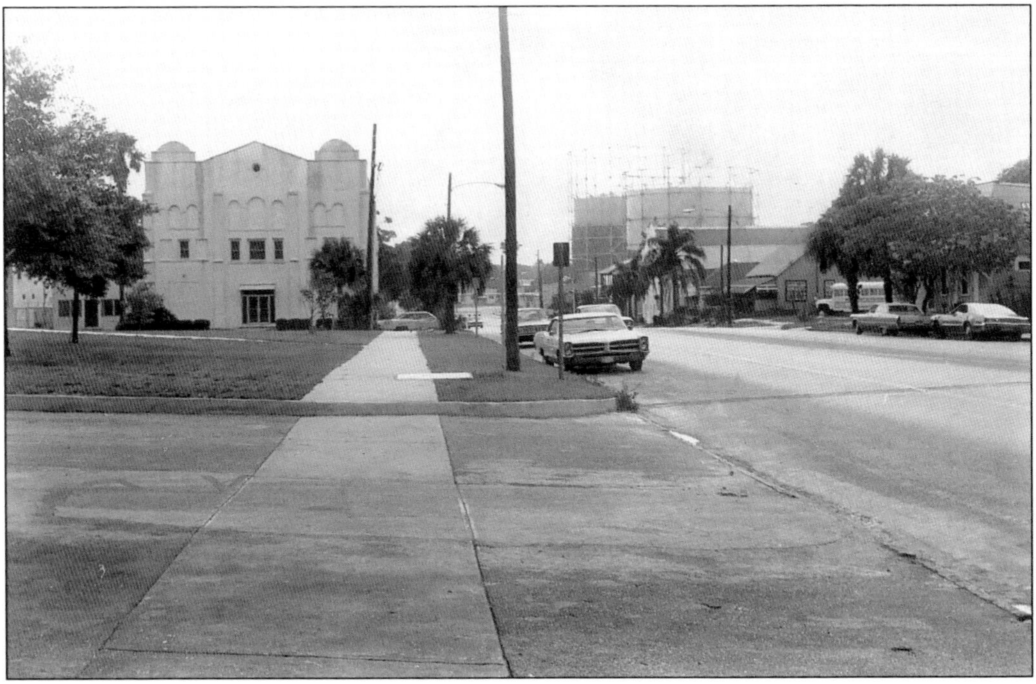

This is a picture of Bethel Metropolitan Baptist Church when it was located on 3rd Avenue. In the background is the Gas Plant area, which later became Tropicana Field.

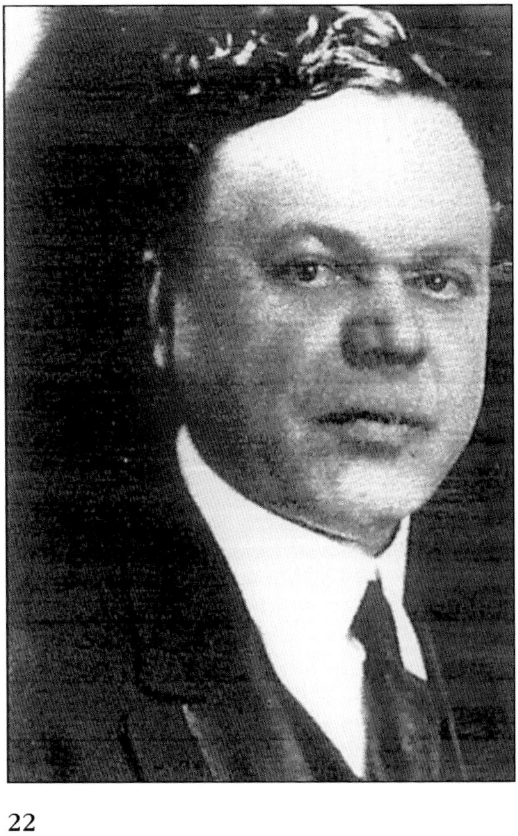

Rev. John W. Carter served as pastor of Bethel Metropolitan Church, above, from 1932 to 1947, during the church's construction. He also was principal of Gibbs High School from 1932 to 1933.

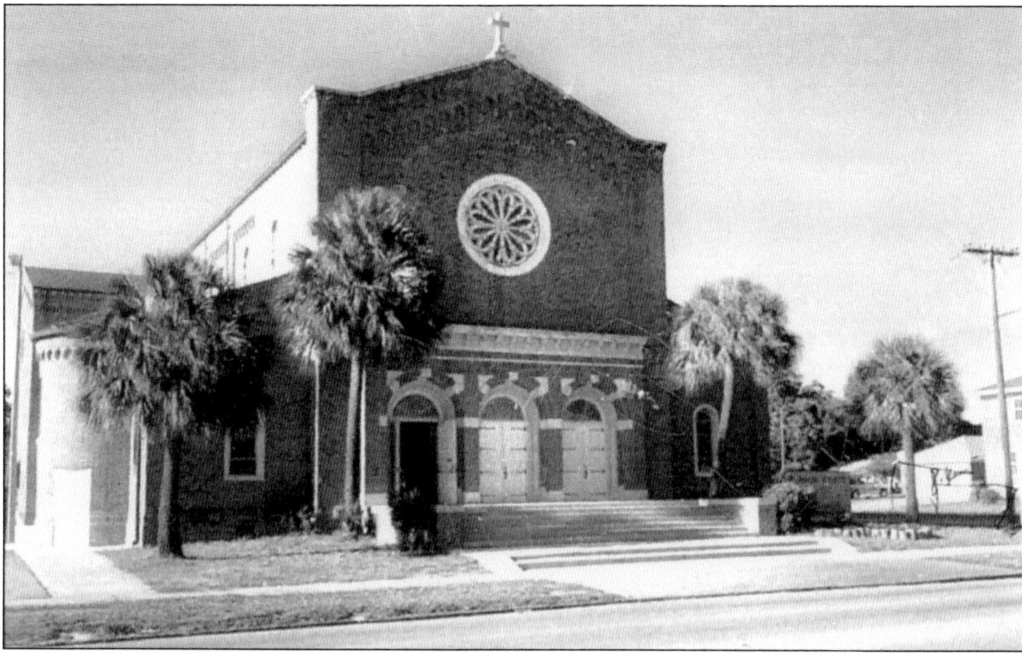

St. Joseph Catholic Church is located at 2025 22nd Avenue South. Father Callist Nyambo serves as priest.

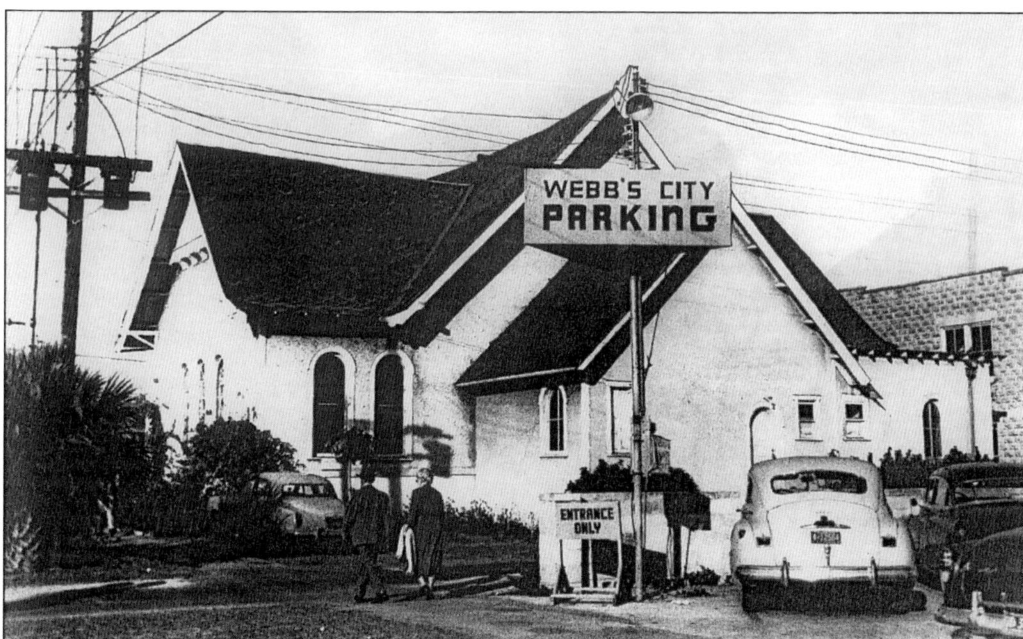

First Baptist Institutional Church was located at 774 2nd Avenue South in 1955. In a *St. Petersburg Times*'s article written on January 12, 1955, it was reported as being purchased by Webb's City and located across from Webb's Trading Post. In 1924, the pastor of First Baptist Institutional Church was Rev. W.C. Brown. *The Business World Magazine* in 1924 described it as having "polite ushers and soul-stirring singing."

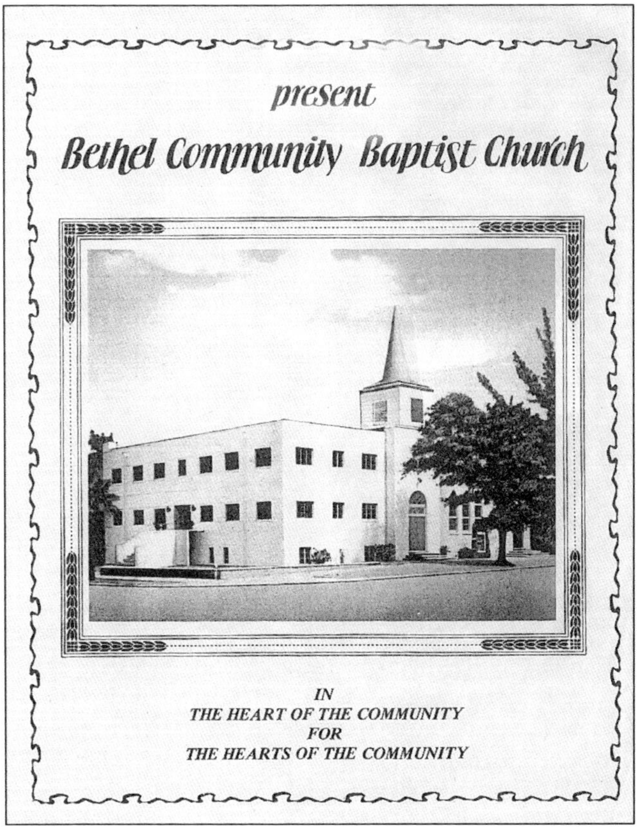

At left is a picture of Bethel Community Baptist Church when it was known as "Second Bethel." The church was founded in October 1923 by Rev. W.H. Pelham and Deacons L.A. Berry and Griffin.

Rev. Enoch Davis, below, served as pastor of Bethel Community Baptist Church for more than 50 years.

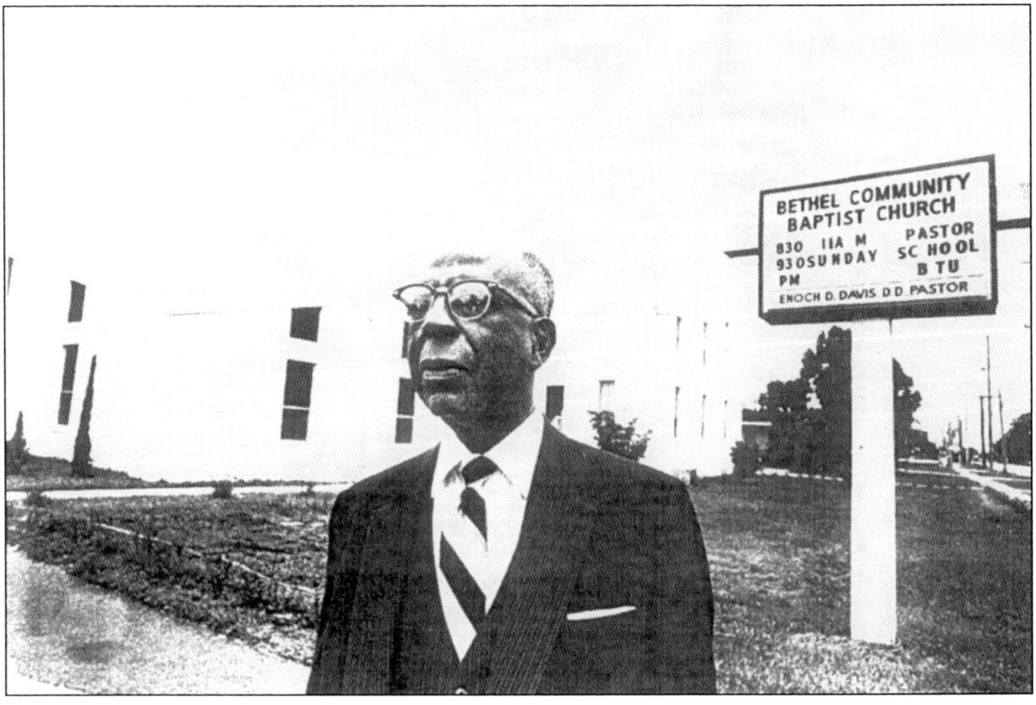

Dr. Annie E. Heath, right, is pictured with her daughter, Mrs. Rubye Heath Wysinger, center, and family friend Mrs. Helena Jenkins during a 1959 visit. She was guest speaker on Women's Day at Bethel A.M.E. Church.

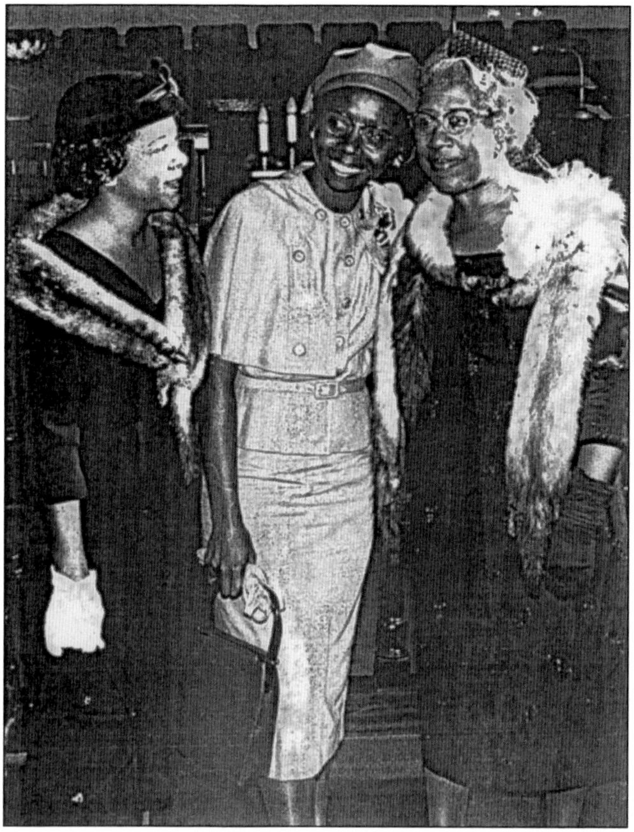

Bethel A.M.E. Church, located at 912 3rd Avenue North, was founded in 1894 under the leadership of Rev. J.S. Braswell. A thriving business district and residential neighborhood grew up around the church. The area took its name from the church and is known as Methodist Town. Bethel A.M.E. Church was designated as a local historic landmark in 1988.

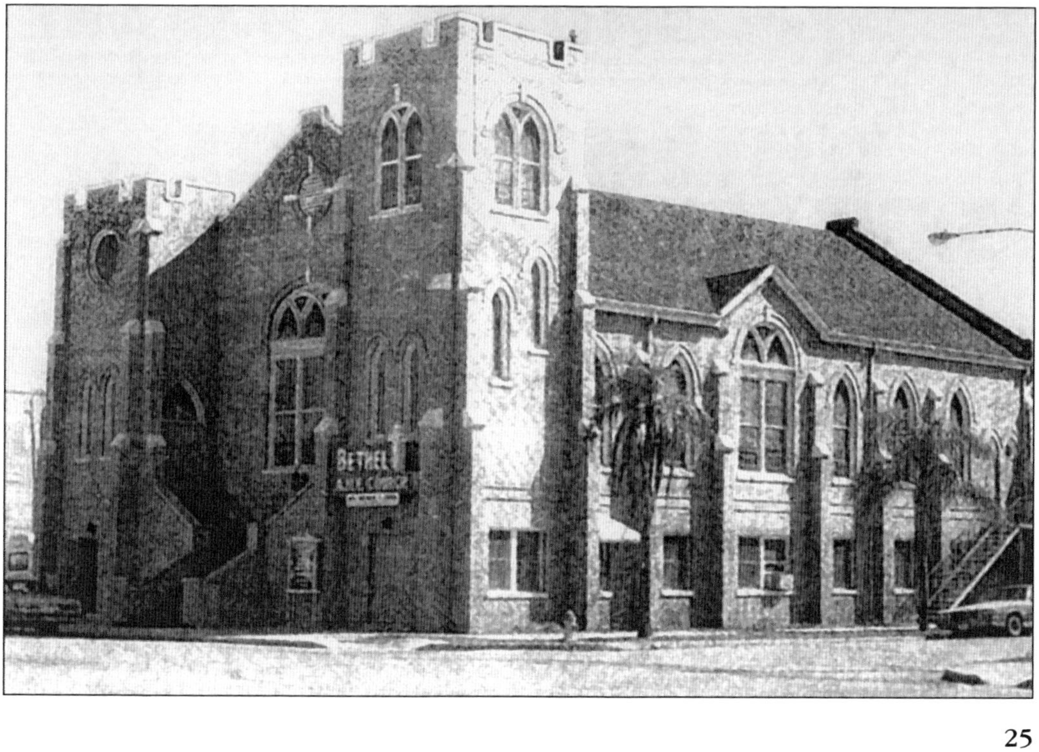

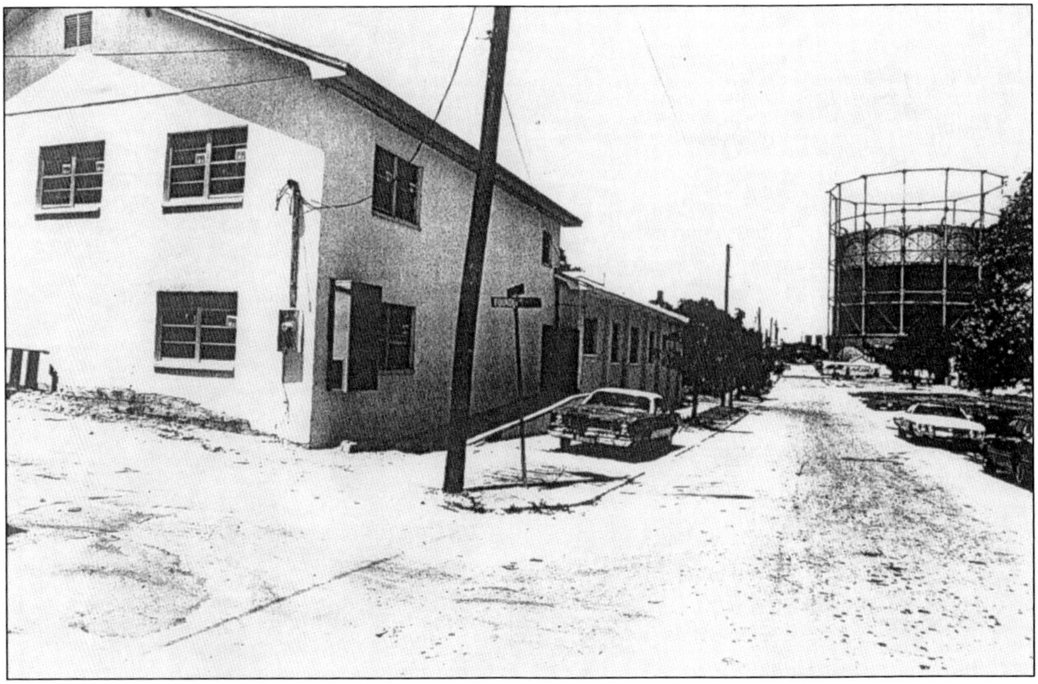

Prayer Tower Church of God in Christ in 1979 was located in the Gas Plant area. In that year officials of the church were upset that their church and the nearly completed annex would be demolished in redevelopment plans for the Gas Plant area. The church was founded in 1919 as the 14th Street Church of God in Christ at 1400 14th Street South.

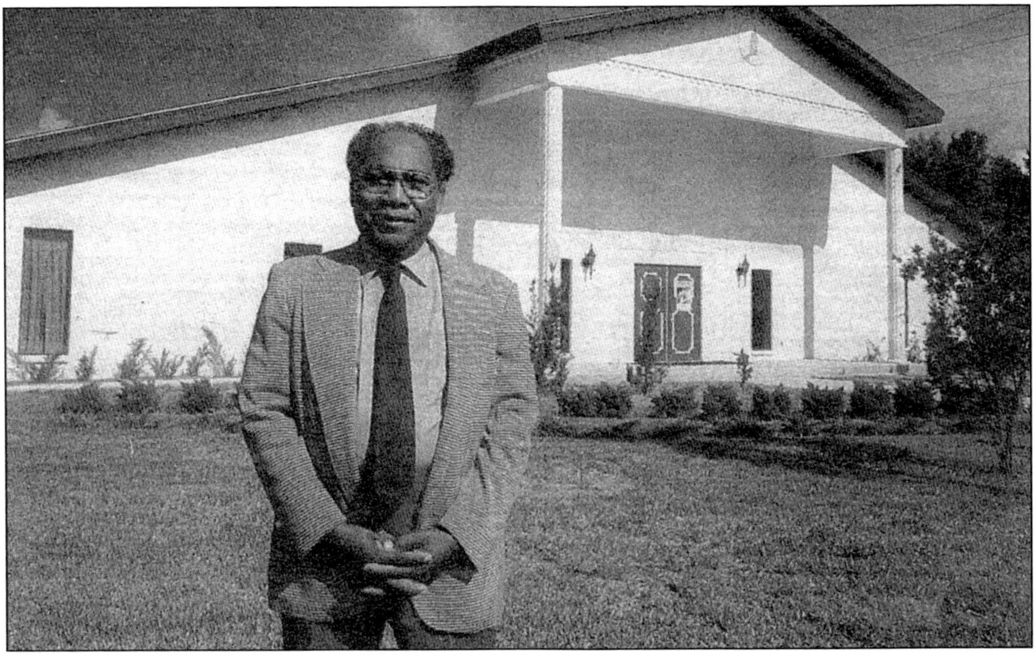

Pictured above is Elder Clarence Welch standing in front of Prayer Tower at its new location at 1137 37th Street South, St. Petersburg.

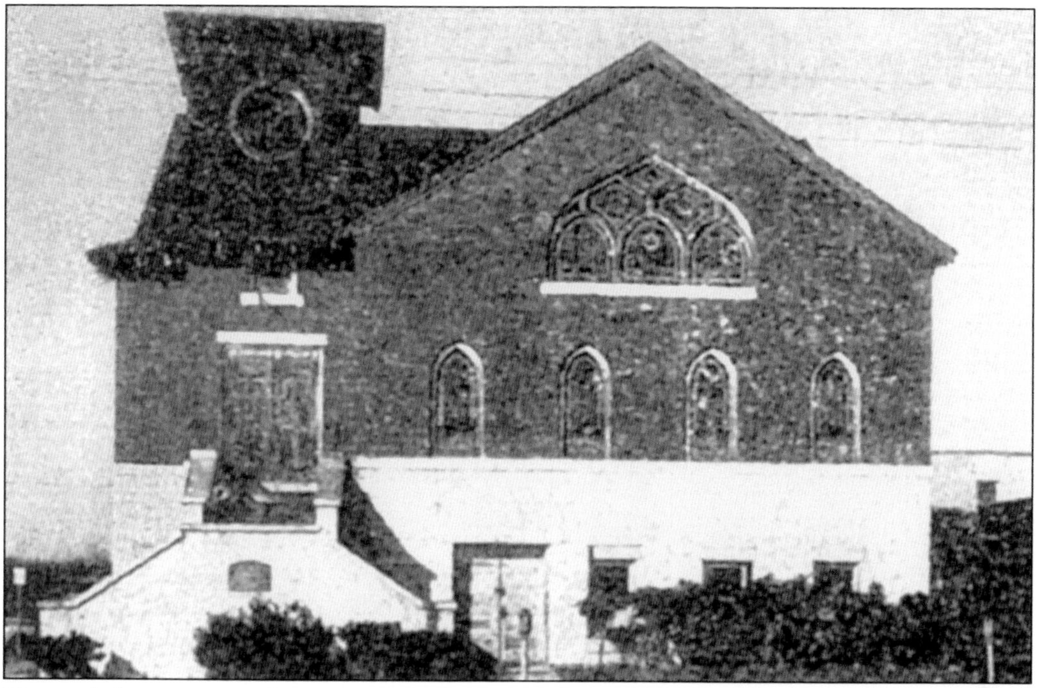

Pictured above is McCabe Memorial Methodist Church. The obituary for Mrs. P.A. Daniels in the 1924 issue of *The Business World Magazine* states that Reverend Daniels and his wife moved to St. Petersburg in 1905 from Gainesville, Florida and founded and built McCabe M.E. Church. It also states that Mrs. Daniels "labored with her husband in his effort and prayed for his success and at all times gave him encouragement." Reverend Daniels died in 1917. In 1924 the pastor of McCabe was Rev. D.S. Selmore.

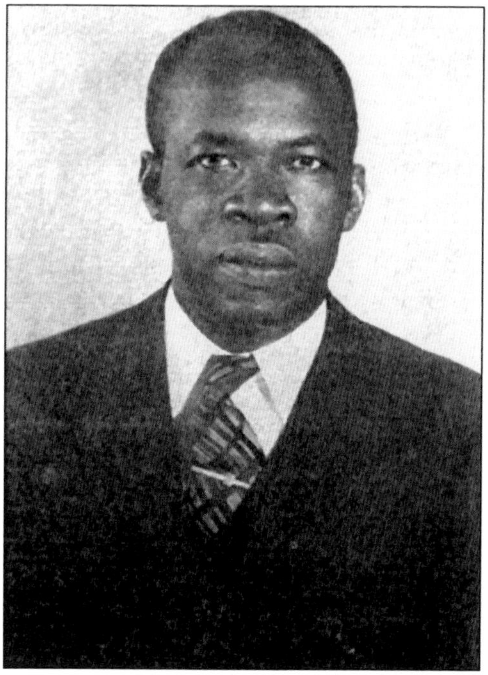

Rev. S.D. Bankston came to McCabe Memorial Methodist Church on June 24, 1951. Prior to this, he had served in Asbury, Savannah; Steward Memorial, Daytona Beach; and Trinity, West Palm Beach. He began his pastorate at McCabe with the message "Push out into deep water, and all of you let down your nets for a haul." (Luke 5:4.)

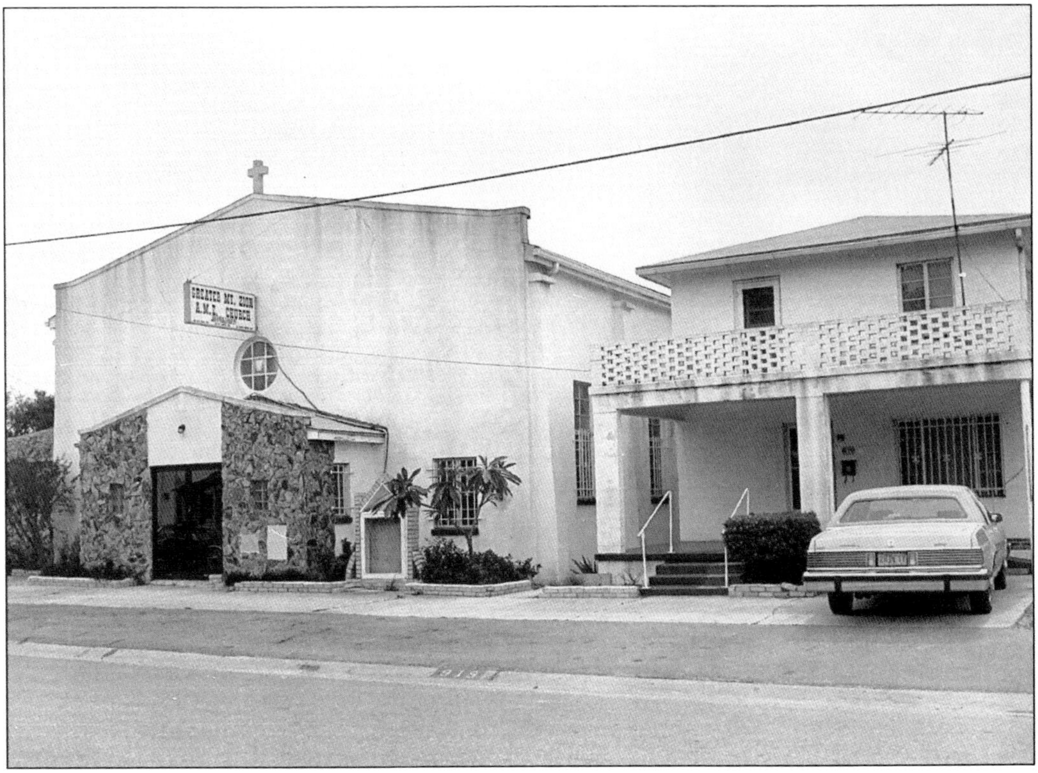

Pictured above is Greater Mt. Zion A.M.E. Church located at 919 20th Street South.

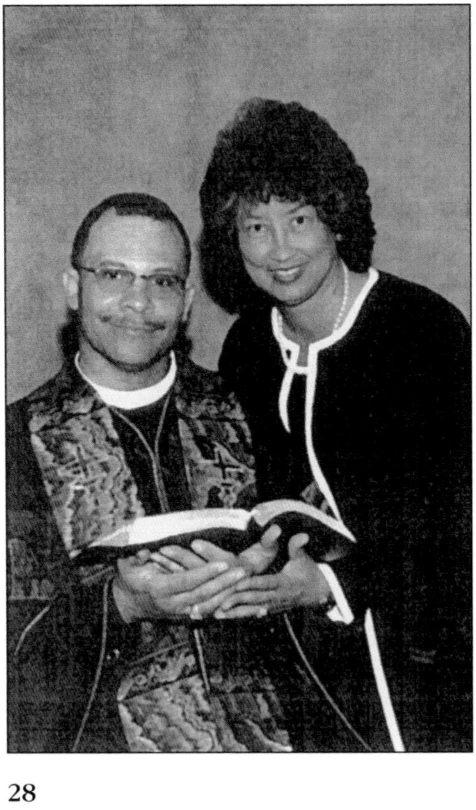

Pictured, left, is Rev. Clarence Williams and his wife, Andrea. Mt. Zion A.M.E. Church dates back to 1925. The first meeting to organize the church was held at Just-Rite Cleaners Pressing Club. Rev. Williams has been pastor since 1999.

Three

EDUCATION

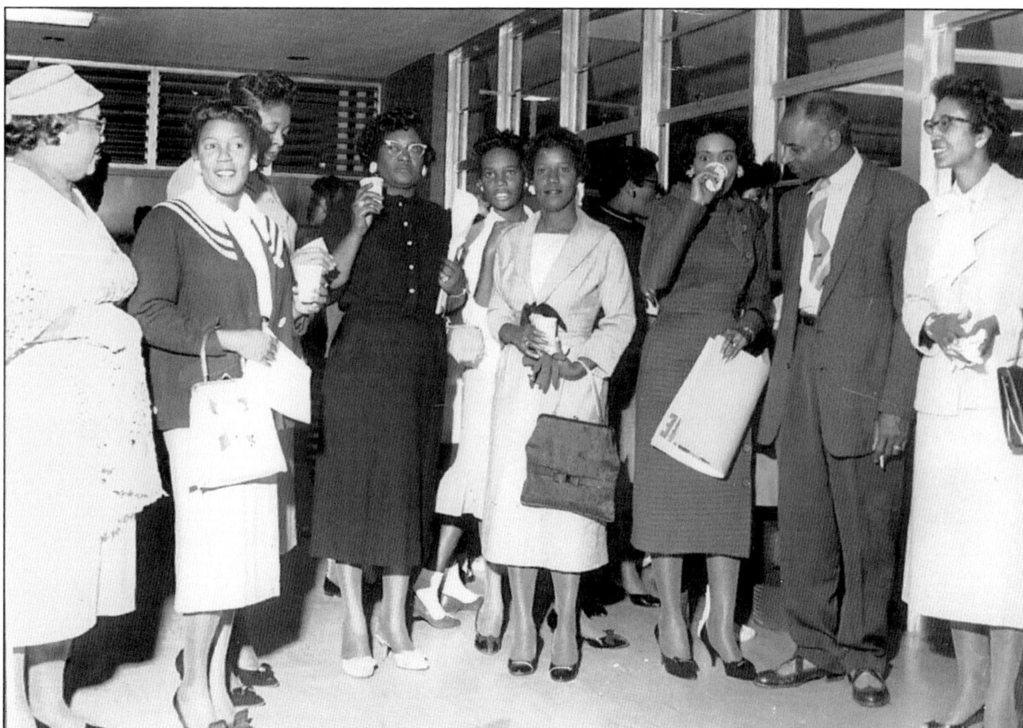

The picture above was taken in 1958 and depicts faculty members celebrating Education Week. Inez Adams (fourth from the right, in front) was married to Calvin Adams, one of the first African-American reporters for the *St. Petersburg Times*. Located at 701 16th Street South, 16th Street School was dedicated on Sunday, November 2, 1952. It served students from kindergarten through eighth grades. John H. Hopkins was the principal for the elementary school, and Frederick Burney was principal for the junior high. Josephine McGarrah Donald was secretary and held that post for over 34 years. The 16th Street band was directed by Samuel Robinson and had a reputation for excellence. The school now bears the names of former principal John H. Hopkins.

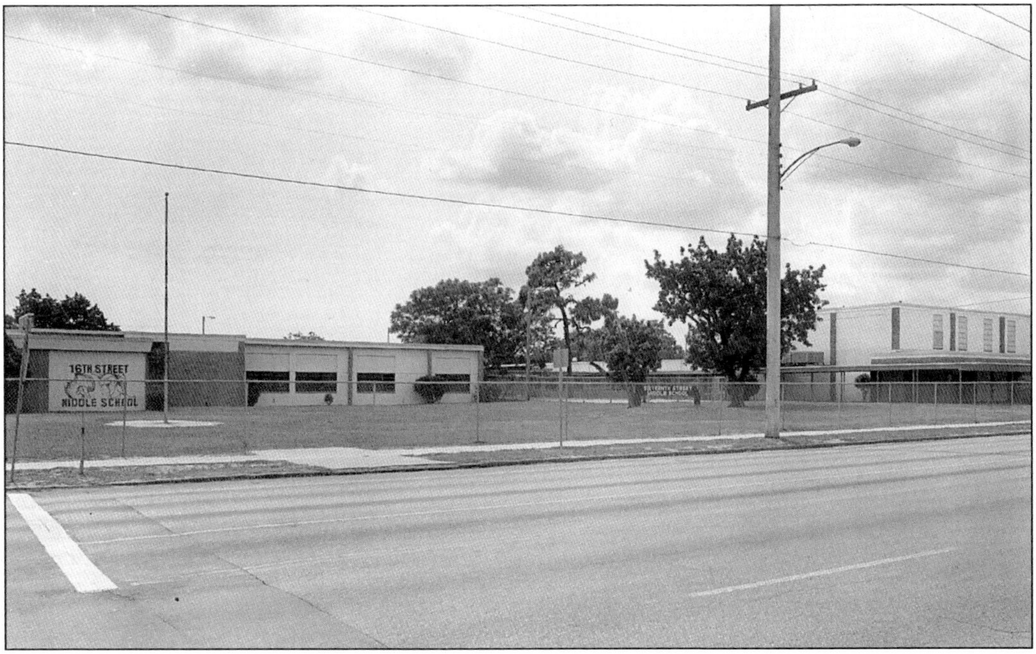

Pictured above is the 16th Street School before a new facility was built at this site.

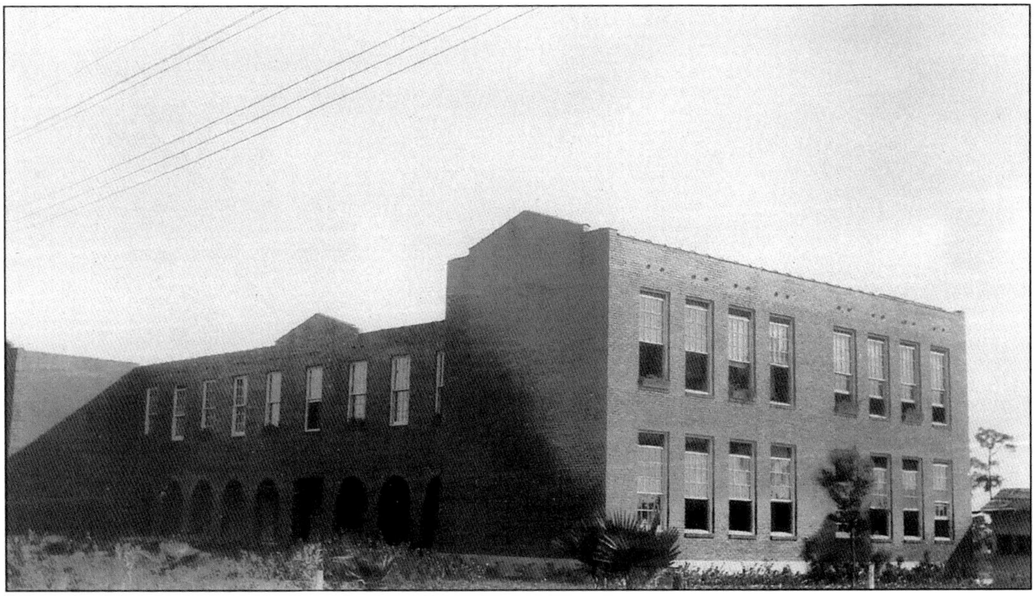

Pictured here is Jordan Elementary School, which opened on September 1, 1925. The principal was George W. Perkins who had a staff of 21 teachers and 1100 students. Jordan pioneered in radio broadcasting a school chorus, having the first home economic classes for boys, PTA organization, free night school for adults, double sessions, and reading clinic for blacks. In 36 years the school has had only four principals, including G.W. Perkins (1925–1929), Marie Pierce (1929–1951), Emmanuel Stewart (1951–1957), and Louis W. McCoy (1958–1962).

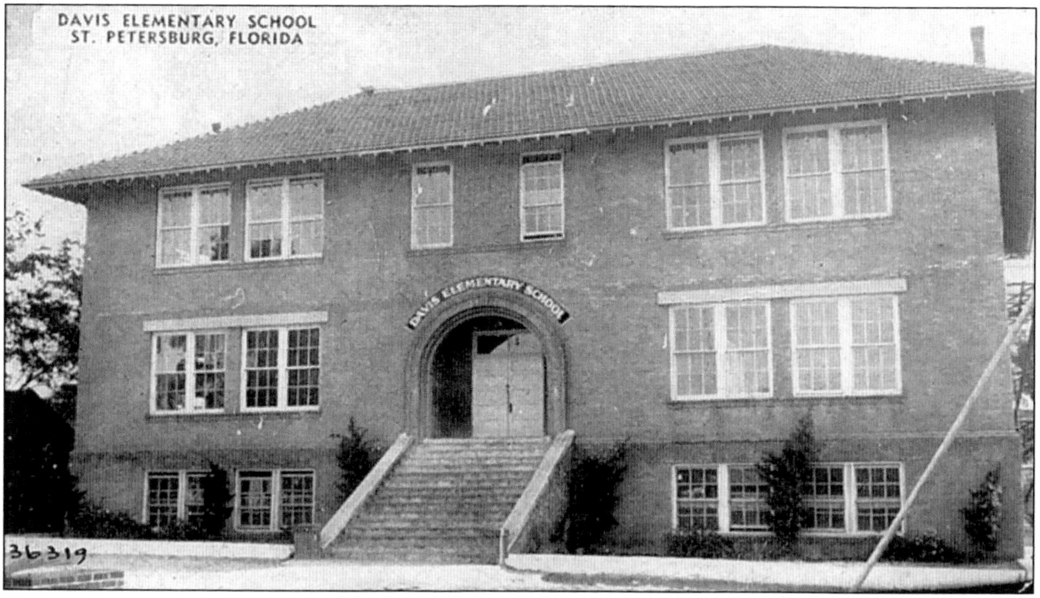

Pictured above is Davis Academy. In 1913 the school board agreed to pay half the cost of a student's transportation to school if the district in which the child lived would pay the other half and if the child lived more than three miles from the nearest school. Later that year, the board established a fixed rate of three cents per mile. Davis Academy was the first school in St. Petersburg built for black students. In addition to reading, writing, and arithmetic, the school offered courses in domestic science and manual training to the younger students.

Mary McLaughlin, pictured at right, was both a student and a teacher at the early Davis Elementary (originally Davis Academy) at 10th Street and 3rd Avenue South. According to *A Tradition of Excellence*, a publication of the Pinellas County School System, she remembered cooking lunches and serving them to white guests. She stated, "I figured that was all in our training, you know. We would prepare little meals and then we'd invite guests, and I learned that those guests paid a fee—a small fee—which helped to purchase the stuff that we worked with."

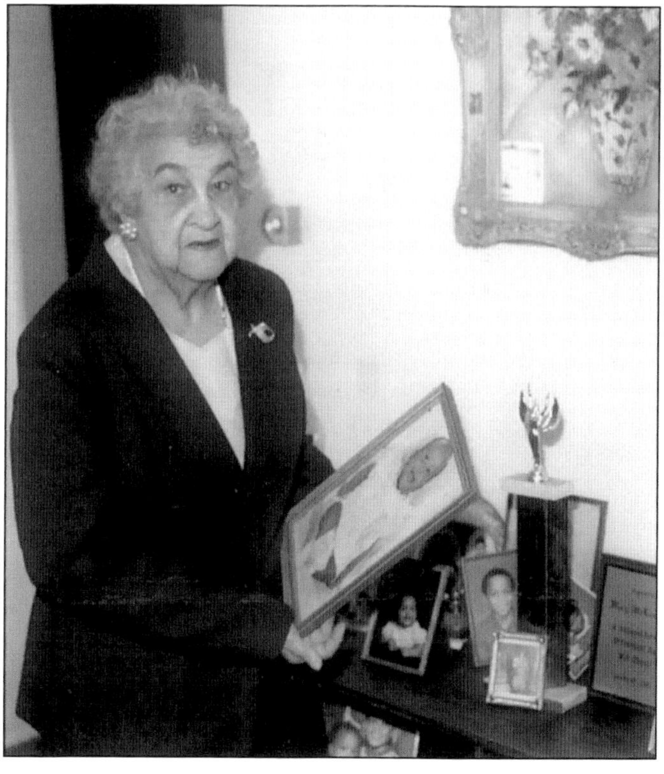

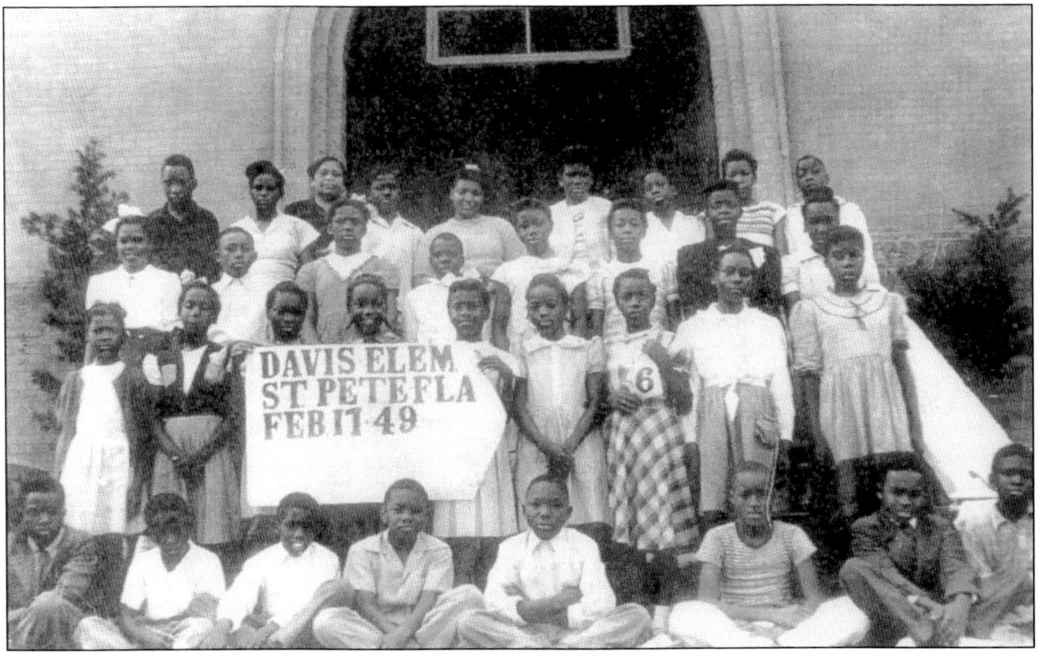

Davis Elementary students are photographed on February 17, 1949. According to school business records, Davis Elementary opened in 1911.

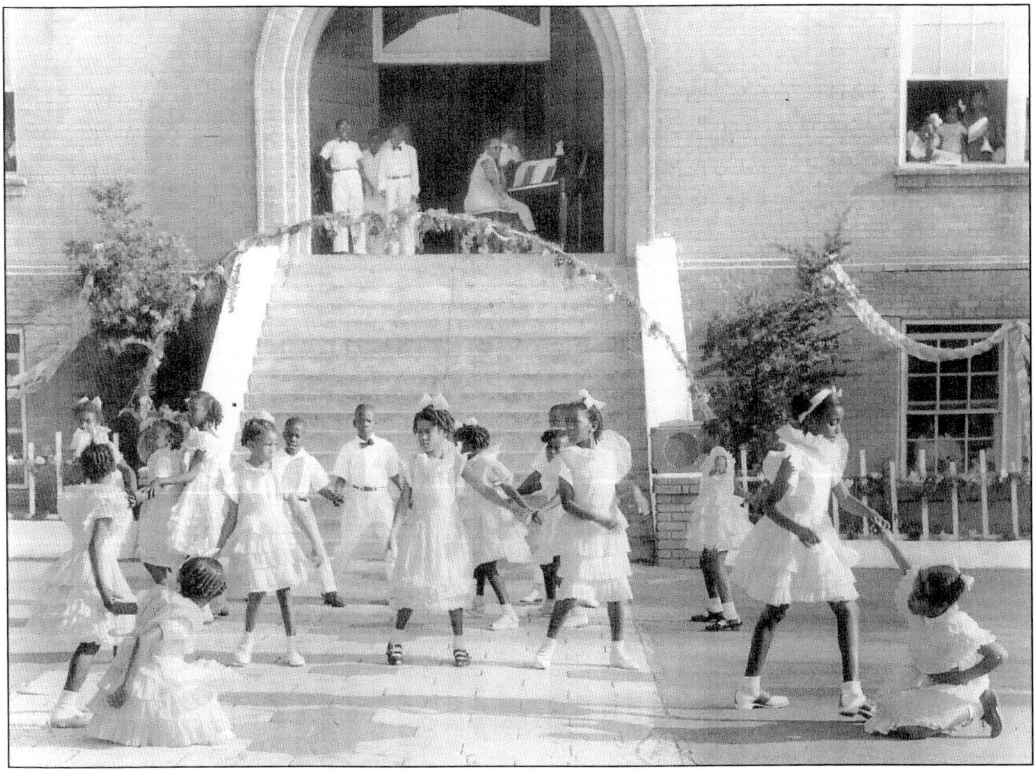

Davis Elementary students celebrate May Day on May 5, 1950.

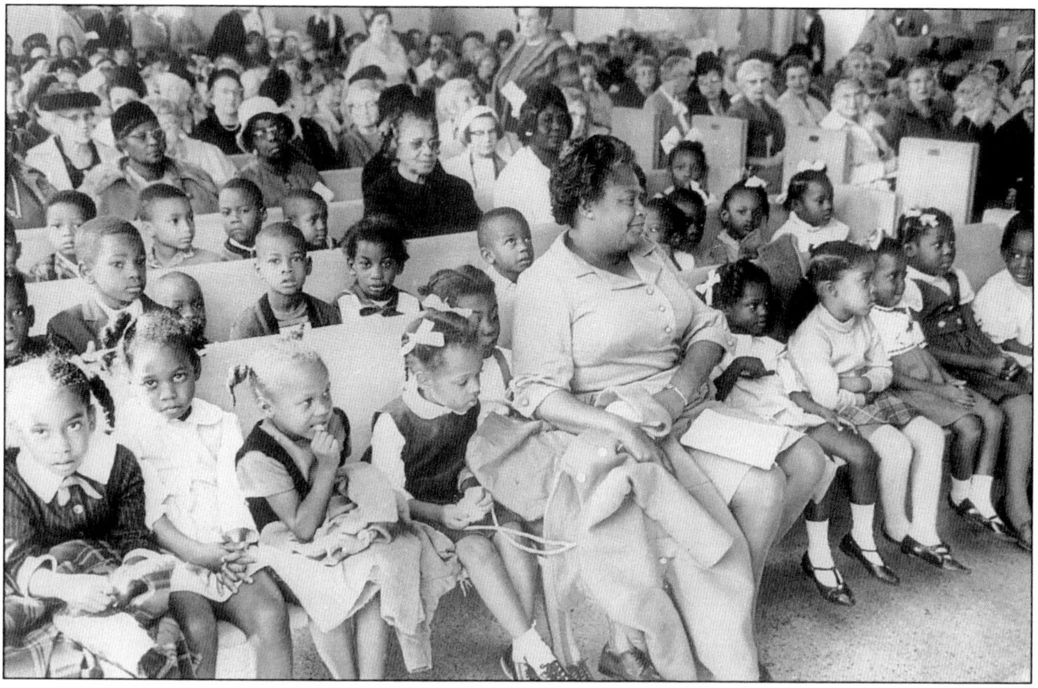

Students from the Happy Workers Day Nursery and Kindergarten sit obediently amongst a group of adults. The school was founded by Mrs. Willie Lee McAdams in 1929. It was the first preschool for African-American children in St. Petersburg.

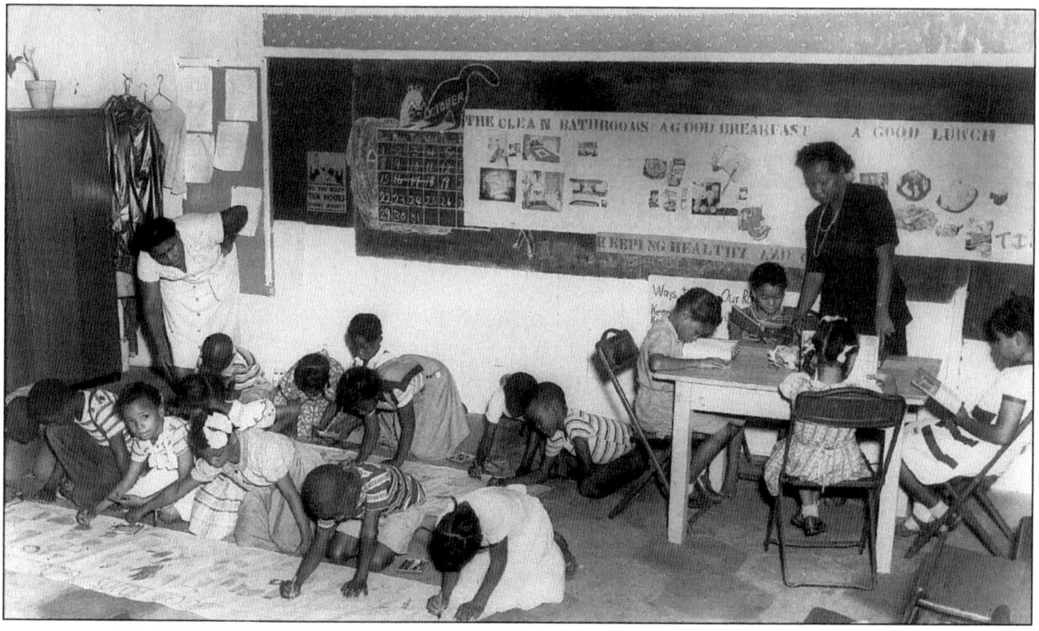

Students in a second grade class at Davis Elementary are shown here. The students at the reading table are being supervised by Mrs. E. Jackson, and the students drawing and coloring are being supervised by Mrs. I. Beasley.

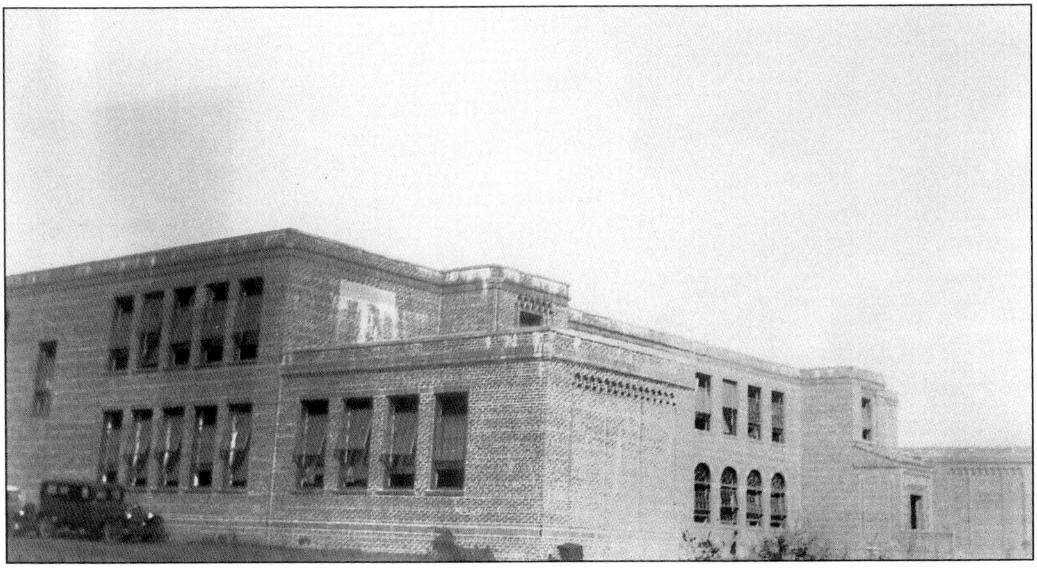

Gibbs Senior High School is pictured in 1935. The school was named after Jonathan C. Gibbs, an African American who was secretary of state for Florida in 1868 during Reconstruction. In 1873, he was appointed State Superintendent for Public Instruction. He died mysteriously only a year and a half into his term.

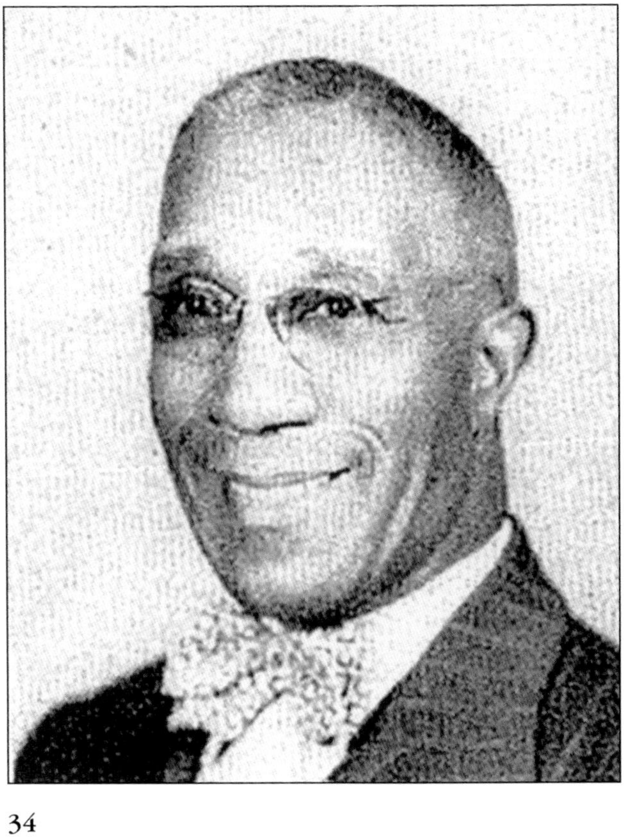

Mr. Lewis Dominis was an educator, an artist, and the first football coach of the Gibbs High School Gladiators.

Mrs. Mary A. Polk taught at Gibbs Senior High School. She was also married to a former principal of the school, Andrew Polk.

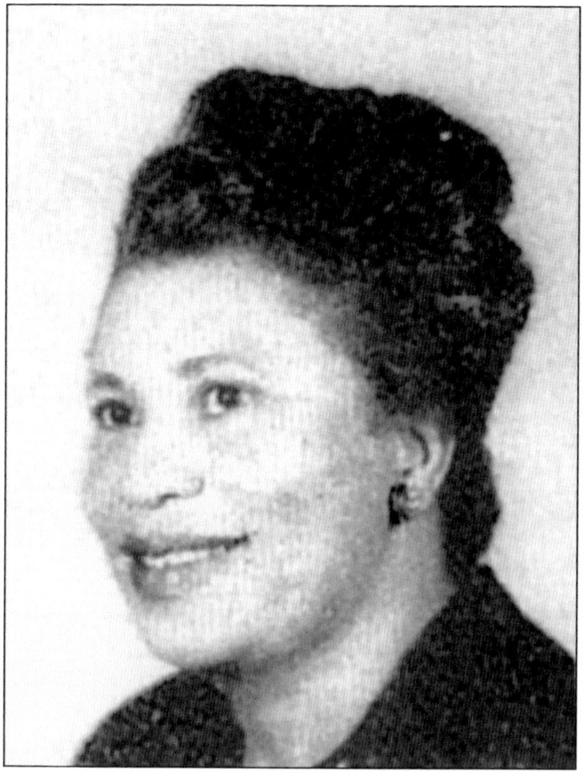

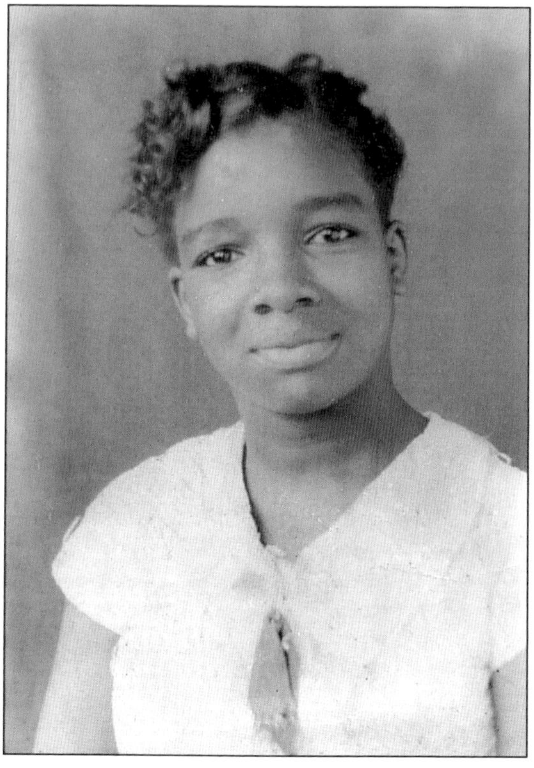

Vermell Johnson was a seventh grade student at Gibbs High School. This picture was taken in the mid-1930s.

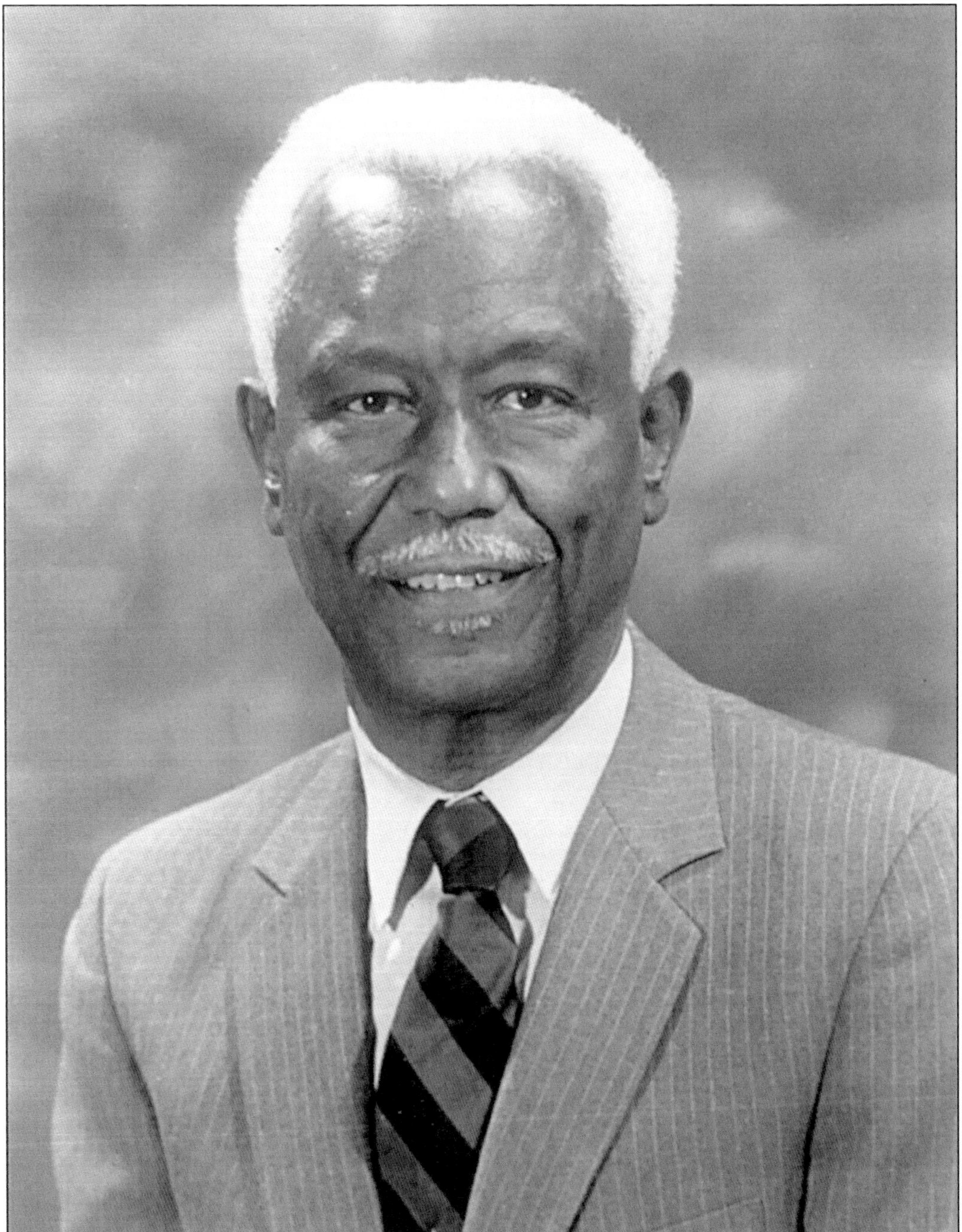

Emanuel Stewart was principal of Gibbs High School from 1958 to 1969. During his administration, Gibbs received its accreditation and became a member of the Southern Association of Colleges and Schools. Aside from his administrative duties, he found time to participate in various civic and social affairs. Some of his affiliations include Alpha Phi Alpha fraternity, Phi Delta Kappa fraternity, the Ambassadors Club, and church, where he serves as deacon. In 1987, Stewart was named St. Petersburg's first African-American "Mr. Sun."

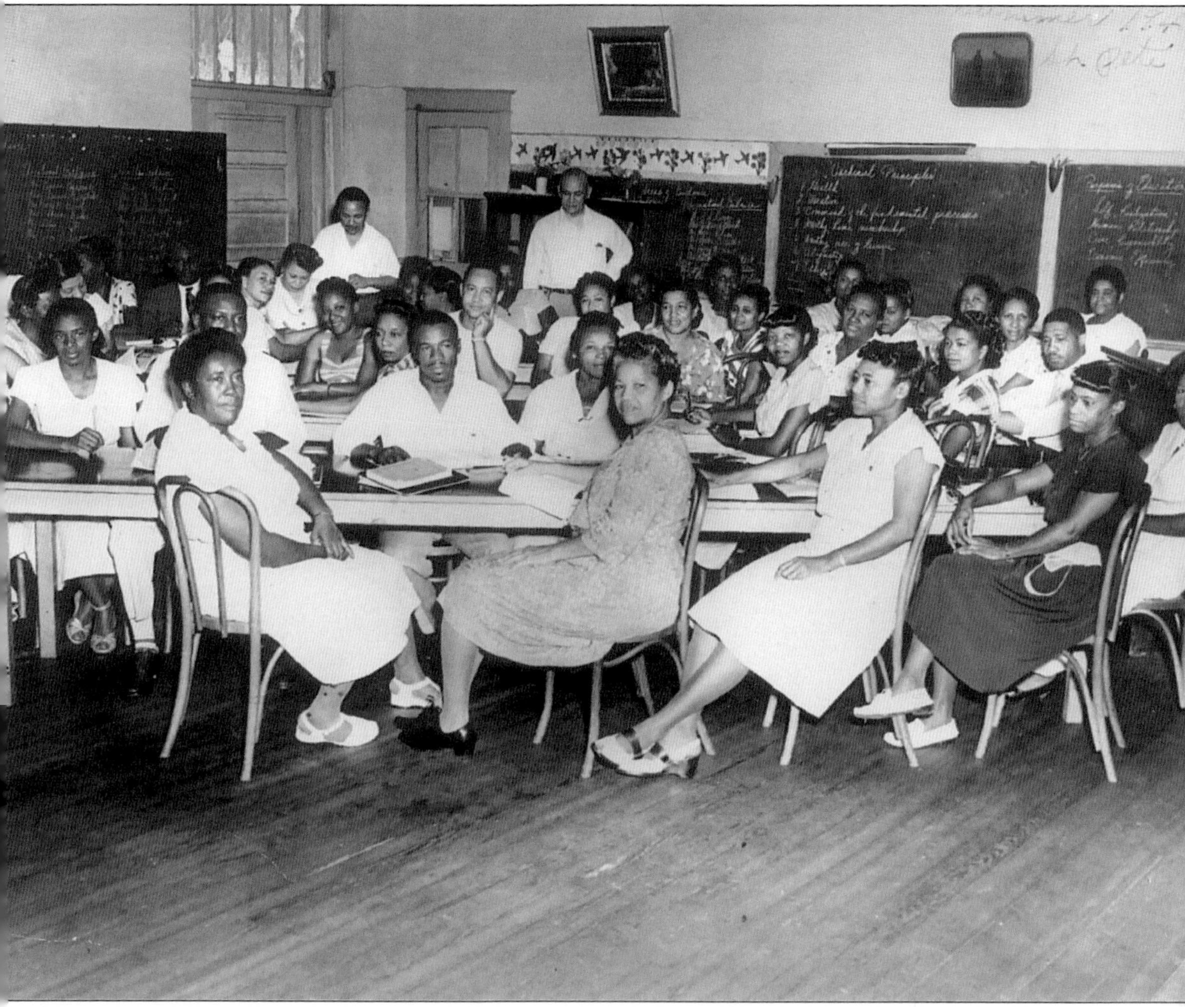

This workshop for Pinellas County African-American teachers includes some from St. Petersburg as well as other areas of Pinellas County. It occurred during the summer of 1949 at Davis Elementary School. The workshop was facilitated by Richard Moore, who is standing in the rear at the right. Dr. Moore later became president of Bethune-Cookman College in Daytona Beach.

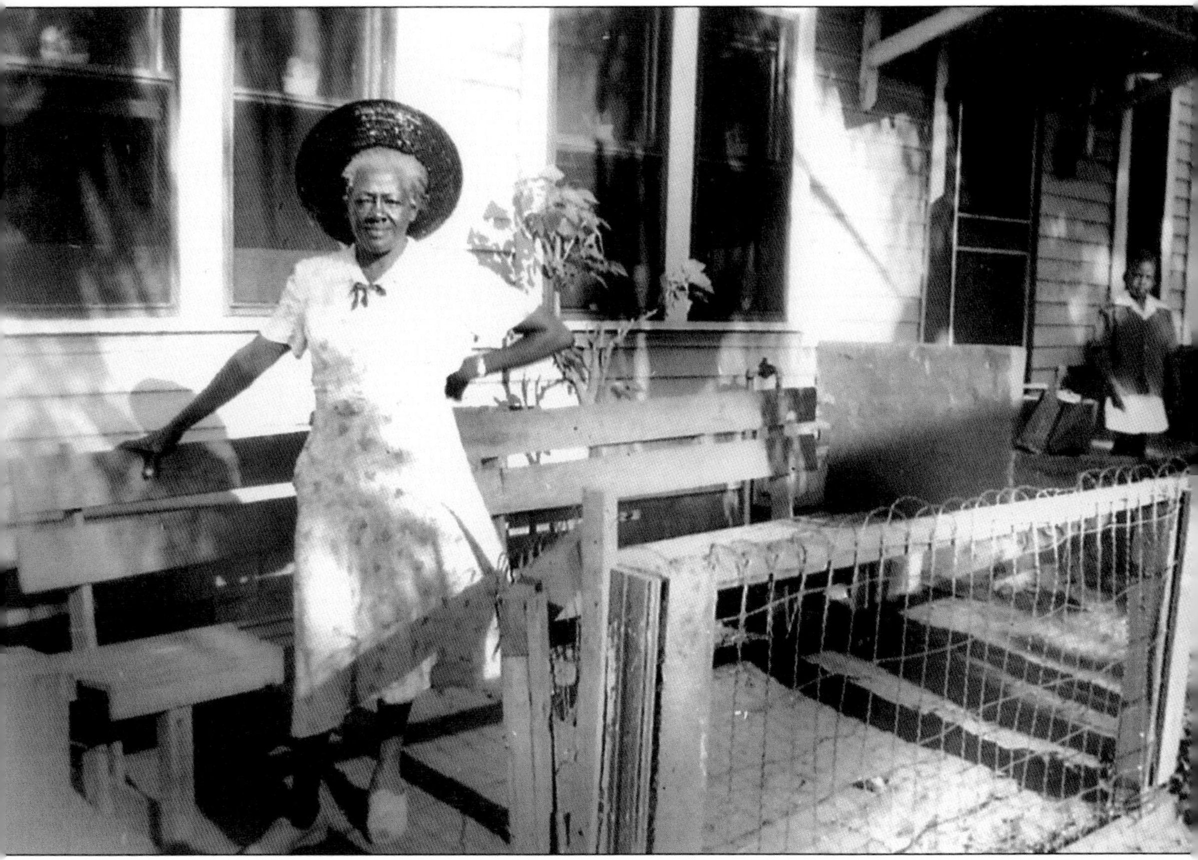

Pictured above is the McCray Foundational School, which was located at 12th Street South between Fifth and Dixie Avenues. The school opened in 1927 and was operated by Rev. Grant H. McCray Sr. and his wife, Arline. Standing to the left is one of the teachers, Miss Braboy. The student in the background is Wayne Johnson. The motto of the school was "Where little lives are properly molded." The cost of tuition and meals when the school opened was 25 cents per week.

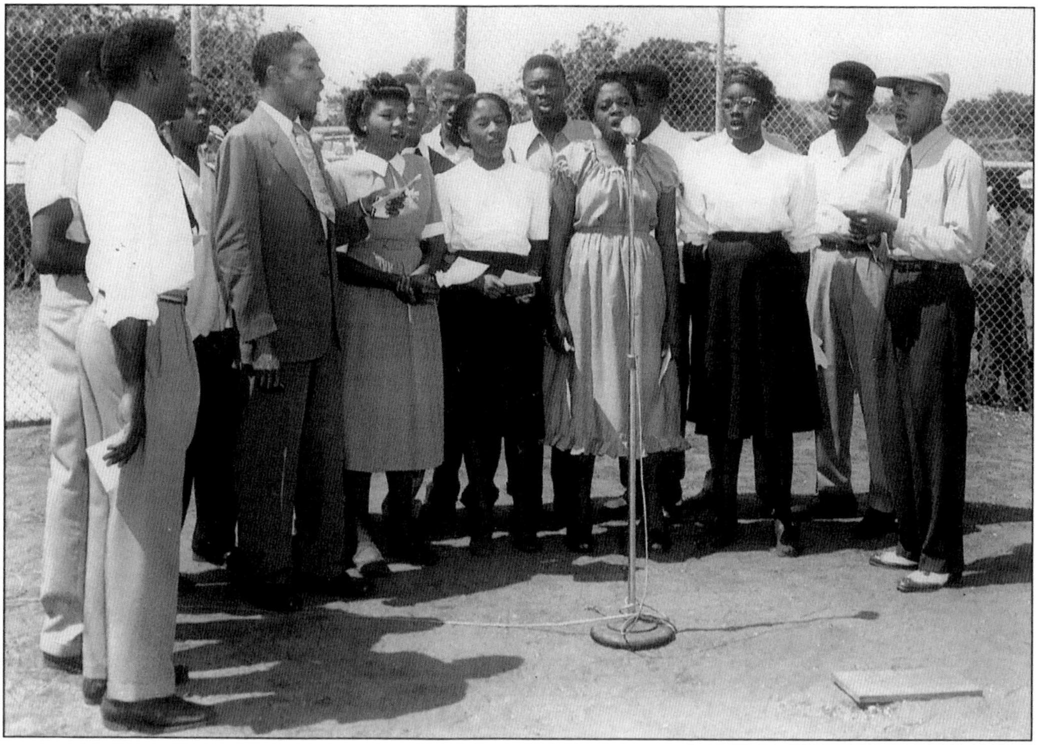

Singing in harmony is the Gibbs High School Glee Club.

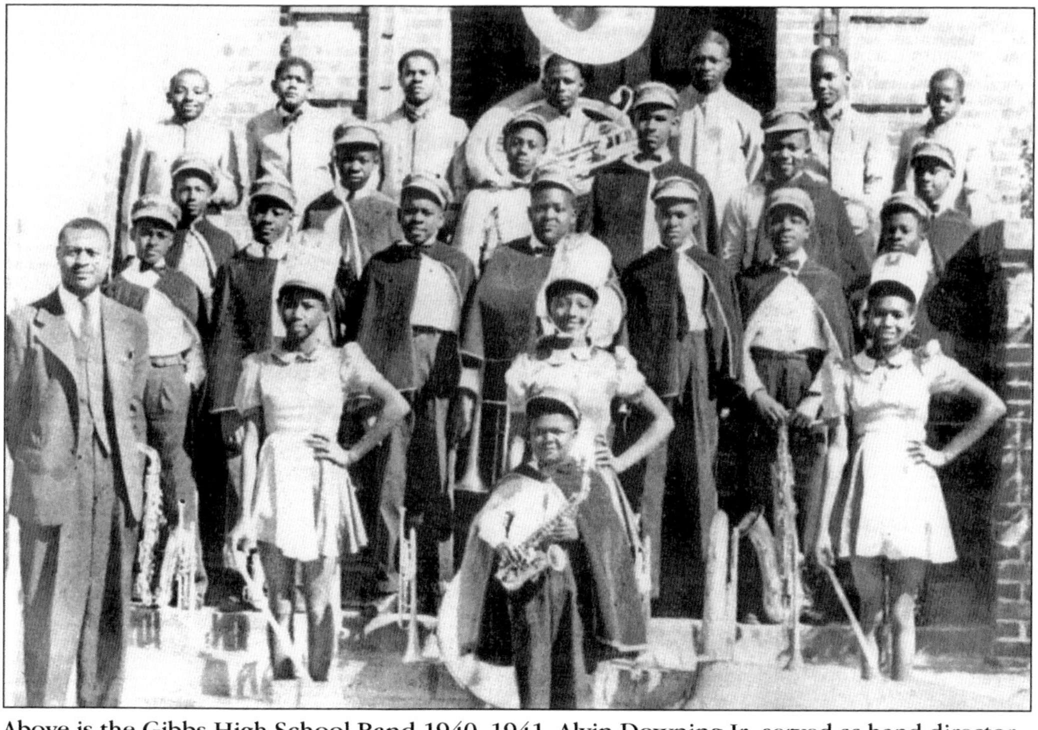

Above is the Gibbs High School Band 1940–1941. Alvin Downing Jr. served as band director.

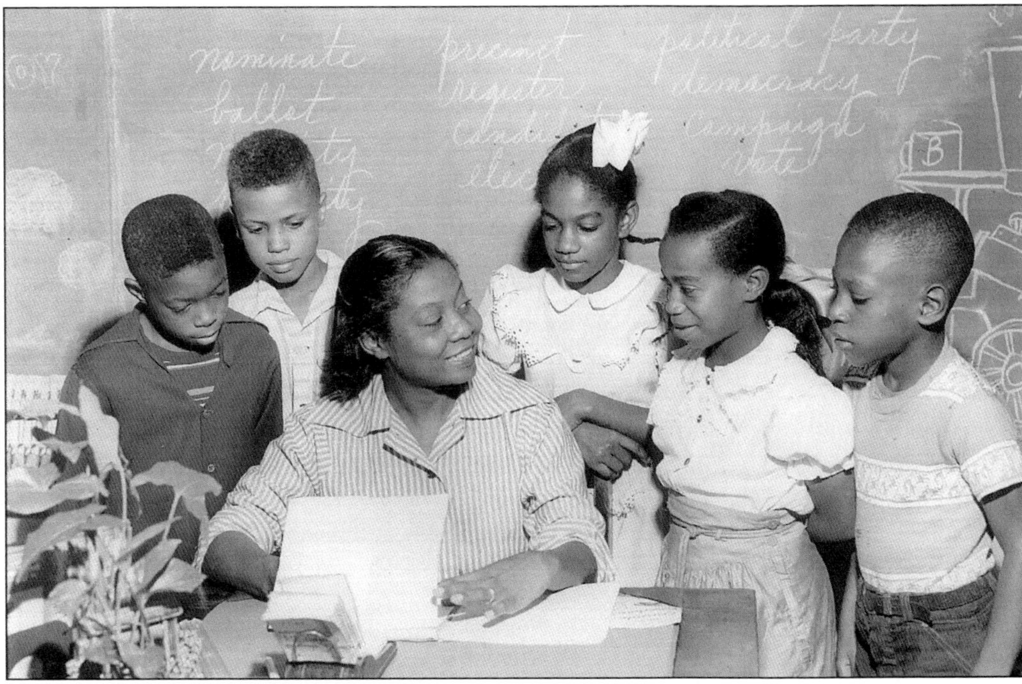

Jordon Elementary teacher Mrs. Mary R. Brown is pictured with students, from left to right, Willie James Williams, Joseph Albury III, Mary Louise Williams, Lillian Johnson. and Carl Dixon in this 1951 photograph.

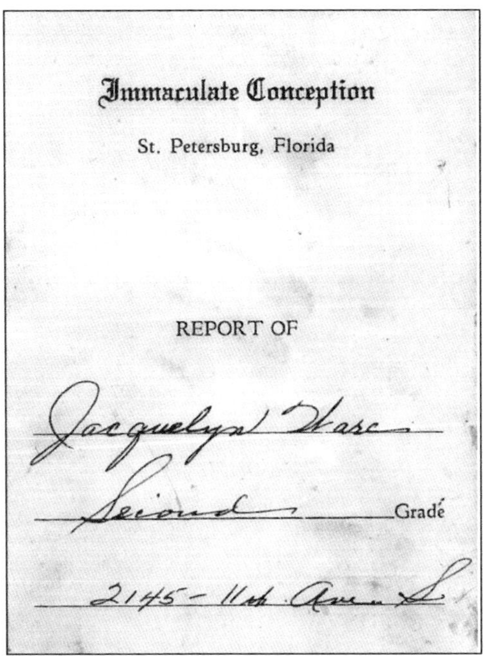

Immaculate Conception

St. Petersburg, Florida

REPORT OF

Jacquelyn Ware

Second Grade

2145 - 11th Ave. S.

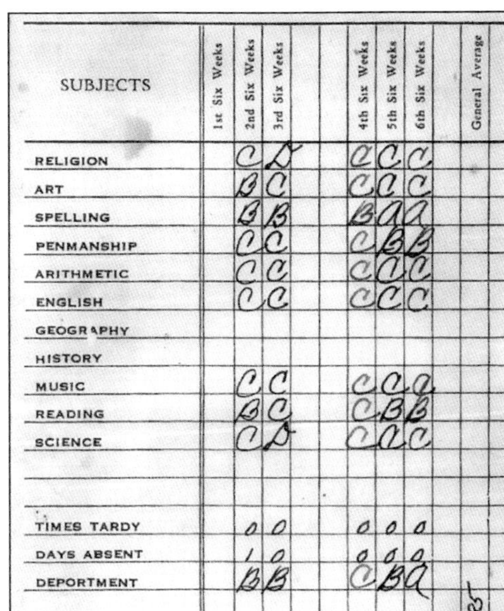

SUBJECTS	1st Six Weeks	2nd Six Weeks	3rd Six Weeks	4th Six Weeks	5th Six Weeks	6th Six Weeks	General Average
RELIGION		C	D	C	C	C	
ART		B	C	C	C	C	
SPELLING		B	B	B	A	A	
PENMANSHIP		C	C	C	B	B	
ARITHMETIC		C	C	C	C	C	
ENGLISH		C	C	C	C	C	
GEOGRAPHY							
HISTORY							
MUSIC		C	C	C	C	C	
READING		B	C	C	B	B	
SCIENCE		C	D	C	C	C	
TIMES TARDY		0	0	0	0	0	
DAYS ABSENT		1	0	0	0	0	
DEPORTMENT		B	B	C	B	A	25

REMARKS:

This is a record card issued to Jacqueline Ware, a second grade student at Immaculate Conception School. The school, which was operated by the Catholic Church, was located next to 16th Street Middle School.

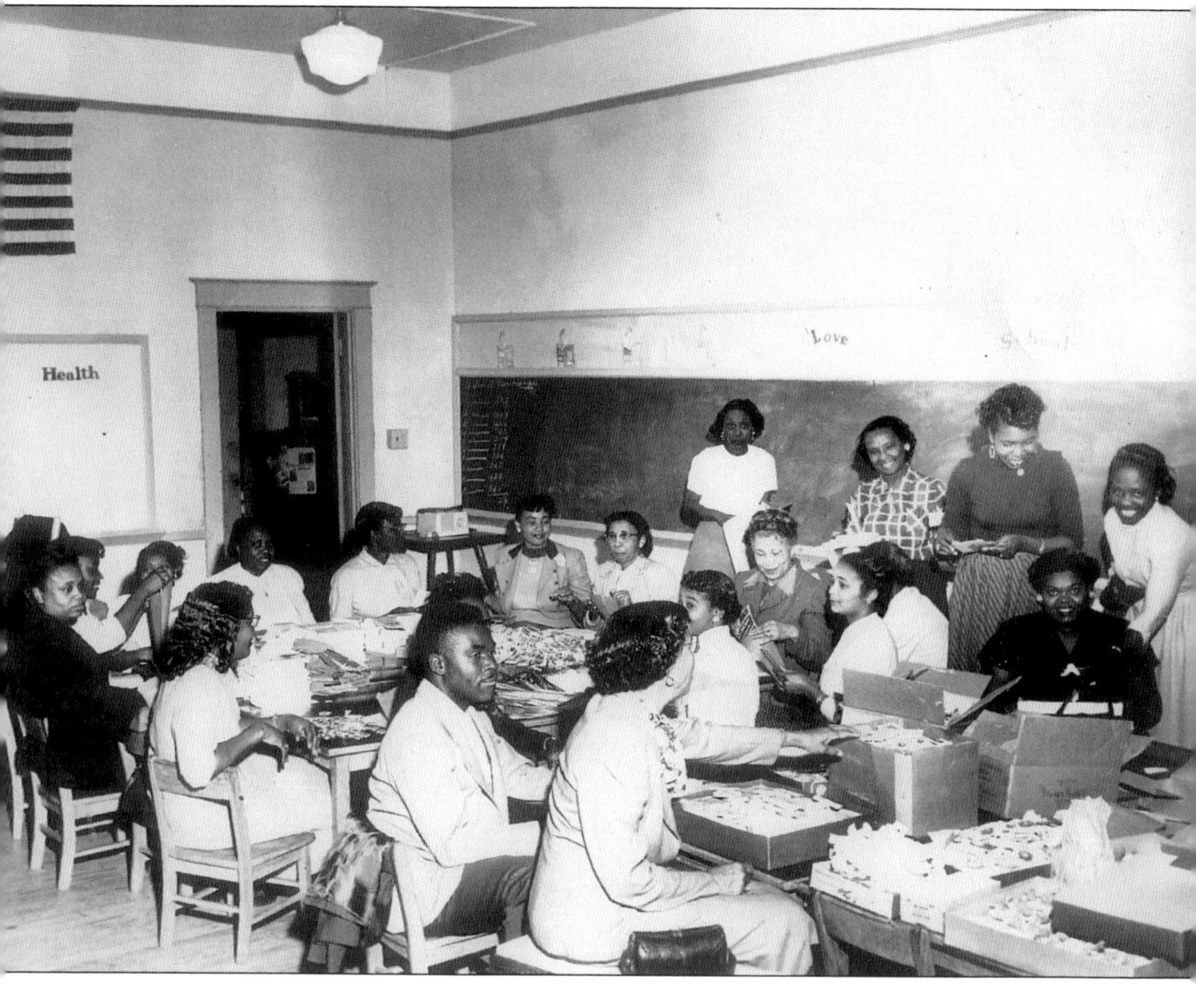

A Florida State Teachers Association Meeting is seen here held at Davis Elementary School.

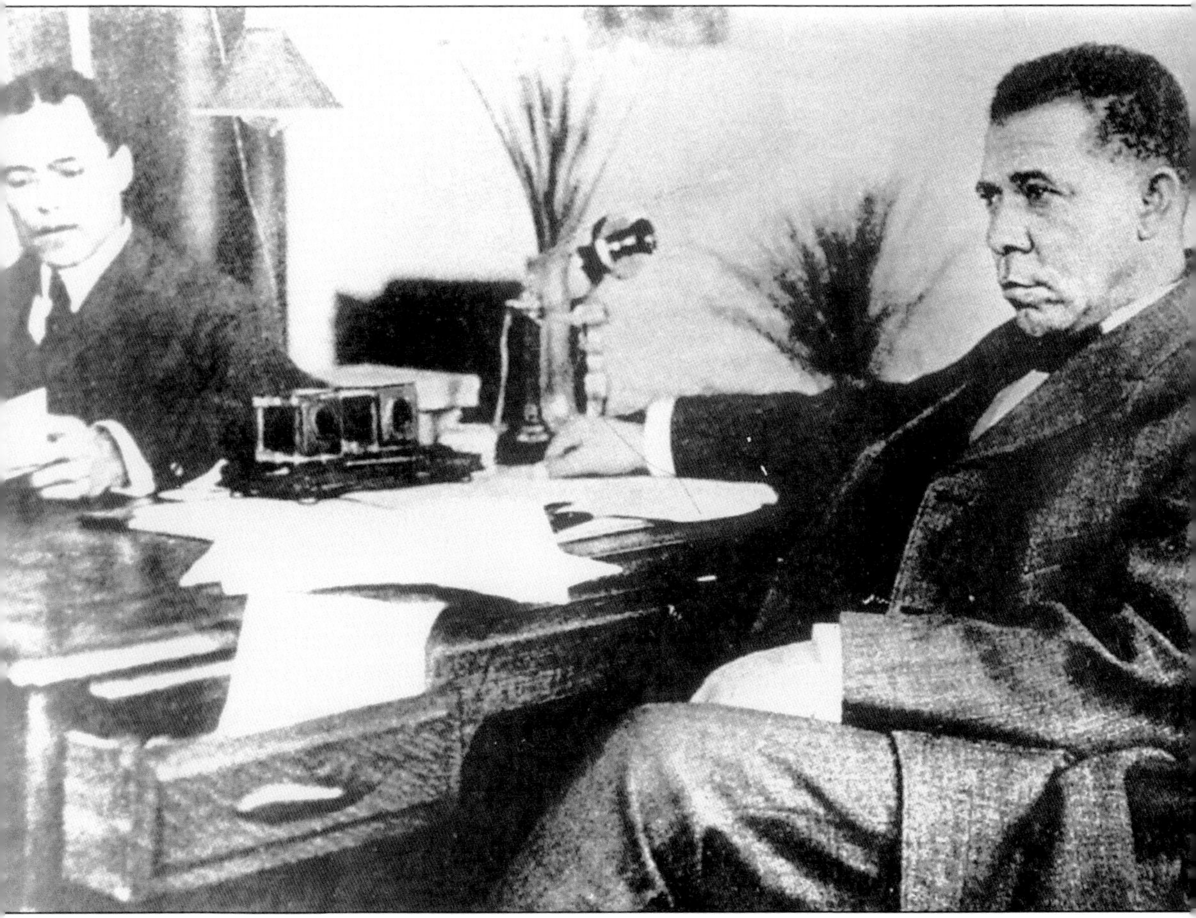

Booker T. Washington, famed African-American educator and principal of the Tuskegee Normal and Industrial Institute in Tuskegee, Alabama, is pictured on the right in this photograph. Washington corresponded with Pinellas County School Superintendent Dixie M. Hollins on several occasions.

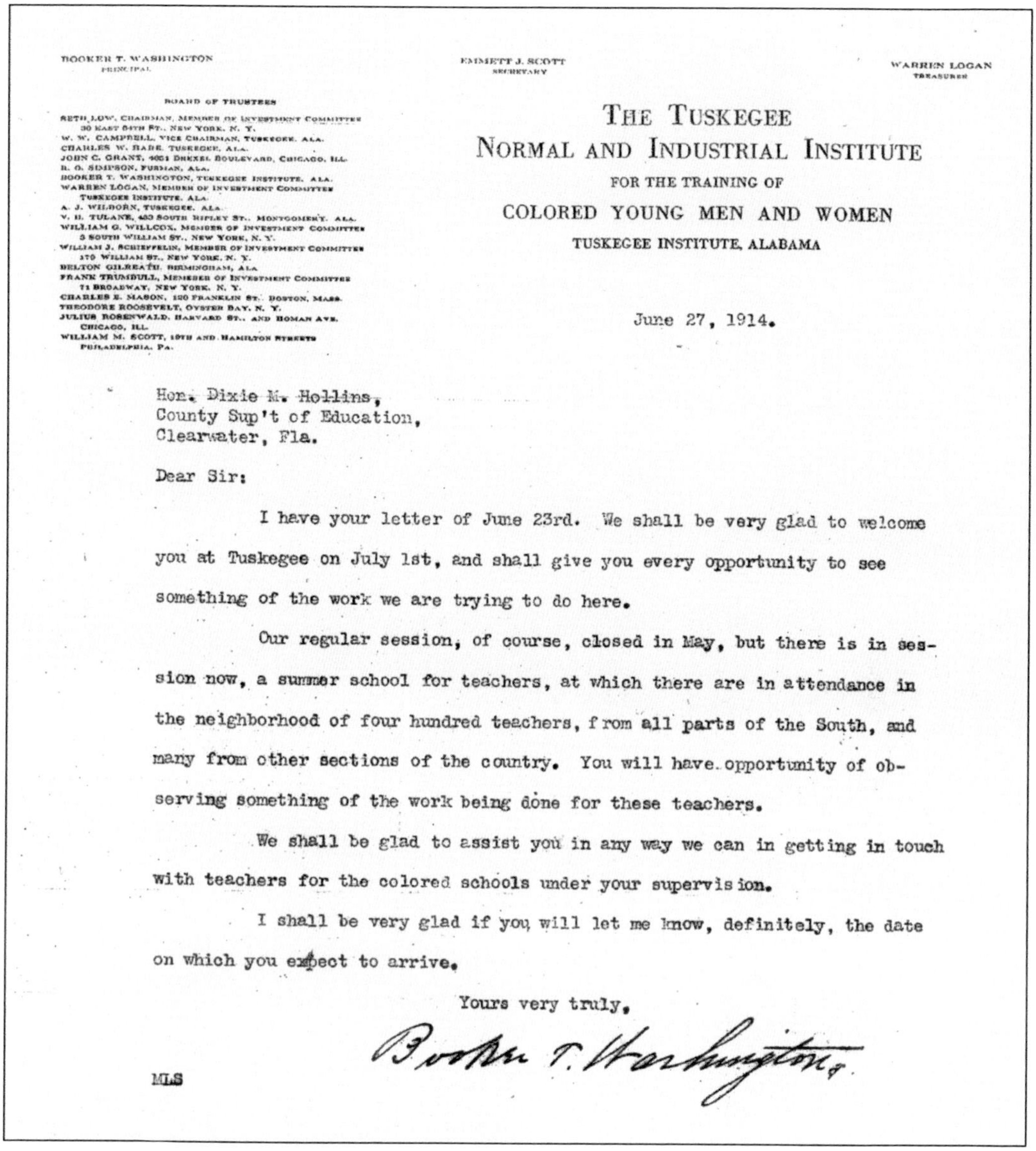

BOOKER T. WASHINGTON
PRINCIPAL

EMMETT J. SCOTT
SECRETARY

WARREN LOGAN
TREASURER

THE TUSKEGEE
NORMAL AND INDUSTRIAL INSTITUTE
FOR THE TRAINING OF
COLORED YOUNG MEN AND WOMEN
TUSKEGEE INSTITUTE, ALABAMA

June 27, 1914.

Hon. Dixie M. Hollins,
County Sup't of Education,
Clearwater, Fla.

Dear Sir:

I have your letter of June 23rd. We shall be very glad to welcome you at Tuskegee on July 1st, and shall give you every opportunity to see something of the work we are trying to do here.

Our regular session, of course, closed in May, but there is in session now, a summer school for teachers, at which there are in attendance in the neighborhood of four hundred teachers, from all parts of the South, and many from other sections of the country. You will have opportunity of observing something of the work being done for these teachers.

We shall be glad to assist you in any way we can in getting in touch with teachers for the colored schools under your supervision.

I shall be very glad if you will let me know, definitely, the date on which you expect to arrive.

Yours very truly,

Booker T. Washington

MLS

In this letter, Booker T. Washington discusses the recruitment of African-American teachers for Pinellas County schools.

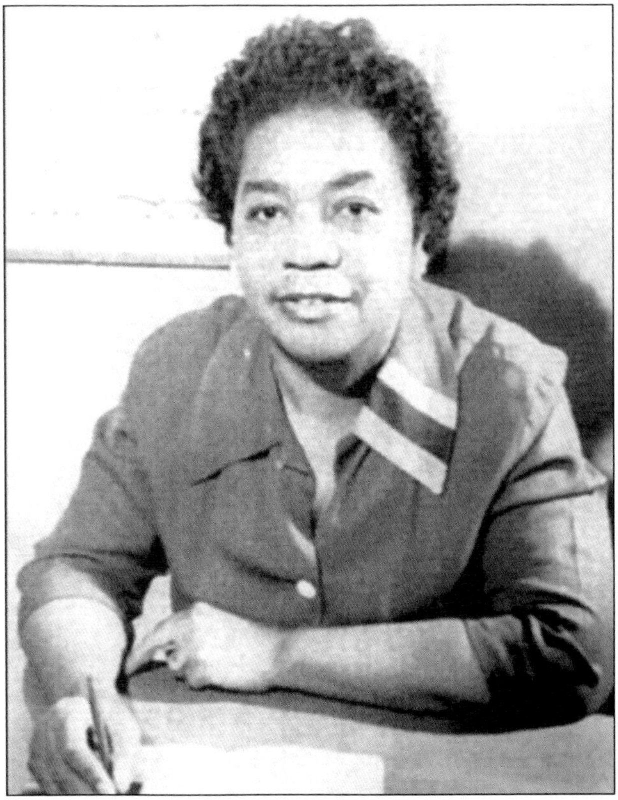

Mrs. Olive B. McLin was a teacher at Gibbs High School who taught her students more than the "three Rs." She promoted the fine arts and counseled her students about standards for dress, grooming, and manners. "O.B.," as she was affectionately called, received her bachelor of arts degree from Florida A&M University and her master's degree from Columbia University.

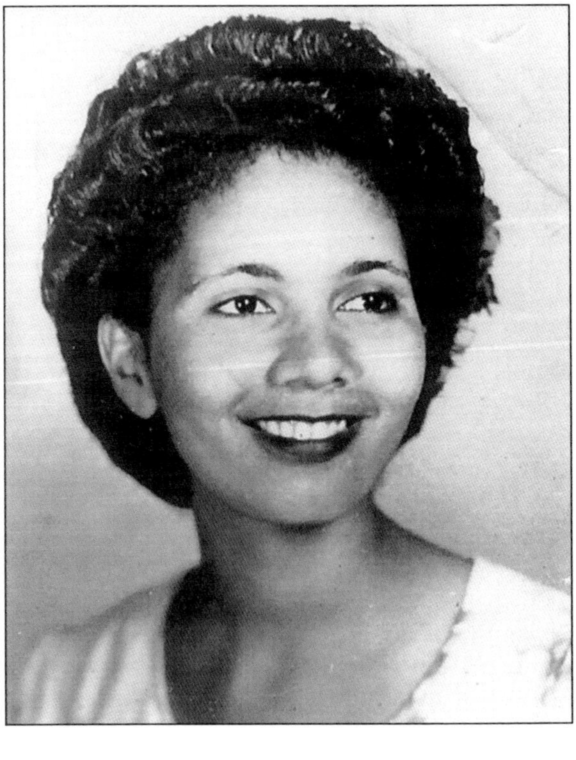

Pictured here is Anna Walker, a home economics teacher at Gibbs High School. Mrs. Walker was the daughter of Andrew Polk, a former principal of Gibbs High School and a professor at Florida A&M University.

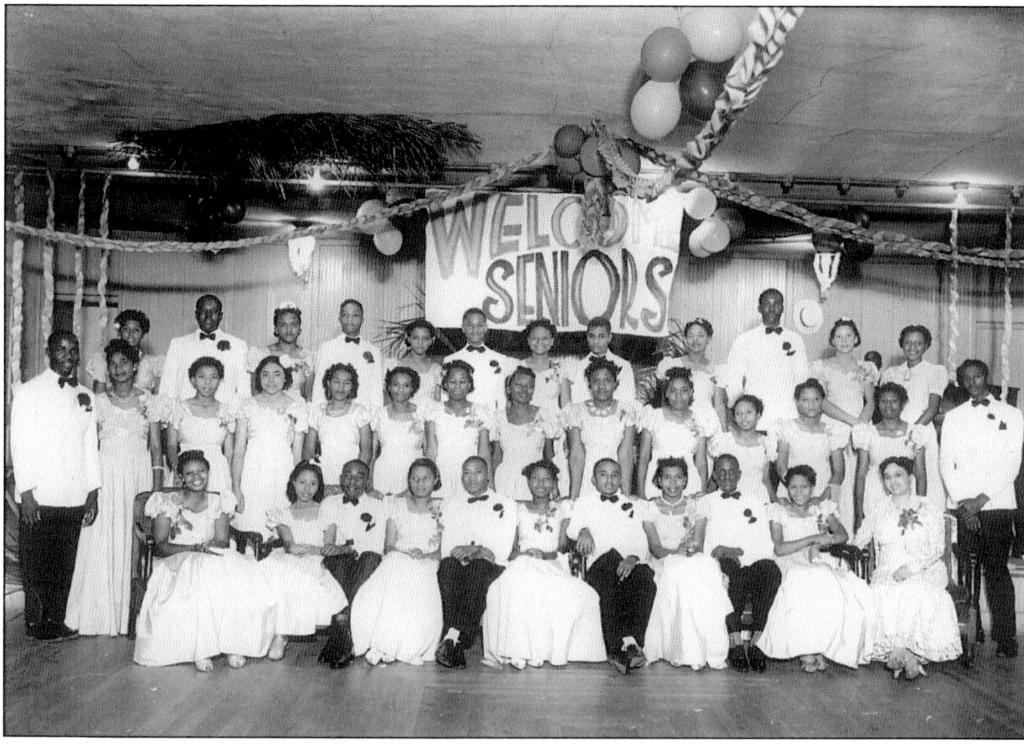

The Gibbs High School prom was held at the Manhattan Casino Club.

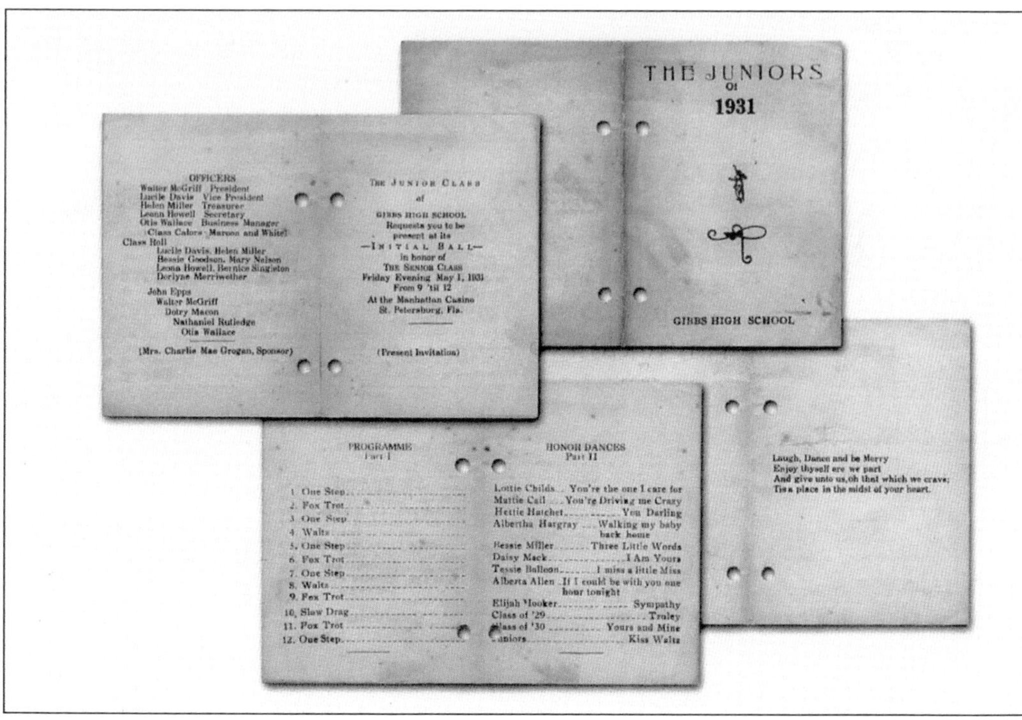

THE JUNIORS
OF
1931

GIBBS HIGH SCHOOL

OFFICERS
Walter McGriff President
Lucile Davis Vice President
Helen Miller Treasurer
Leona Howell Secretary
Otis Wallace Business Manager
(Class Colors Maroon and White)
Class Roll
Lucile Davis, Helen Miller
Bessie Goodson, Mary Nelson
Leona Howell, Bernice Singleton
Derlyne Merriwether

John Epps
Walter McGriff
Dotry Macon
Nathaniel Rutledge
Otis Wallace

(Mrs. Charlie Mae Grogan, Sponsor)

THE JUNIOR CLASS
of
GIBBS HIGH SCHOOL
Requests you to be
present at its
—INITIAL BALL—
in honor of
THE SENIOR CLASS
Friday Evening May 1, 1931
From 9 'til 12
At the Manhattan Casino
St. Petersburg, Fla.

(Present Invitation)

PROGRAMME
Part I

1. One Step........................
2. Fox Trot........................
3. One Step........................
4. Waltz........................
5. One Step........................
6. Fox Trot........................
7. One Step........................
8. Waltz........................
9. Fox Trot........................
10. Slow Drag........................
11. Fox Trot........................
12. One Step........................

HONOR DANCES
Part II

Lottie Childs... You're the one I care for
Mattie Call ... You're Driving me Crazy
Hettie Hatchet.............. You Darling
Albertha Hargray ... Walking my baby back home
Bessie Miller........ Three Little Words
Daisy Mack.................. I Am Yours
Tessie Balloon.......... I miss a little Miss
Alberta Allen . If I could be with you one hour tonight
Elijah Hooker.............. Sympathy
Class of '29.................. Truley
Class of '30 .... Yours and Mine
Seniors.................... Kiss Waltz

Laugh, Dance and be Merry
Enjoy thyself ere we part
And give unto us, oh that which we crave;
Tis a place in the midst of your heart.

This is a copy of a prom invitation for the senior class of 1931 at Gibbs High School.

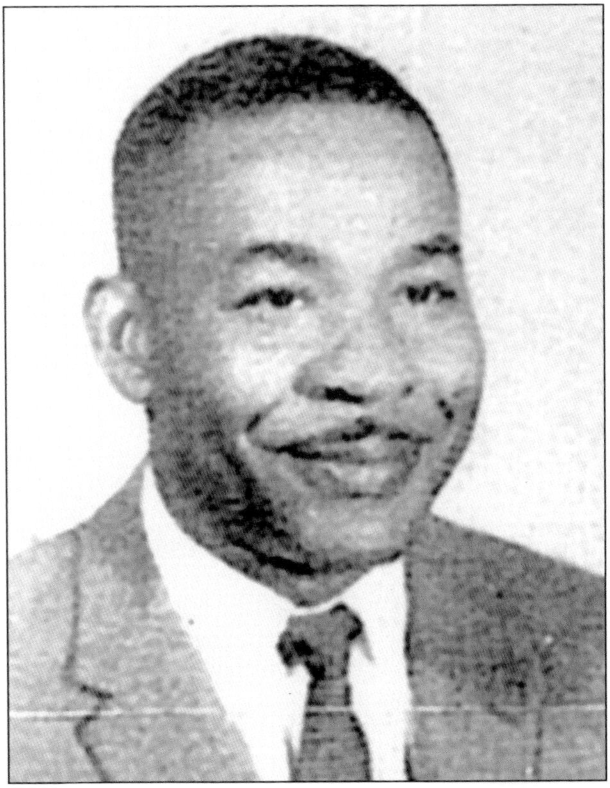

Pictured at left is Frank Pierce, an instructor at Gibbs Junior College.

Pictured below is Dr. Johnny Ruth Clarke, an administrator at Gibbs Junior College.

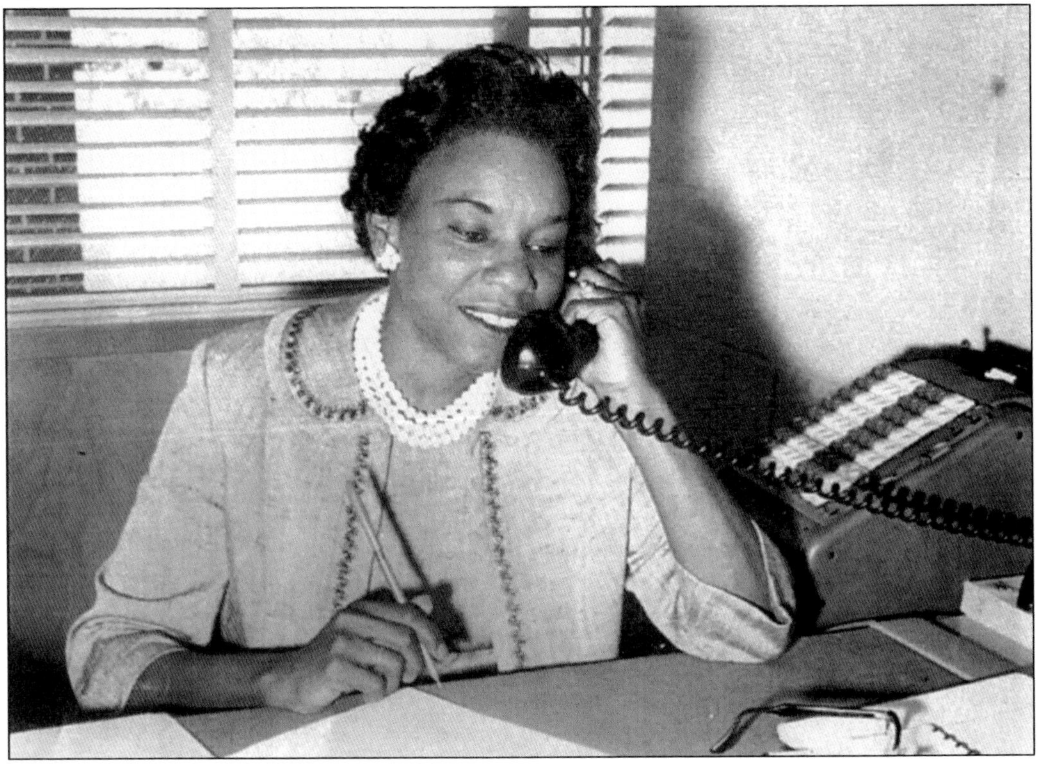

In this 1961 Al Downing taught music and humanities, and he led the band at Gibbs Junior College.

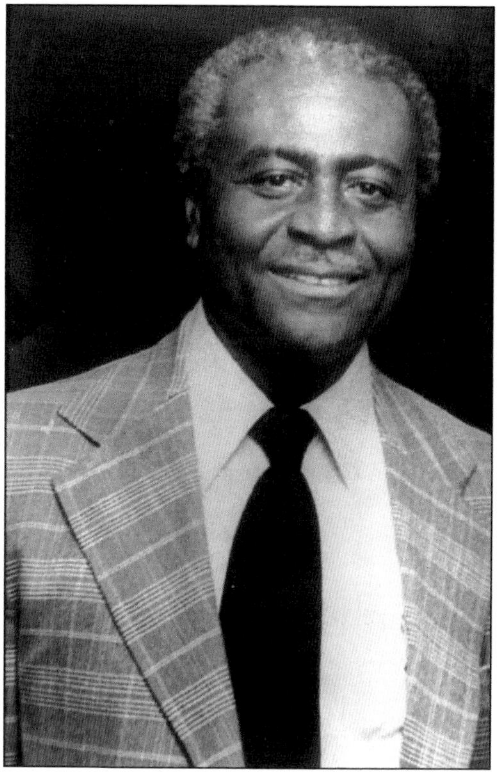

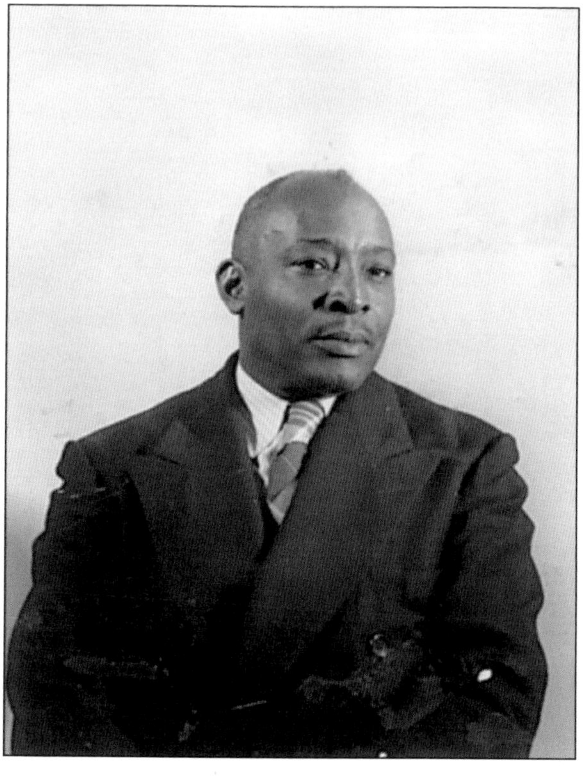

Milton Rooks Sr. was director of community services and an instructor in human growth and development at Gibbs Junior College.

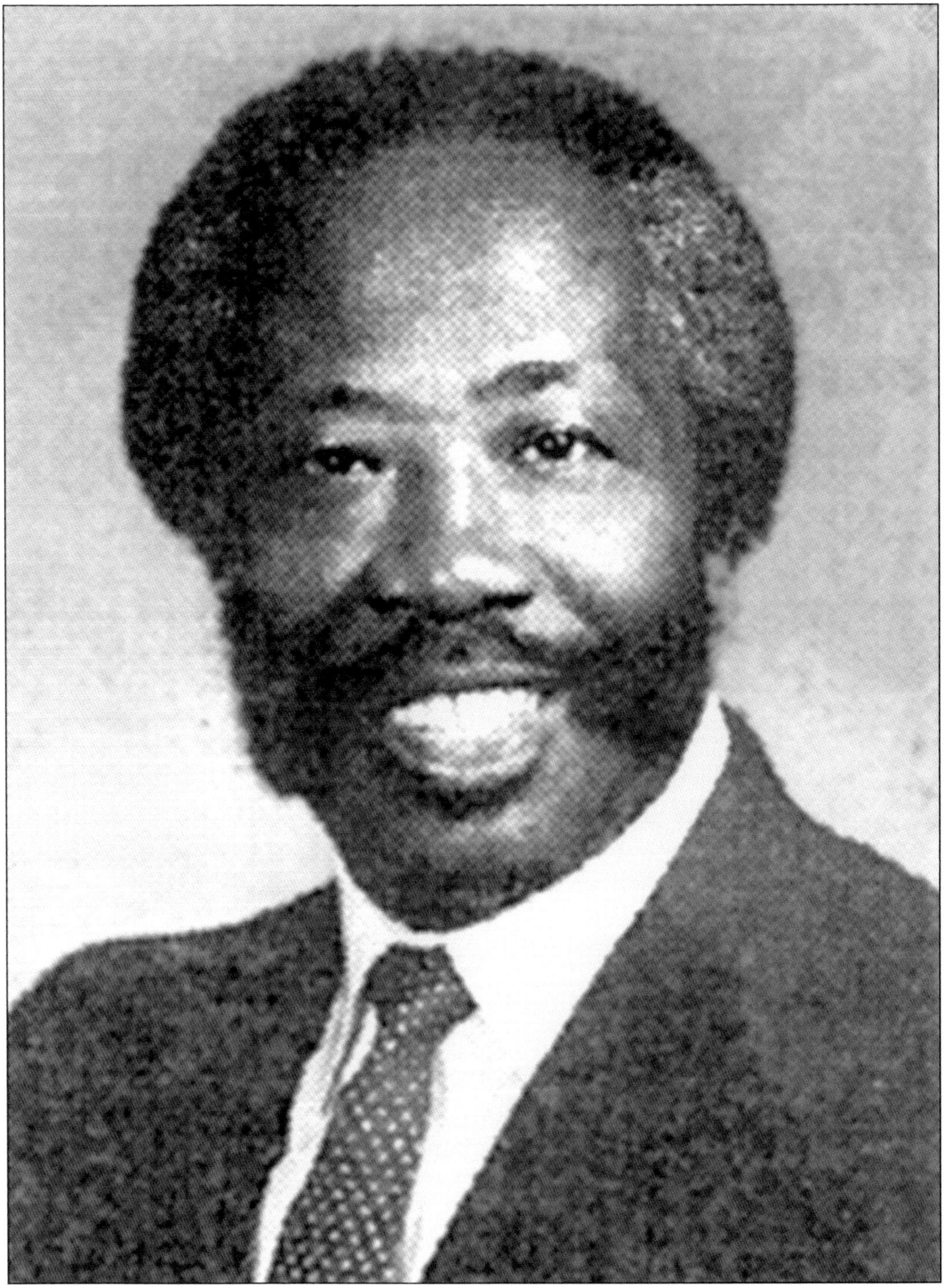

Robert L. Anders served as choral and band director for several schools in Pinellas County. He also is the co-founder of Academy Prep Center for Education and director of the Alumni Singers.

Four

Business and Labor

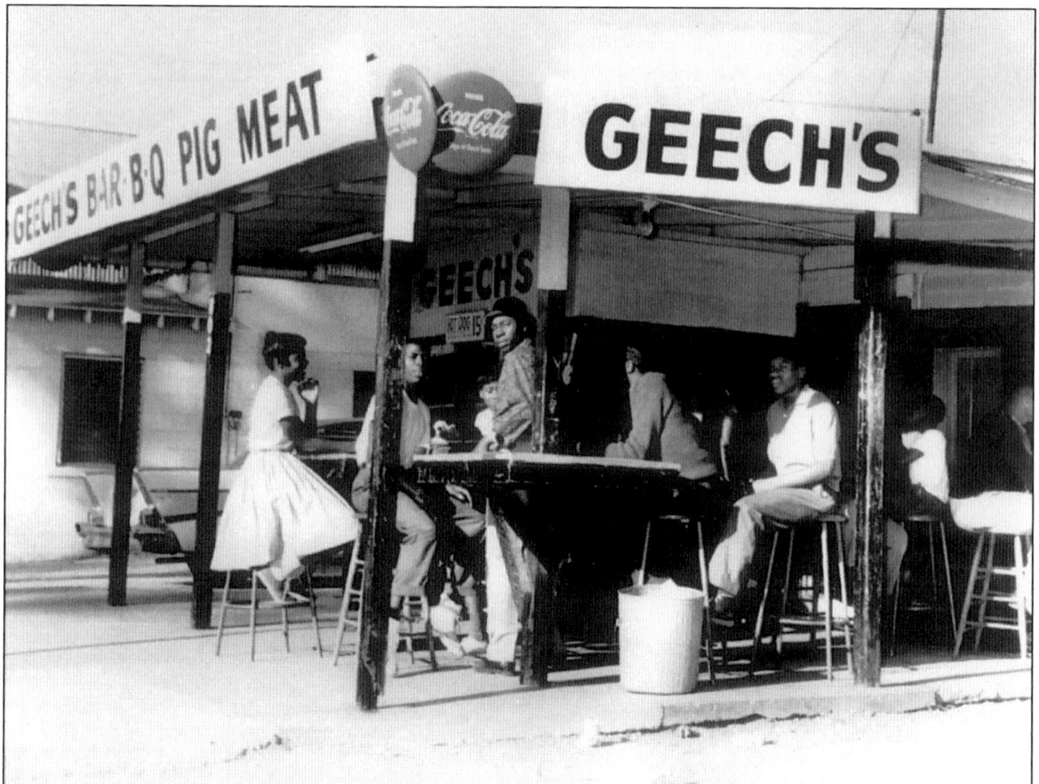

The following were three business districts in the black community of St. Petersburg during the 1930s: 3rd Avenue North between 10th Street North and 11th Street North; 3rd Avenue south between 10th Street North and 11th Street South and 14th Street South; and 22nd Street South between 6th Avenue South and 11th Avenue South. Located in the third business district was Geech's Bar-B-Q Stand, pictured above. This business had a reputation for having the best barbecue in St. Petersburg.

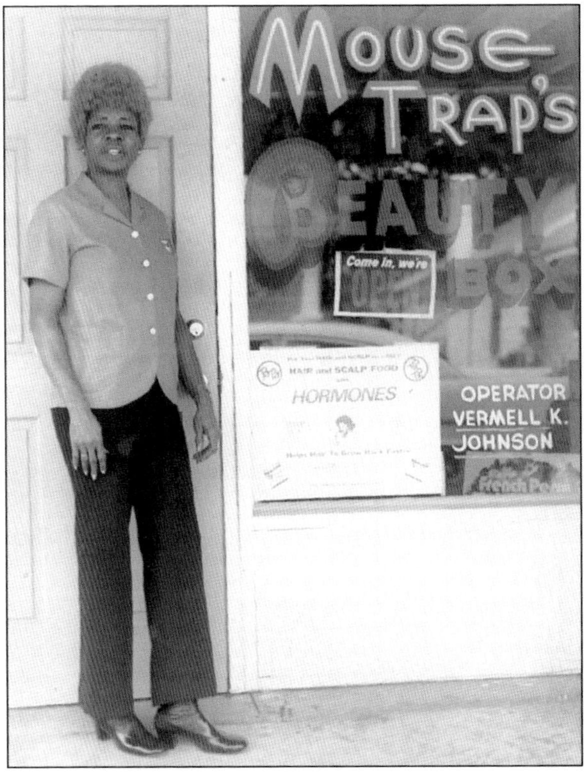

Many of the businesses in the African-American community existed out of necessity. Since many white establishments would not cater to African Americans, businesses like beauty and barber shops, grocery stores, funeral parlors, and restaurants were located in close range of black patrons. Pictured here is Vermell Johnson, standing in front of her beauty shop, Mouse Trap's Beauty Box. This picture was taken in the early 1970s. Johnson also worked at Maas Brothers Department Store.

Members of the Southside Cosmopolitan Beautician Association pose for this photograph taken in the 1970s.

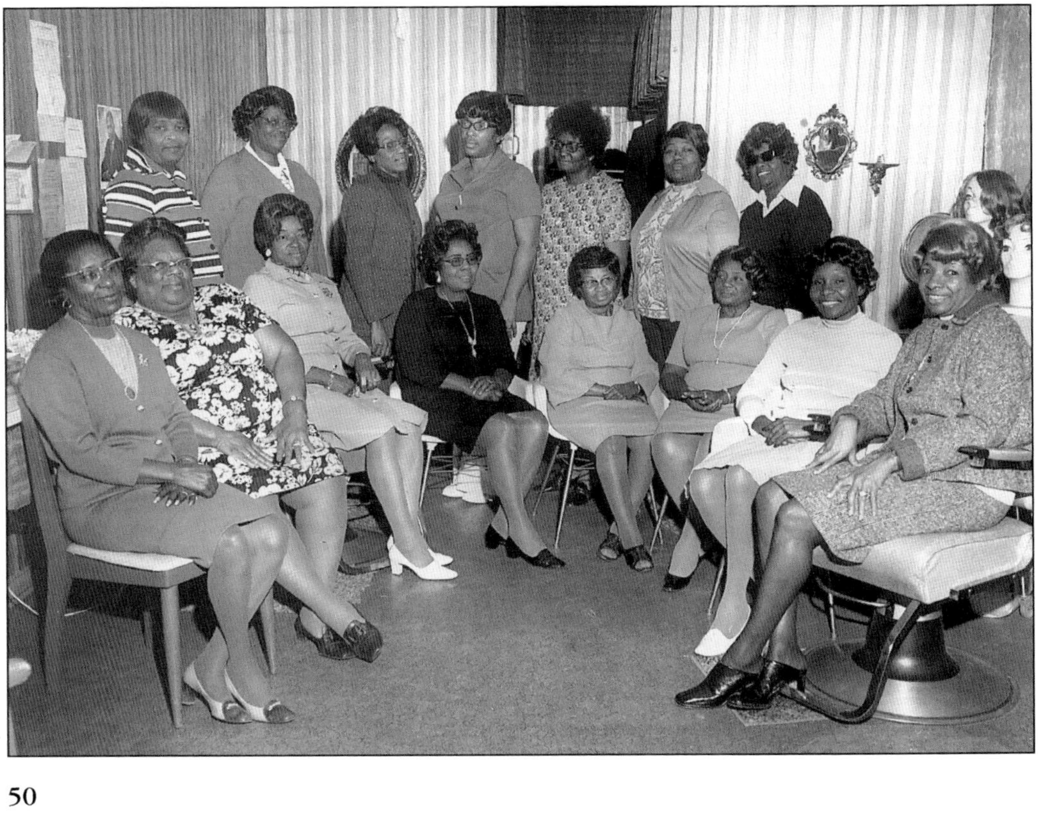

To the right is a picture taken in October 1957 of a cab from the Royal Cab Company.

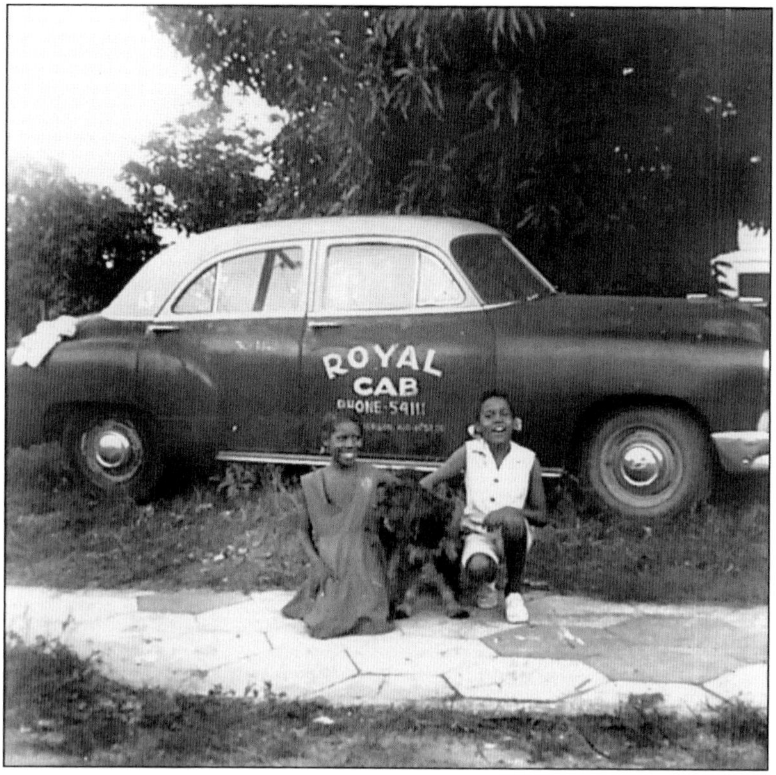

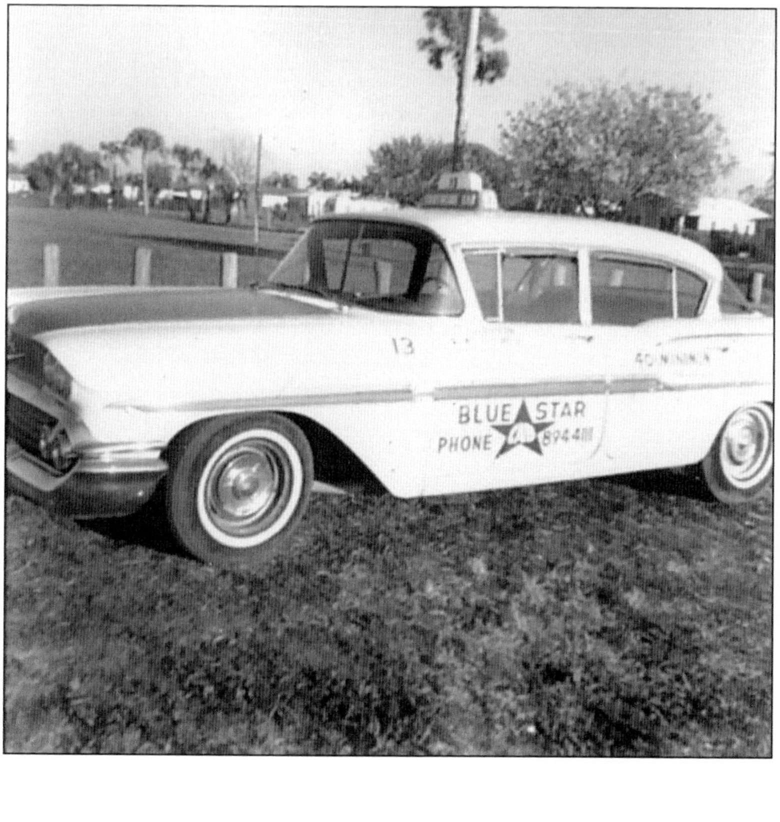

The Royal Cab Company later became the Blue Star Cab Company. Cab #13, pictured at left, was operated by Jesse Henderson. Blue Star Cab was located at 1300 22nd Street South.

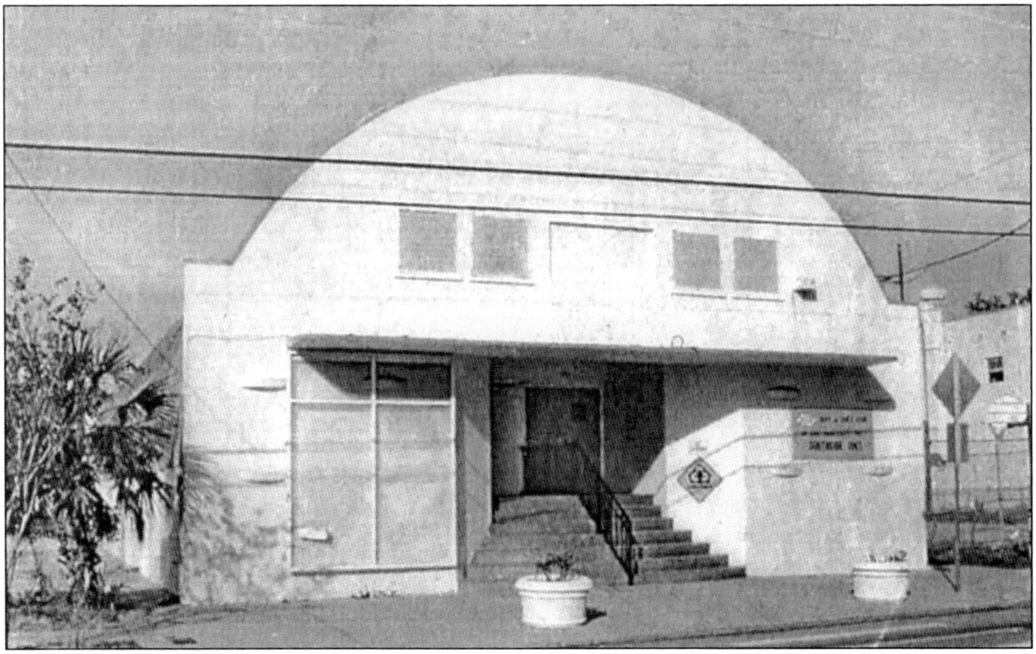

Pictured here is the Royal Theater. It was one of only two theaters in the city that African Americans could attend; the other was the Harlem Theater. The Royal Theater, located on 22nd Street South, was open from 1948 to 1966. The style of the building is Quonset hut, which was used often during World War II to do everything from providing shelter to storing supplies. After the war, the government sold the huts to businesses. The Boys and Girls Club for youth programs currently meets in the building.

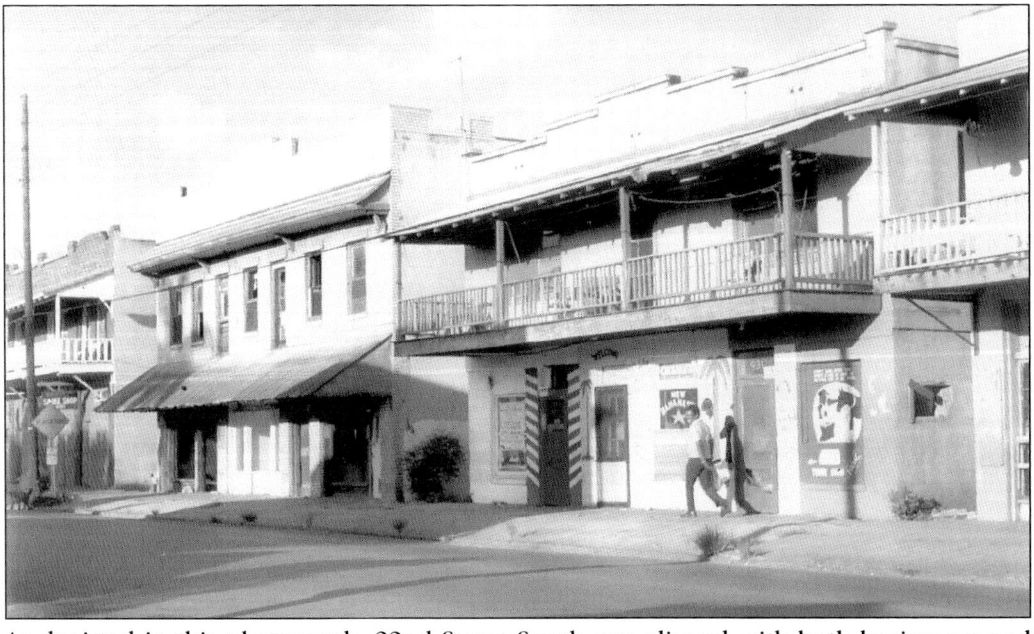

As depicted in this photograph, 22nd Street South was aligned with both businesses and residences. This photograph was taken during the 1960s.

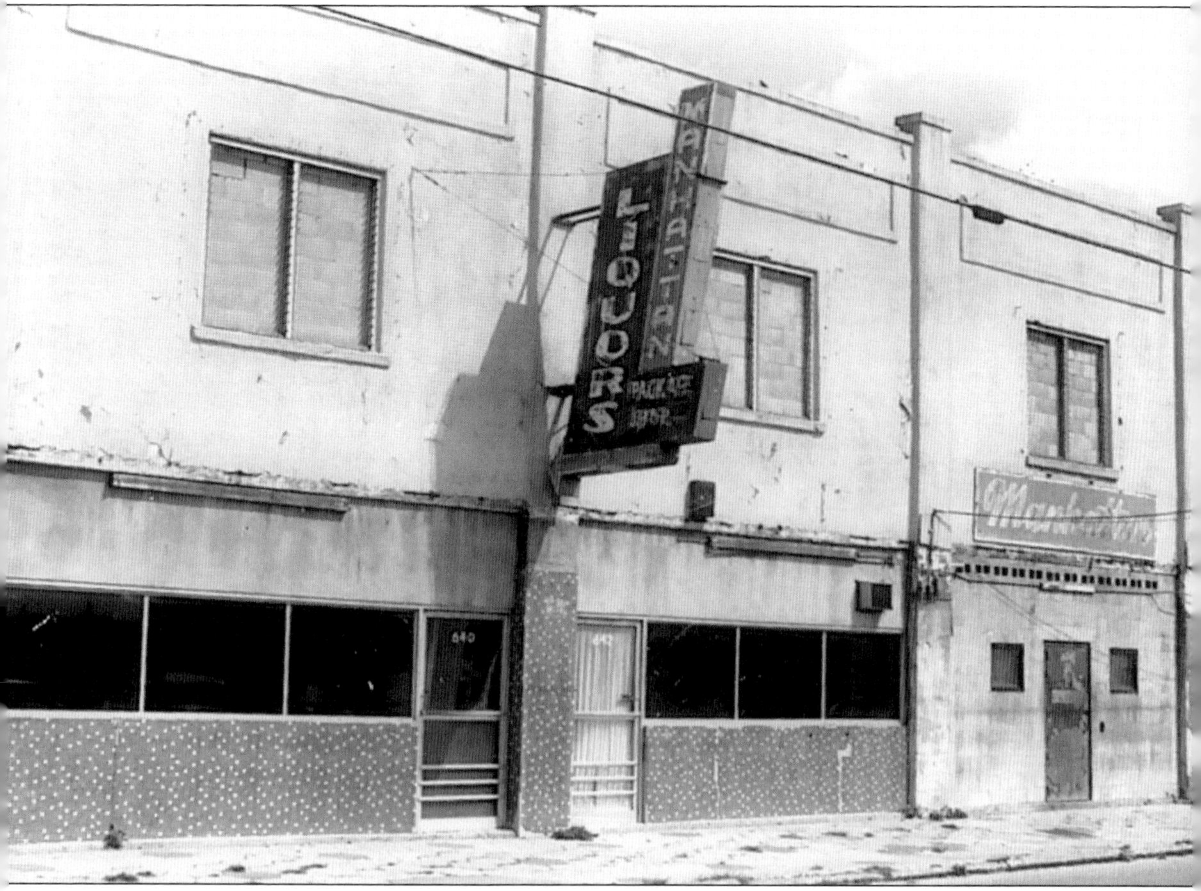

For several decades, 22nd Street South, also known as "the Deuces," was the main street in the African-American community. Elder Jordan originally named the business the Jordan Dance Hall. Later, it was renamed the Manhattan Casino. The Manhattan Casino featured many well-known performers. Some of them were Duke Ellington, Louis Armstrong, Cab Calloway, Count Basie, James Brown, and Little Richard. It also played host to many bands from Florida such as the Gibbs High School Revelers, the Sunset Royals, the Manzy Harris Band, and Al Williams and the Versatiles. In the late 1960s the Manhattan Casino closed, but it was designated a local historic landmark in 1994.

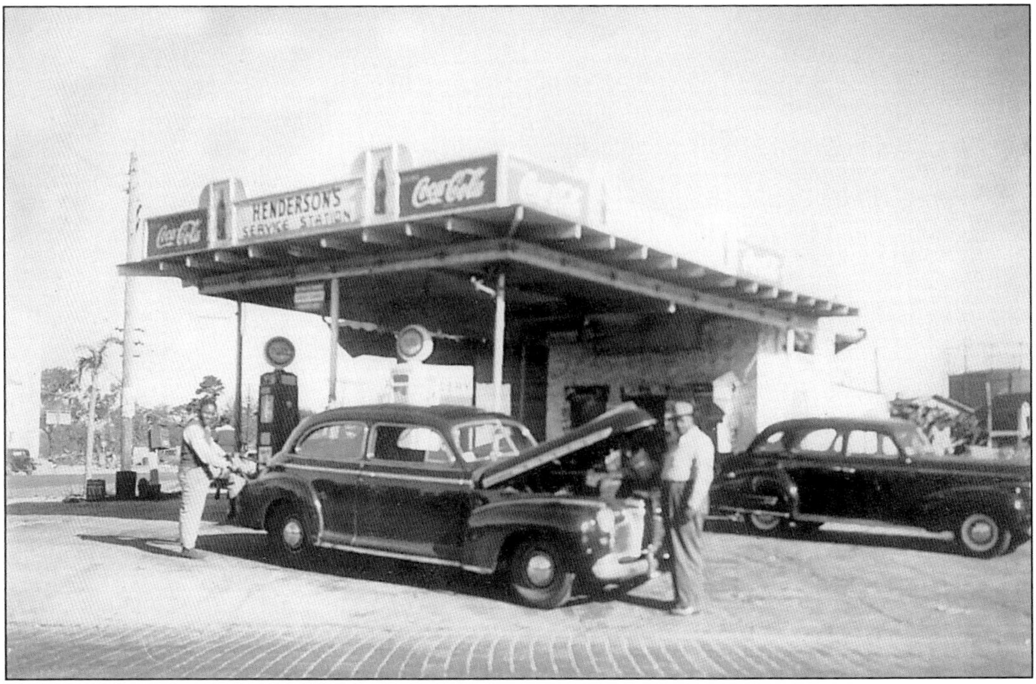

Pictured above is Henderson's Service Station, located at 14th Street and 5th Avenue South in the Gas Plant area. This picture was taken in 1943. Jesse Henderson is standing in the front of the car with the hood raised.

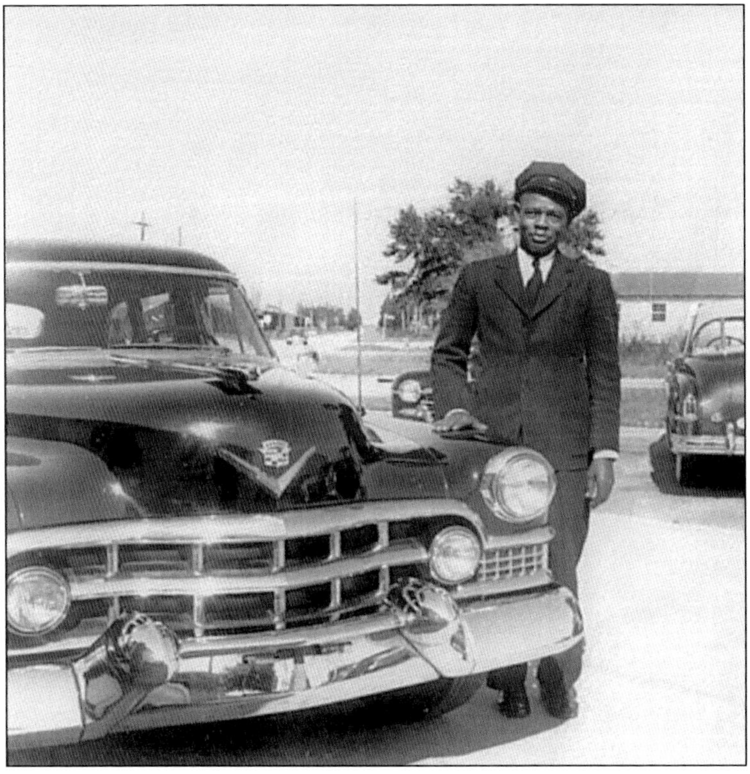

Robert T. Brown stands next to the vehicle he operated as a private chauffeur during the 1950s.

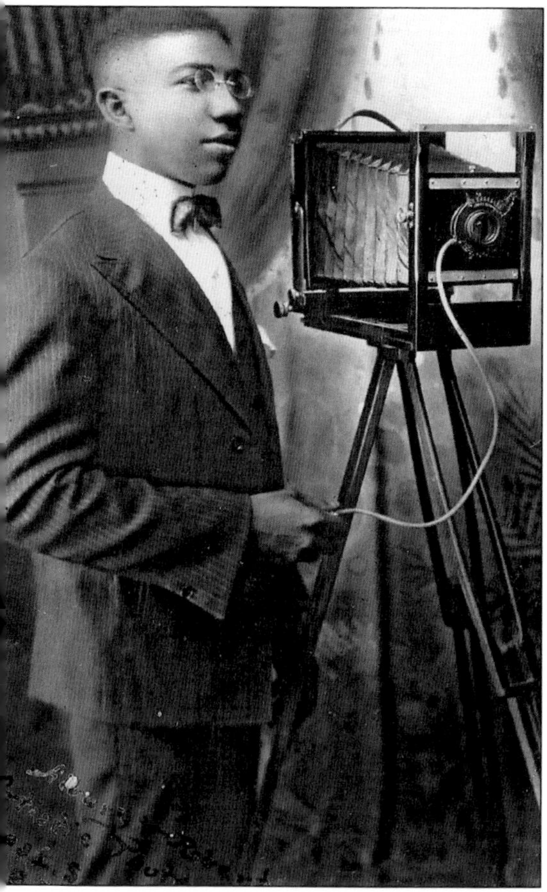

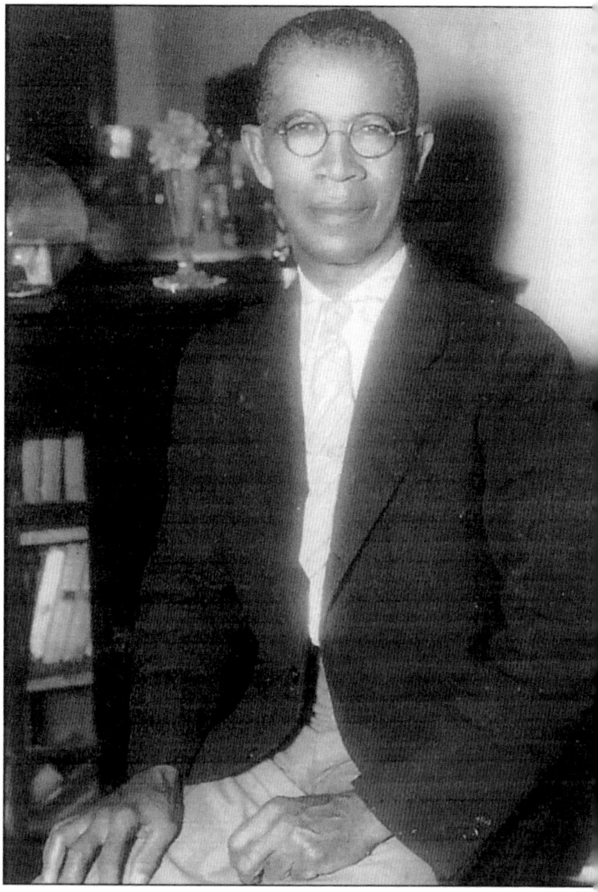

Albert Roberts and Joseph Albury Sr. operated a photography studio in the early 1900s. The above picture to the left features Roberts behind the camera, while the above picture to the right depicts Mr. Albury.

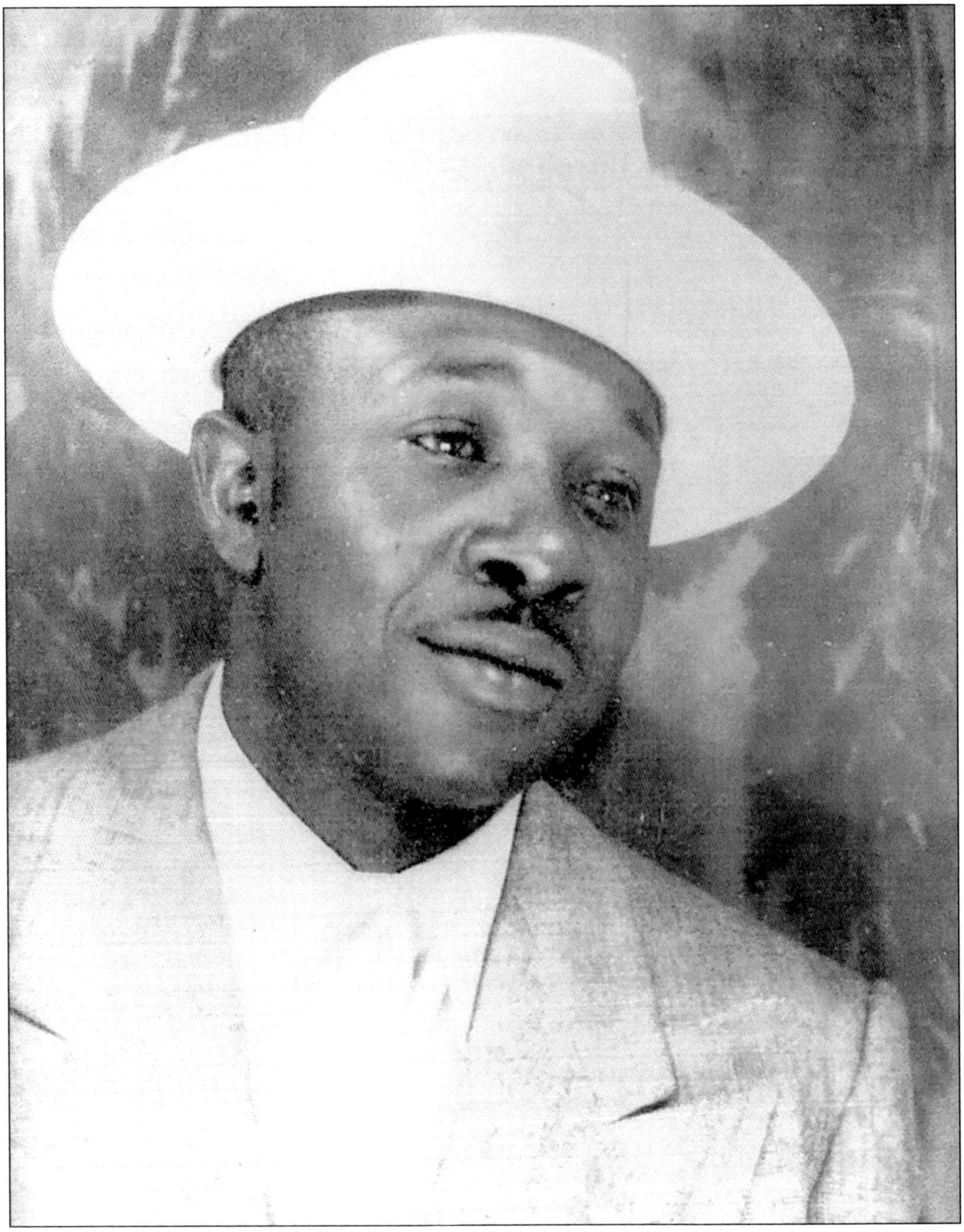

Pictured above is William "Buddy" West, a local barber on 22nd Street South. The original barber shop was located at 631 22nd Street South. Later, the shop was relocated to 920 22nd Street South. This was due to a fire that destroyed pictures and memorabilia kept from Mr. West's days as a promoter of bands that performed together at the Manhattan Casino.

Pictured here is Joe Yates Jr., who operated Yates Barber Shop at 1239 22nd Street South.

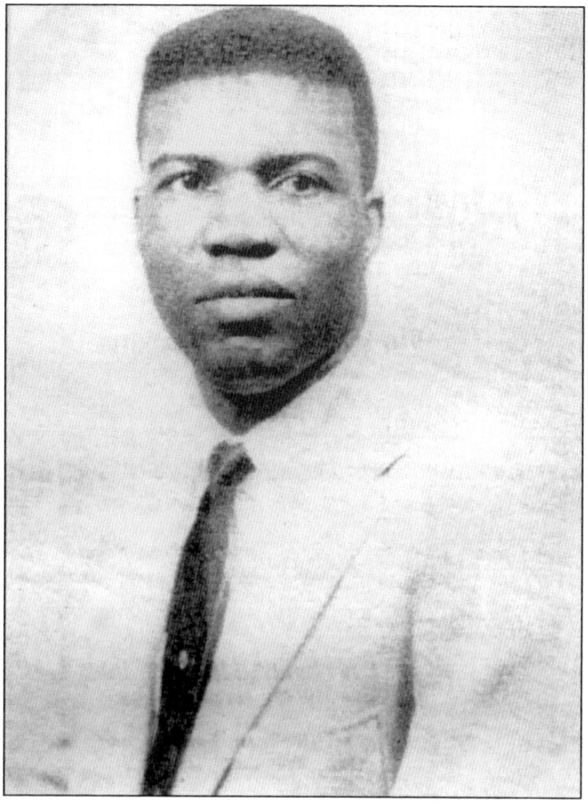

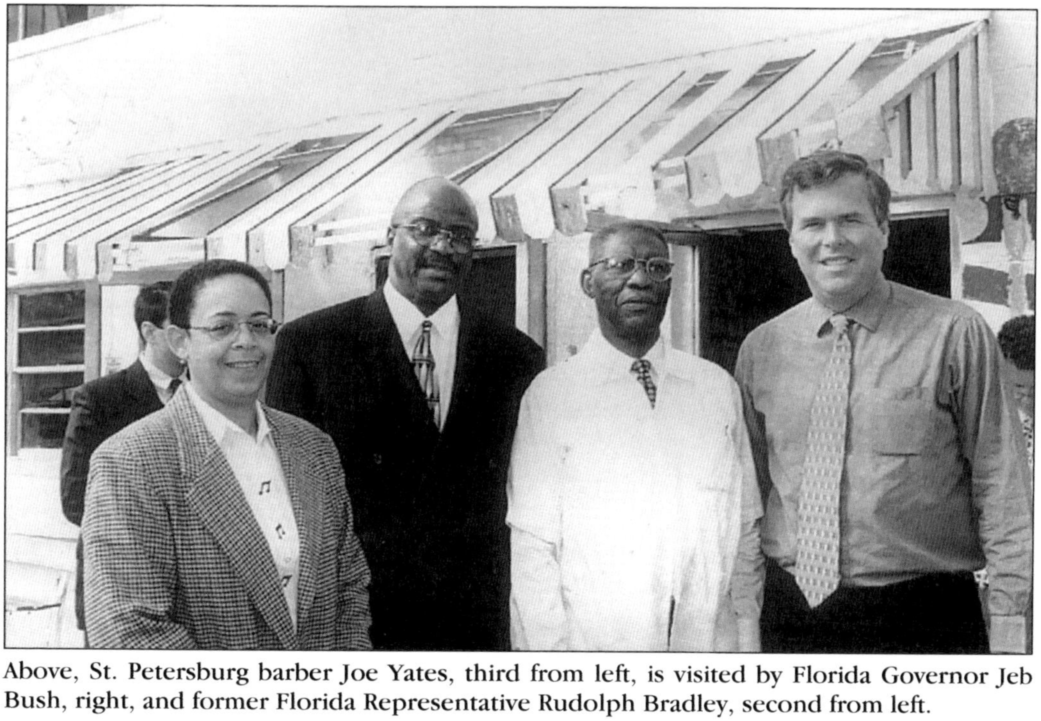

Above, St. Petersburg barber Joe Yates, third from left, is visited by Florida Governor Jeb Bush, right, and former Florida Representative Rudolph Bradley, second from left.

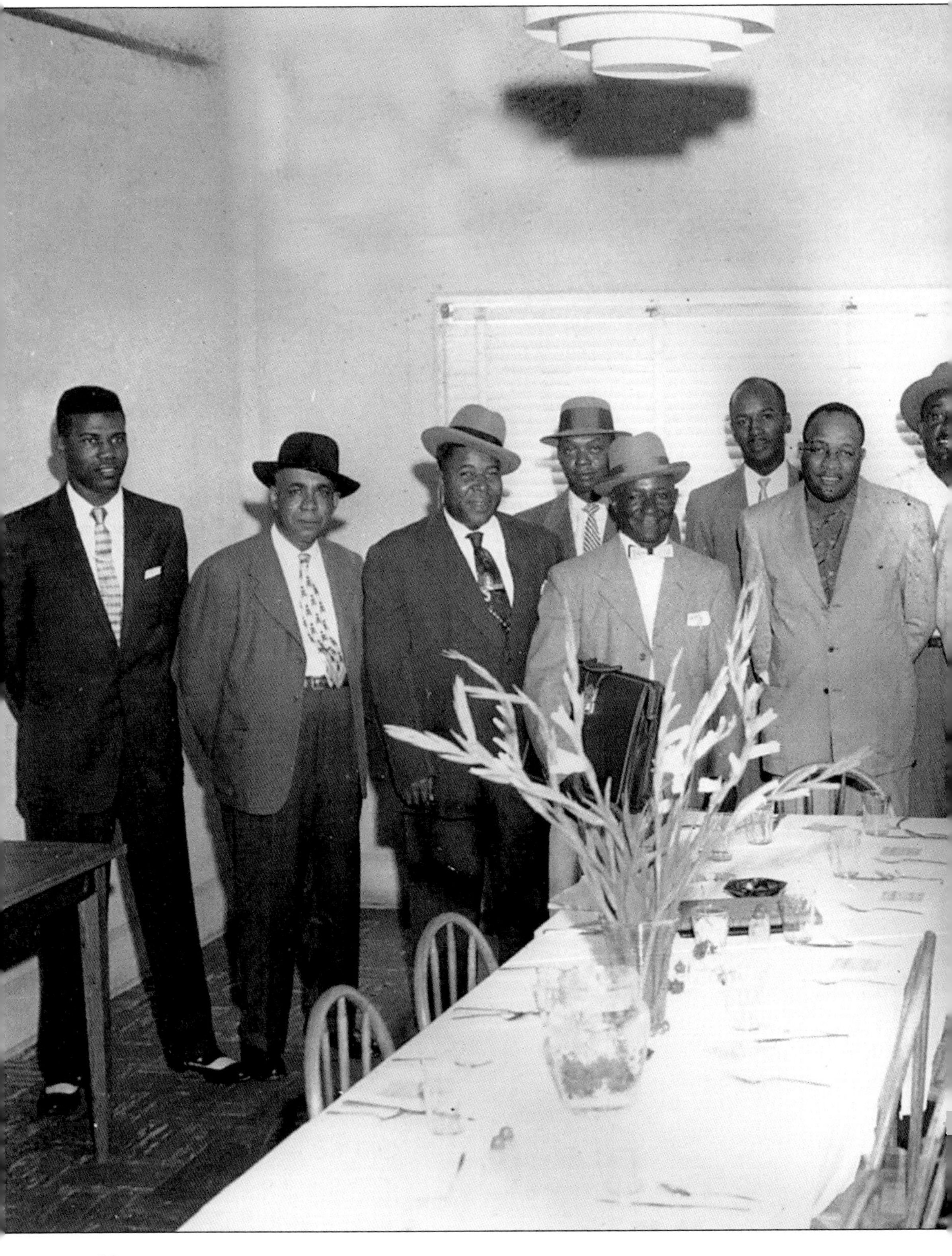

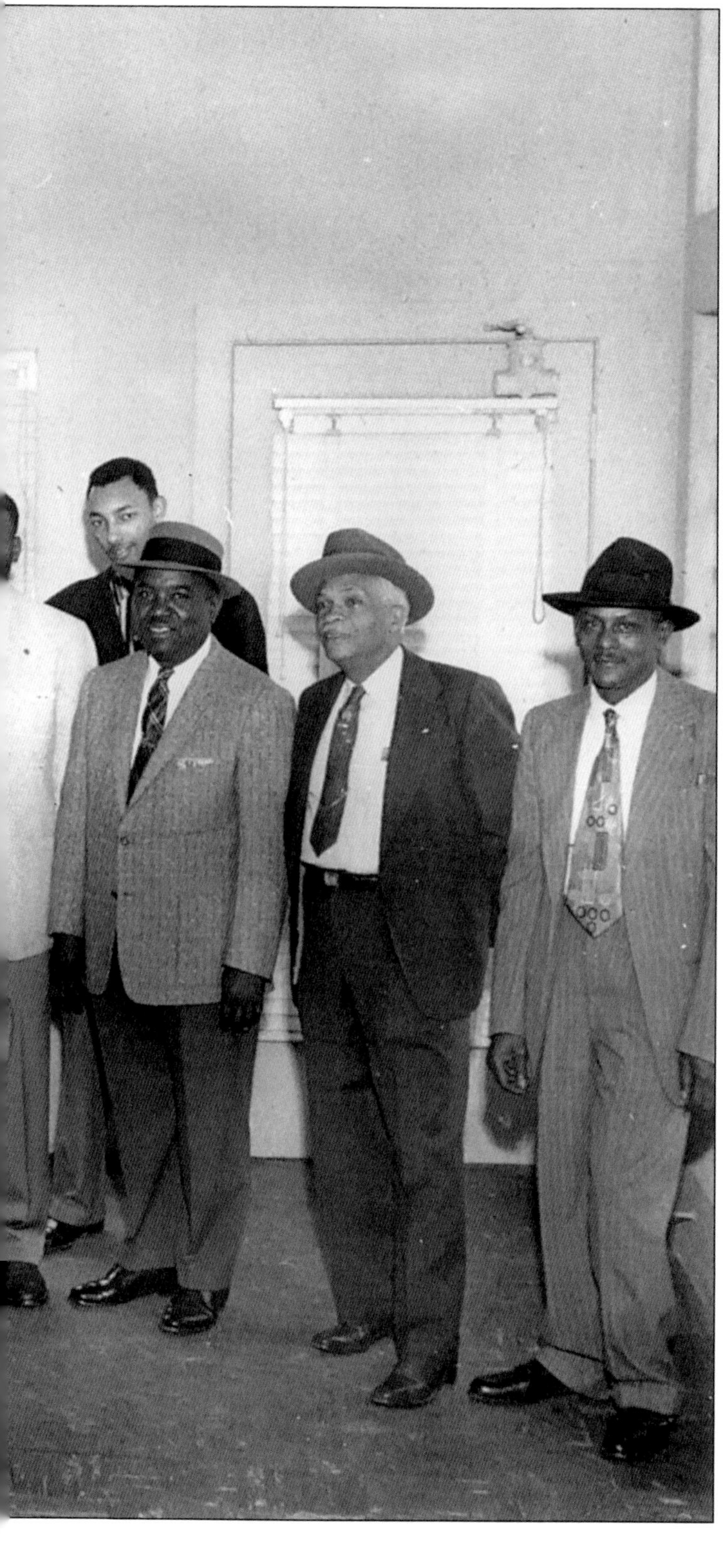

In the late 1950s, the members of the Suncoast Barbers Association gathered to take this picture at one of their meetings. This humanitarian group was comprised of barbers throughout the Tampa Bay area. They sponsored community projects and contributed to blood banks, the United Community Fund, the American Legion Hospital for Crippled Children, the Little League, the Holt Street Recreation Center, nursery schools, and various other causes.

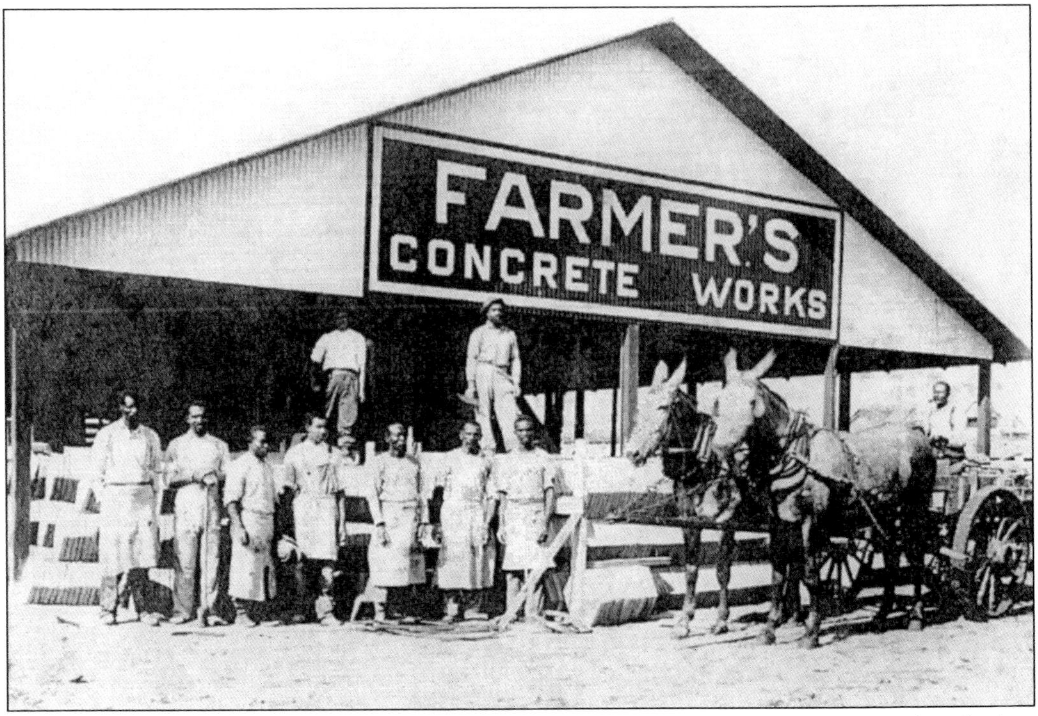

In the early 1900s the largest group of workers in the black community was classified as laborers. Most laborers earned just enough money to pay the rent and meet other basic needs. The photograph above depicts African-American workers at a concrete factory.

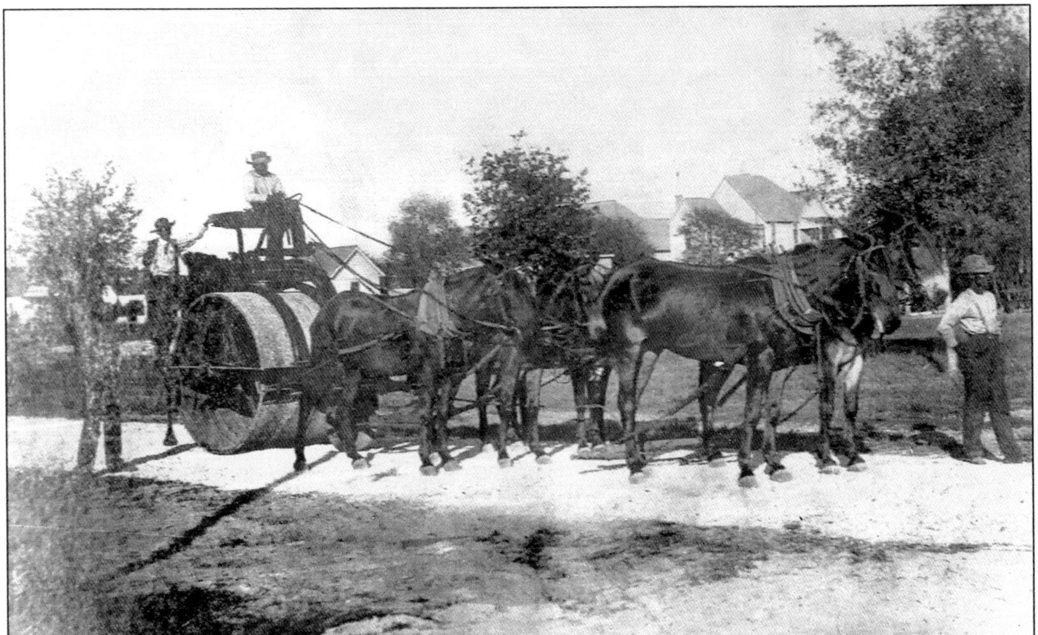

In this picture, African-American laborers pave a road in St. Petersburg. Black males were employed to clear and pave roads throughout Pinellas County.

Five

CAREGIVERS

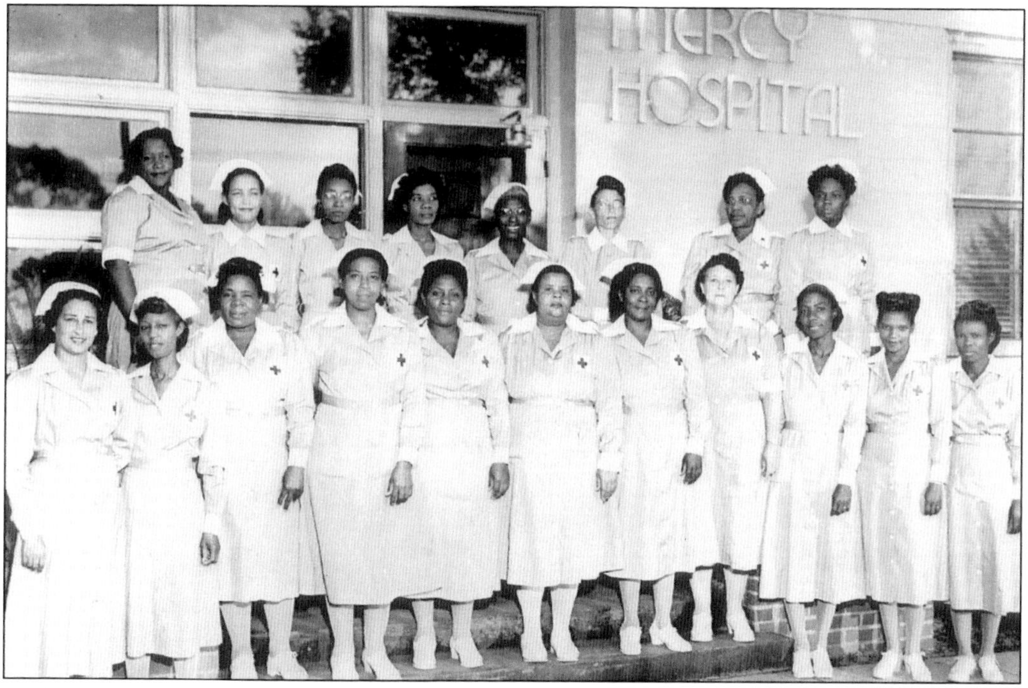

In the 1930s, segregation was practiced in both physician health care and hospital care. Black midwives in the black community assumed many responsibilities that were generally reserved for physicians. They not only delivered babies, but also prescribed remedies for the sick. Those who went to the white physicians had to endure the humiliation of going to the back door. There were two separate hospitals, Mound Park for the whites, located at 701 6th Street South, and Mercy Hospital, located at 1244 22nd Street South. Above are members of the Gray Ladies of Mercy Hospital. The Gray Ladies gave their time for free to aid patients at Mercy Hospital. They wrote for them, kept fresh flowers in their rooms, and did things to make the patients comfortable. Standing from left to right, are (front row) Lucille Sims, Beatrice Lloyd, M. Warren, Margaret Smith, Maggie White, Annie B. Mills, Annie Waller, Inez Ponder, Fannie Ford, Velma Bennett, Mildred Brockinton, and R. Ward; (back row) Irene Richardson, Lizzie Crawford, Willie Smith, Irene Brewington, Annie Danley, and A. Fork.

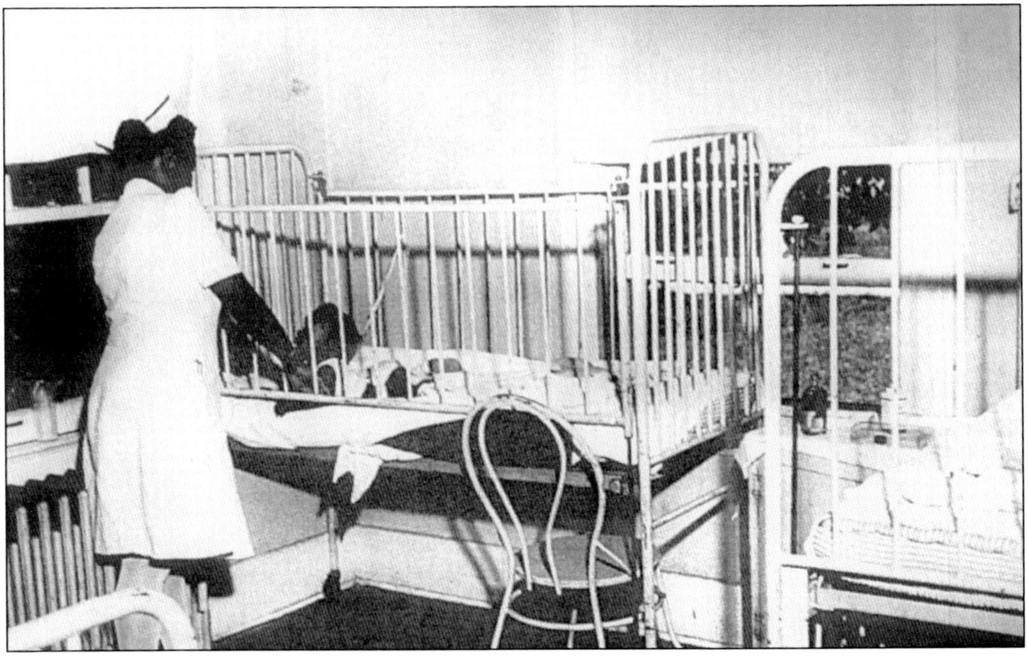

Nurse Taylor tends to a young patient in a ward at Mercy Hospital in the mid-1940s.

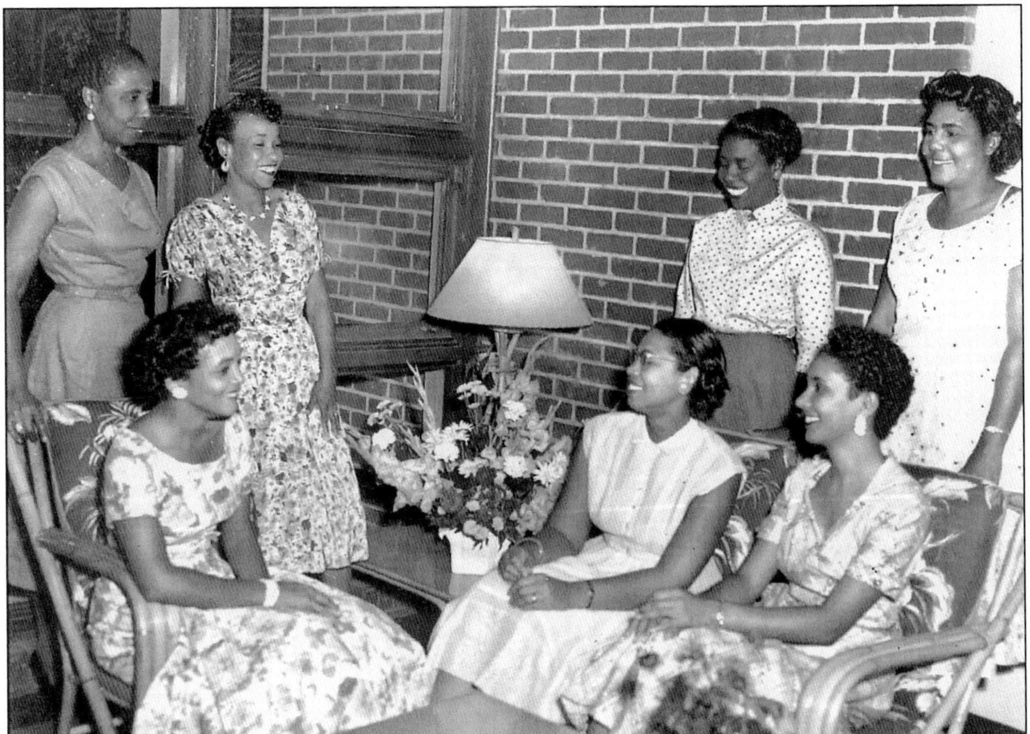

Pictured here is a woman's group that spearheaded a project to air condition Mercy Hospital in 1955. Seated at the extreme right is Anna Polk Walker.

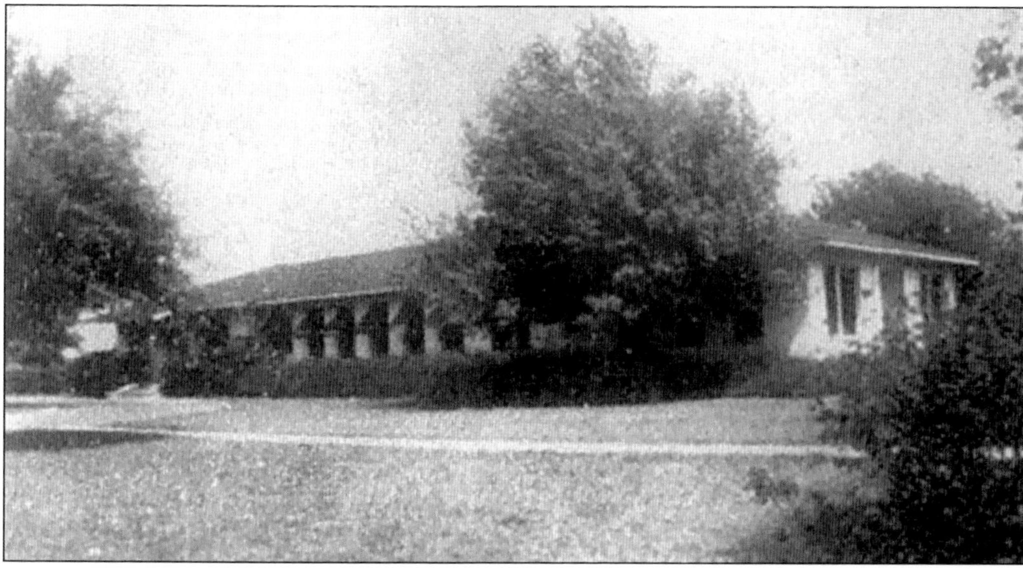

Pictured above is Mercy Hospital in 1945. Mercy Hospital was built in 1922 at 22nd Street and 12th Avenue. When the hospital opened, it only had 16 beds.

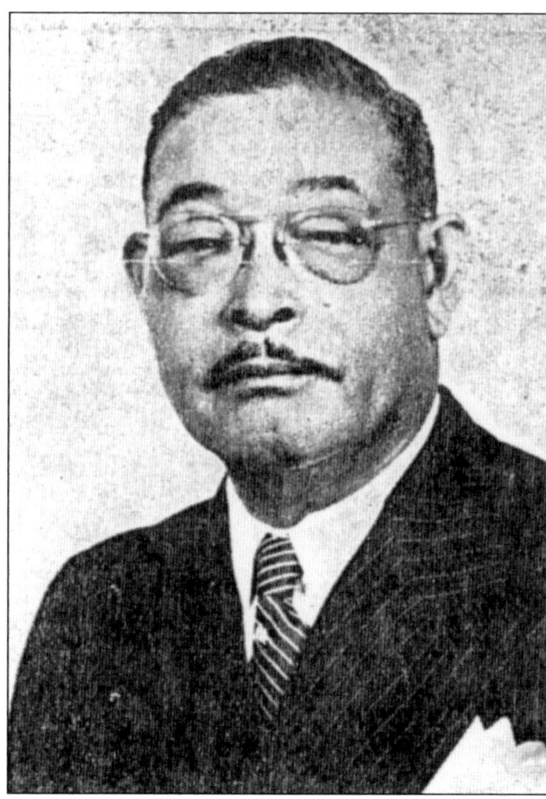

Dr. James M. Ponder was a staff physician at Mercy Hospital. Ponder spearheaded the drive to have Mercy Hospital built for black citizens.

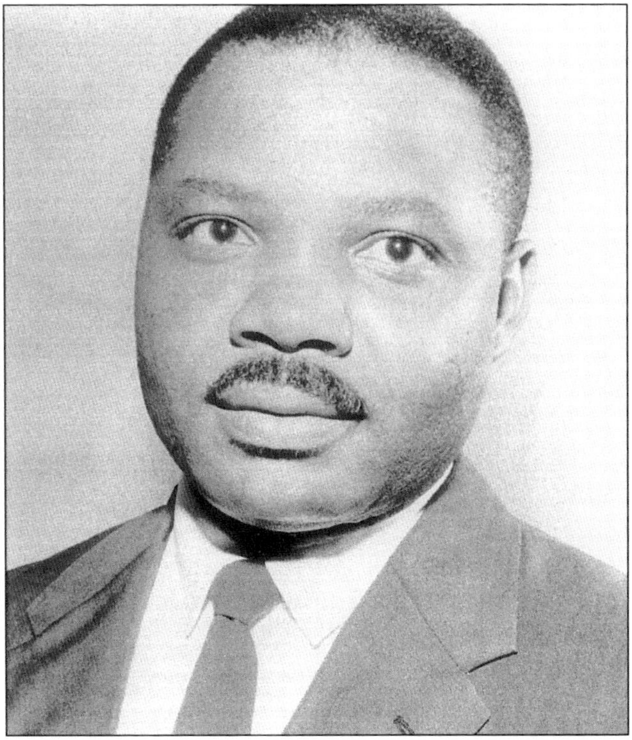

Pictured at left is Dr. Robert Swain, a St. Petersburg dentist. This picture was taken in the 1950s. Dr. Swain was also active in the local NAACP.

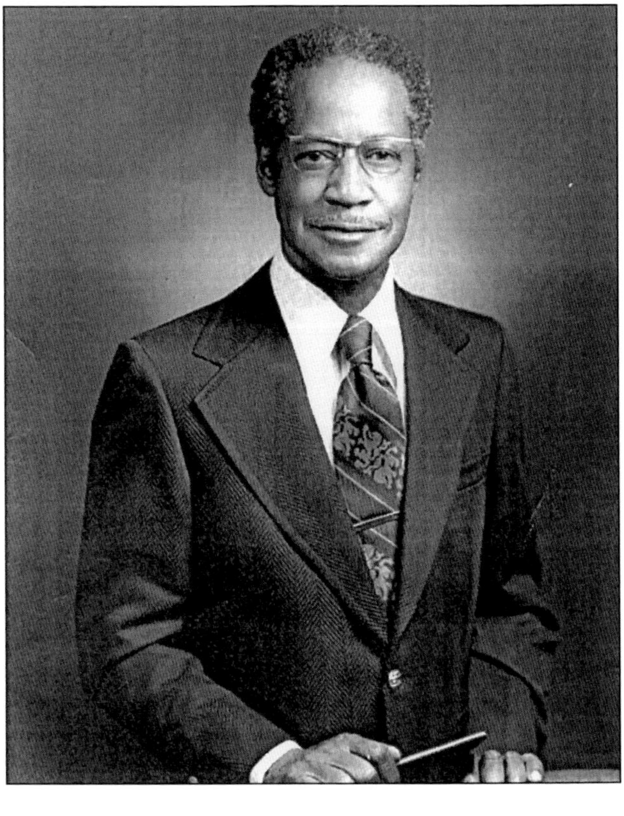

Pictured at right is Dr. Fred Alsup. In 1952 he became the first black doctor in Pinellas County to be accepted to membership in the Pinellas County Medical Society.

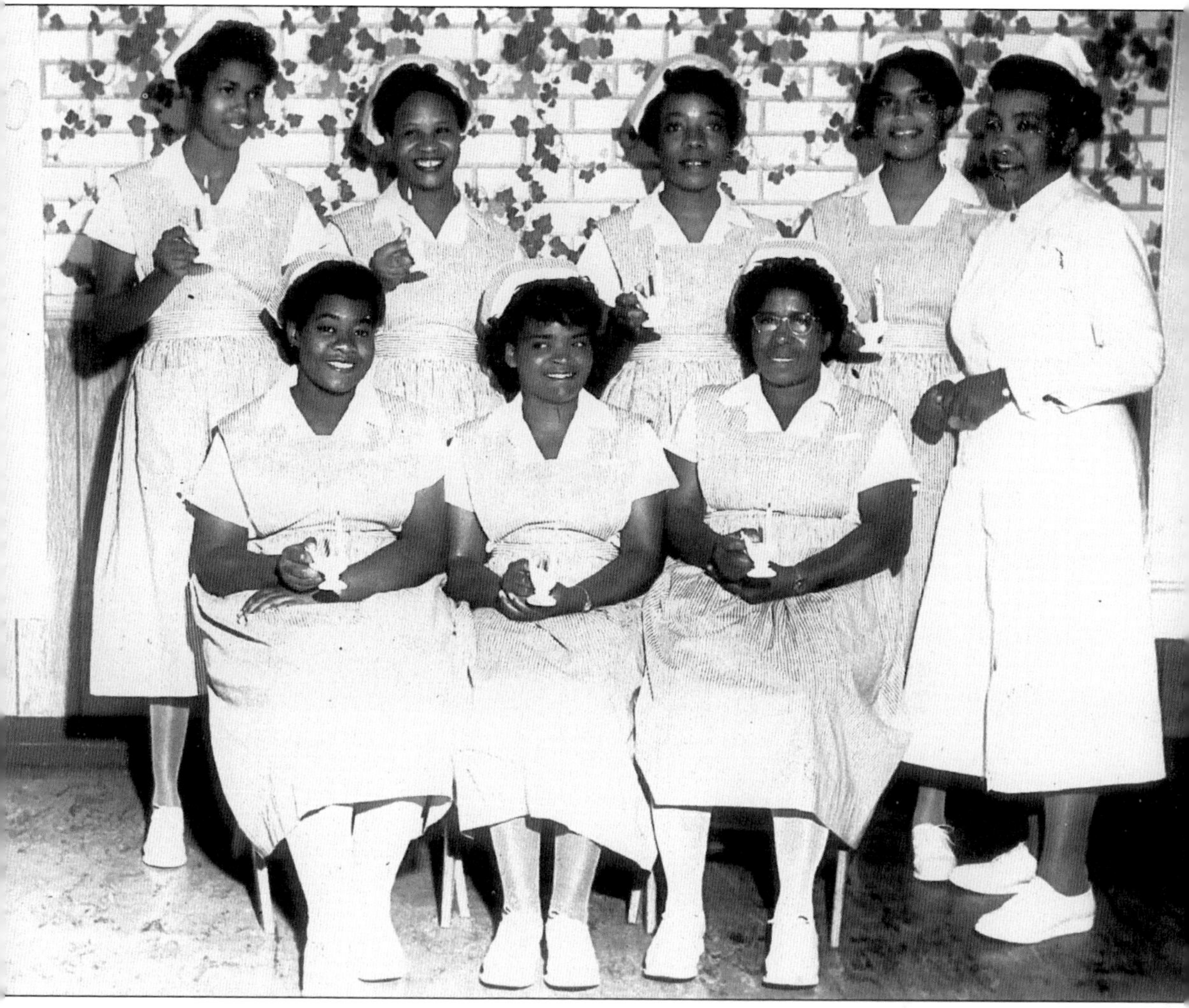

Nurse Mary Brayboy Jones, standing at the extreme right, is depicted here with several nursing assistants.

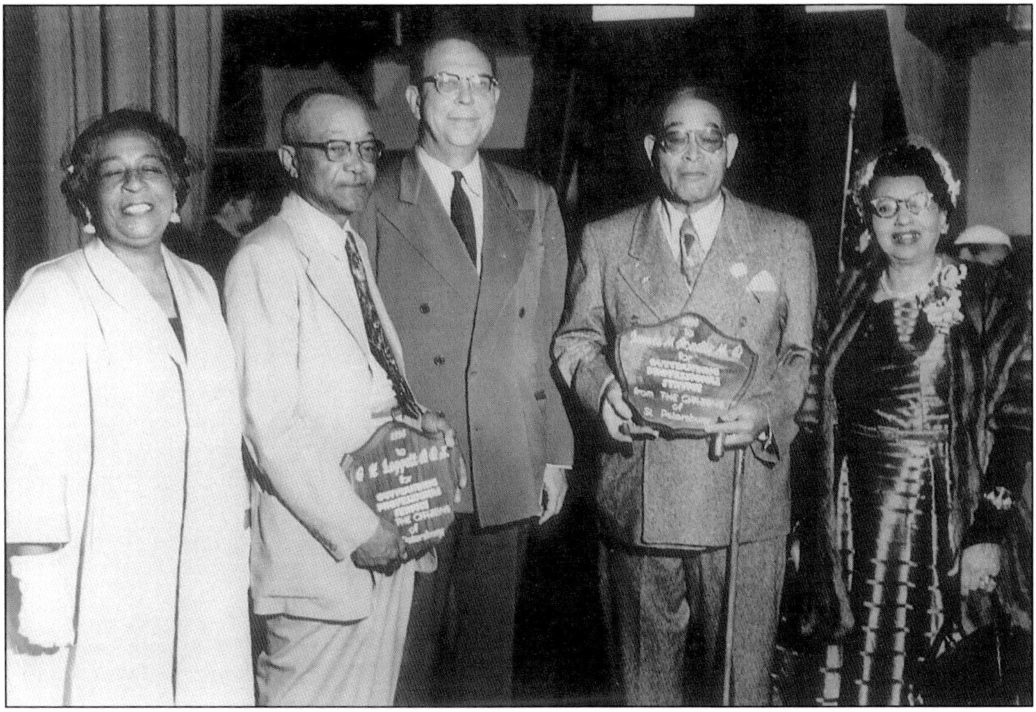

Dr. Gilbert Leggett and Dr. James Ponder receive outstanding service awards in the above picture. Dr. Leggett was a dentist who led the legal action to allow black people to vote in the Democratic Party primary elections in Pinellas County in 1944.

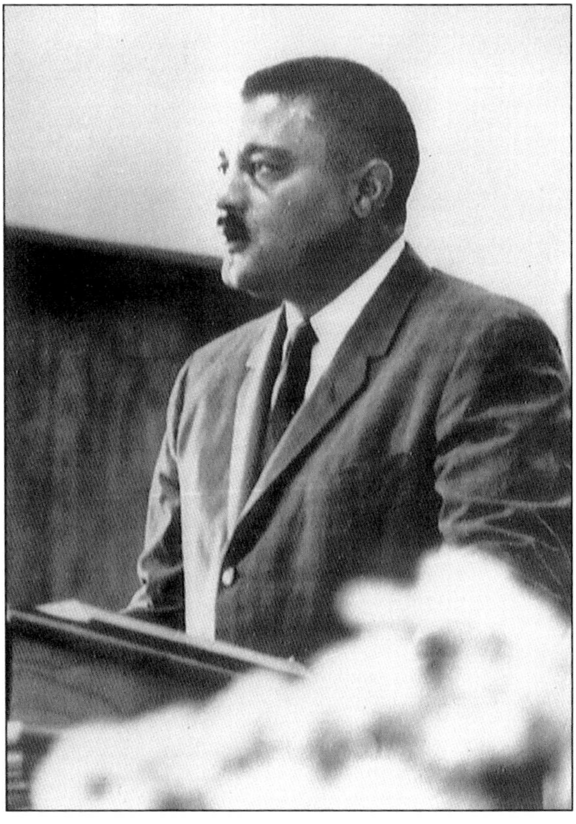

One of the leading post-war African-American medical practitioners in Tampa Bay, Dr. Ralph Wimbish was a towering figure within the medical community. Like many of his fellow African-American professionals, Dr. Wimbish labored under the restrictions imposed by segregation. But eventually, by his own admission he grew "tired of waiting," saying, "I have waited 30 years in this town and nothing has happened yet."

Six

Entertainment

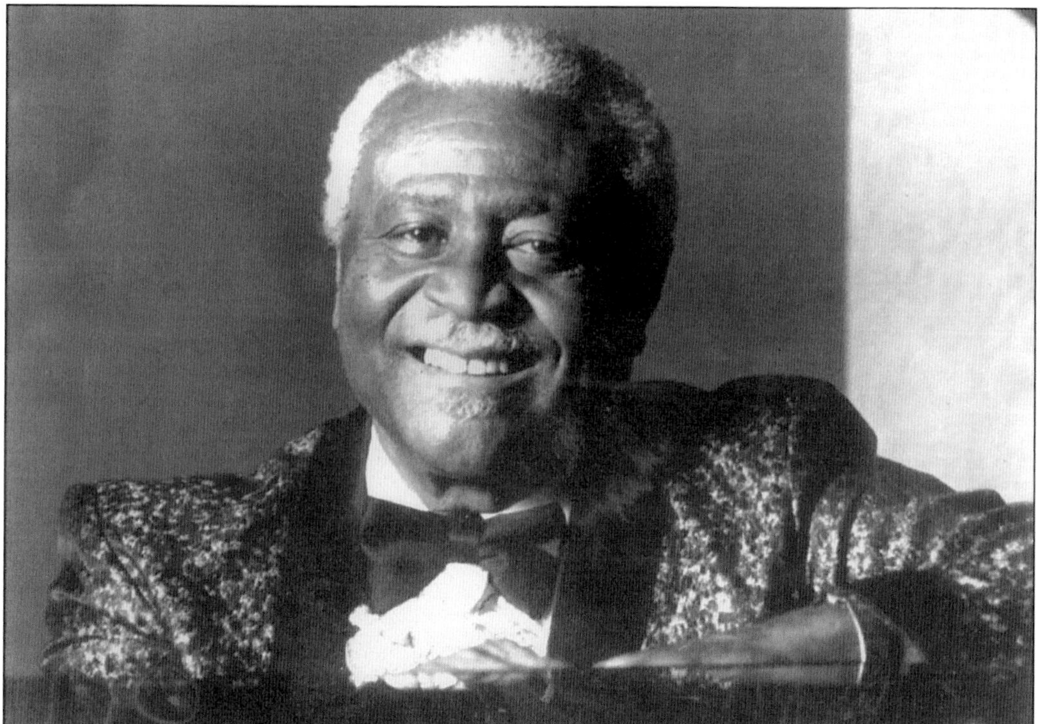

Alvin J. Downing has been credited as being a legend in jazz circles. Born in Jacksonville, Florida, Downing received his Bachelor of Arts degree from Florida A&M University and his Master of Arts degree in music from Catholic University in Washington D.C., and he studied at Potsdam University in New York and UCLA in California. He received the key to the City of St. Petersburg for outstanding community service. After teaching at Gibbs High School, he was drafted into the Army Air Corps. After 20 years of service to his county, he returned from the Air Force with the rank of major. Later, he taught music at the Clearwater Campus of St. Petersburg Junior College. He formed his own jazz group, "Al Downing and the All Stars," which for decades was the most popular and sought-after band among jazz fans in Tampa Bay. Downing died in 2000 at the age of 83.

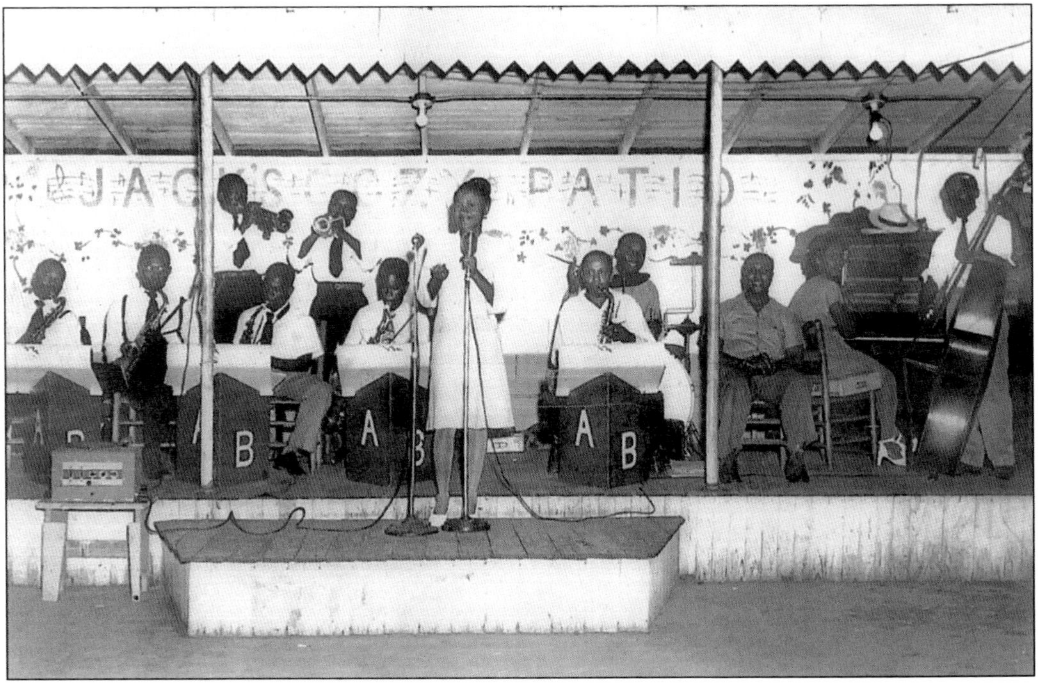

Portrayed above is the Alonzo Brown Band at the Manhattan Casino. Seated, from left to right, are Mr. Tilman, C.J. Robinson, unidentified, Don McRae, Dotry Macon, Fess Clark, and Martha Brown. Standing, from left to right, are Bud Snell, Alan Lewis, Louise Levine, and Alonzo Brown.

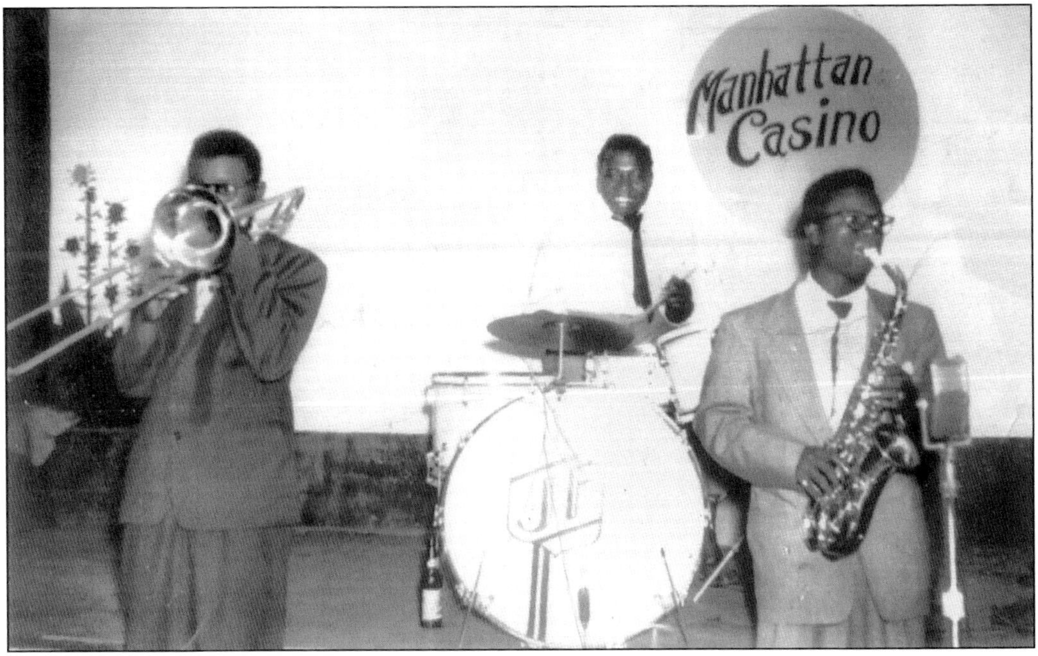

Buster Cooper, an unidentified drummer, and Leroy Barton entertain an audience at the Manhattan Casino.

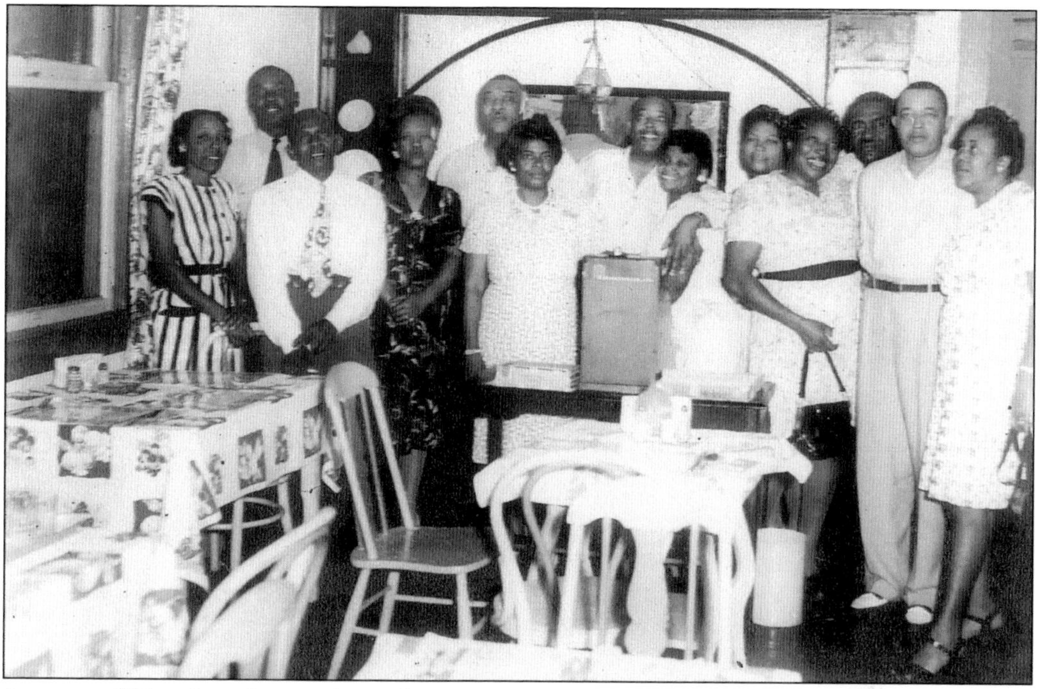

A group of friends gather in the 1940s at the Club 16 for some fun. Card games and dances were often enjoyed at the club.

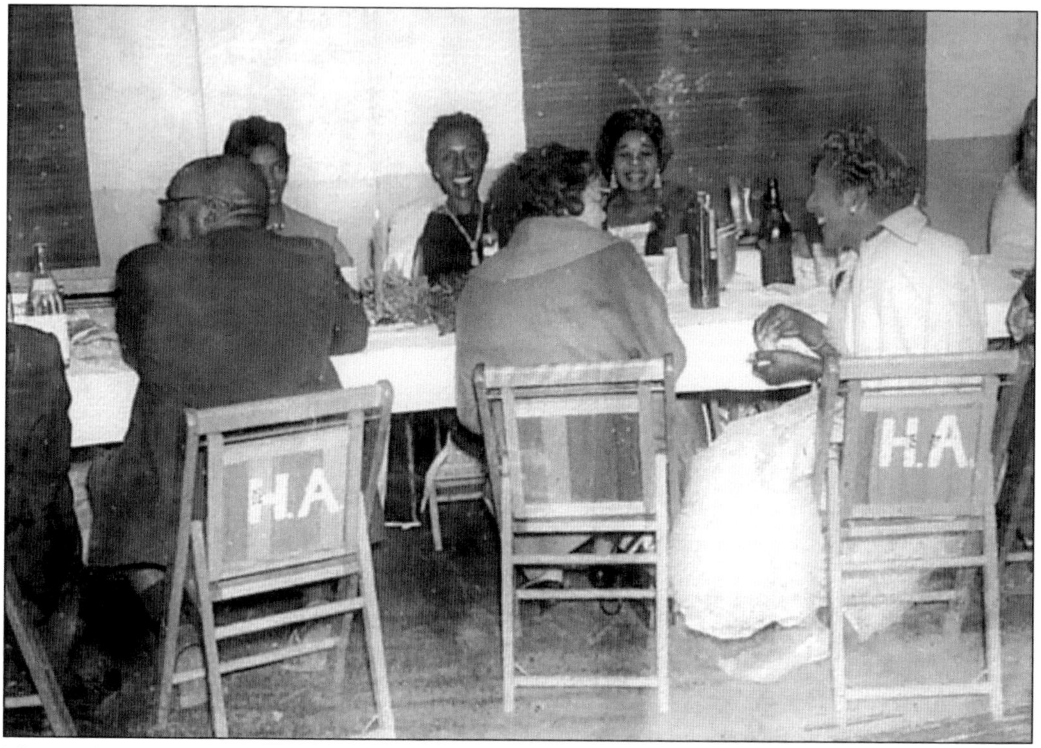

The Jordan Park Club House, pictured above, was also a favorite place for social gatherings.

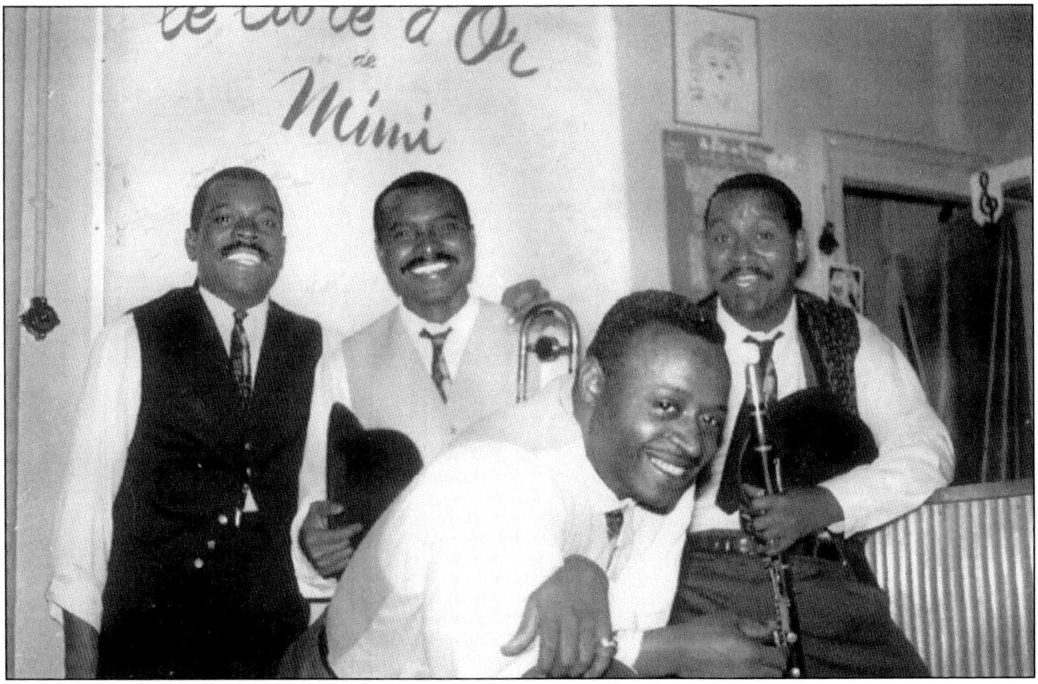

Here, musicians at the Casino "take five." Steve and Buster Cooper, far left, are accompanied by two unidentified musicians.

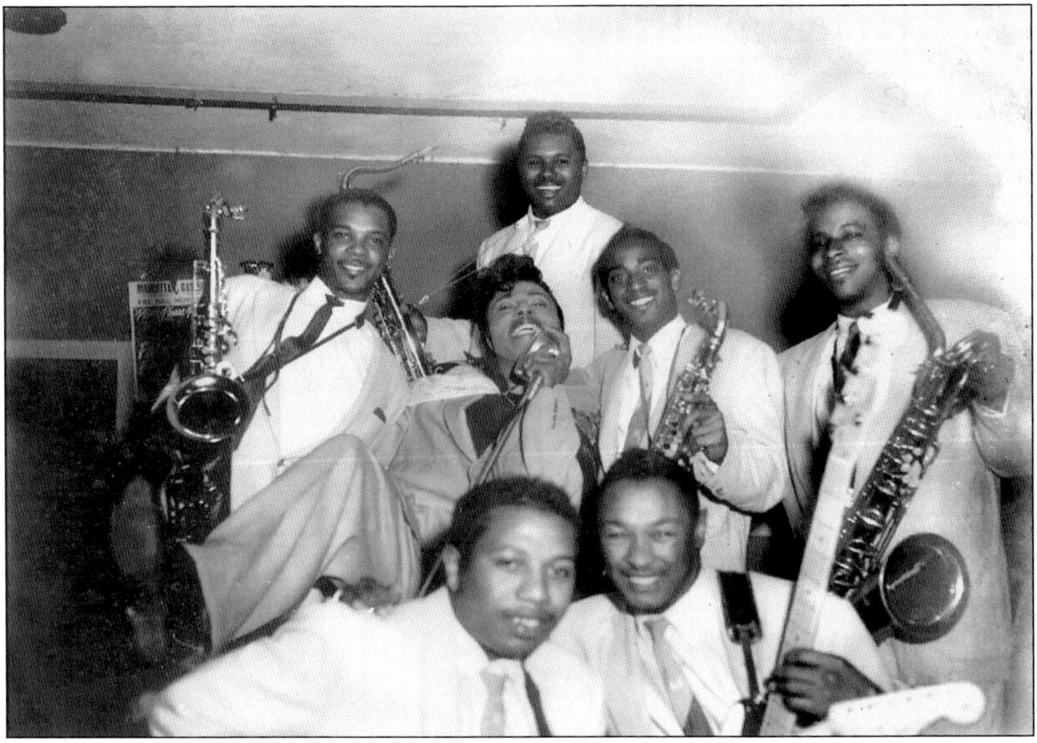

Little Richard is in control of the mike during this jam at the casino.

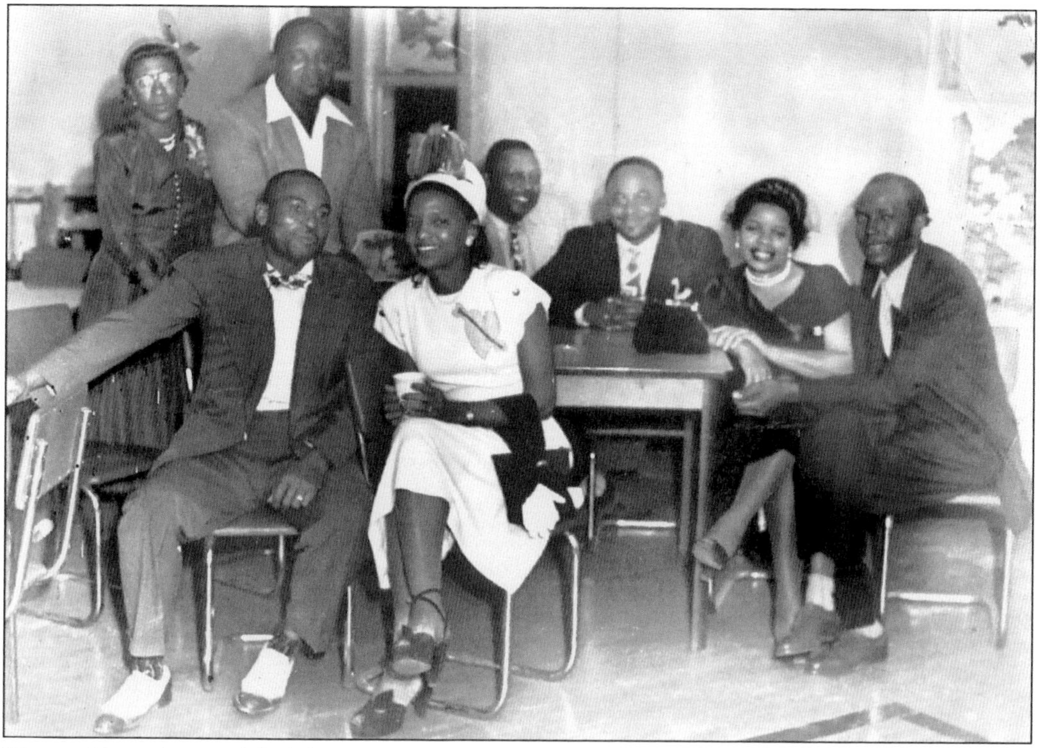

Pictured here is a social club meeting at the casino. Seated at the far left is Jerone Harris and at far right is Willy Dunlap.

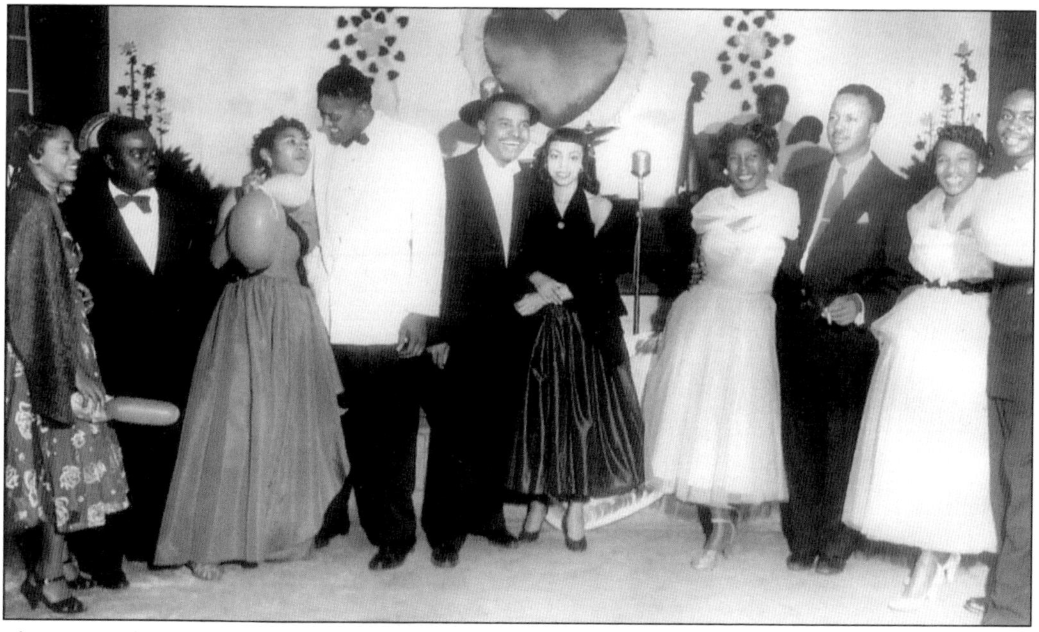

Above, a jubilant group is photographed at a Sweetheart Ball. Pictured from left to right are Fannie Macon Barton, Leroy Barton, unidentified, Edward Fuller, Mr. and Mrs. Buster Cooper, Pauline Givens, Evans Haile, Verdya Dennard, and Sammy Robinson.

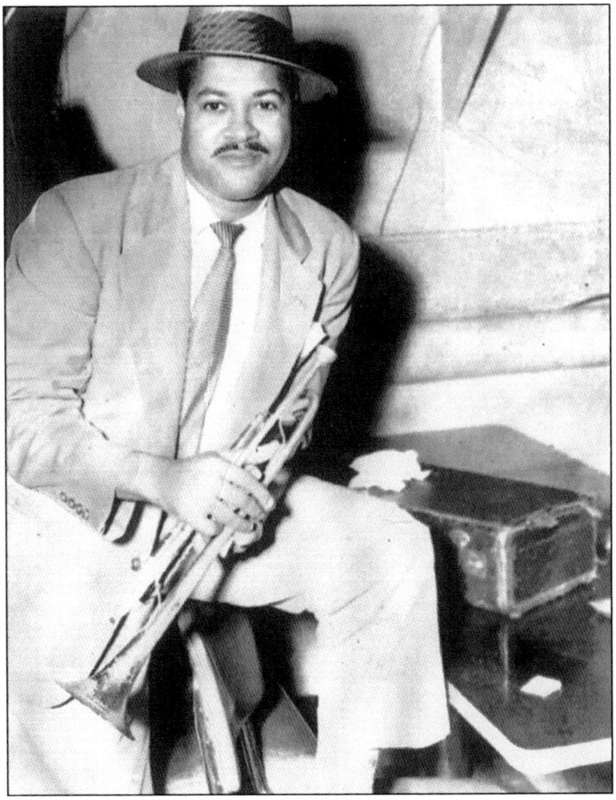

Alfred Williams looks very suave and debonair as he poses in this picture with his trumpet.

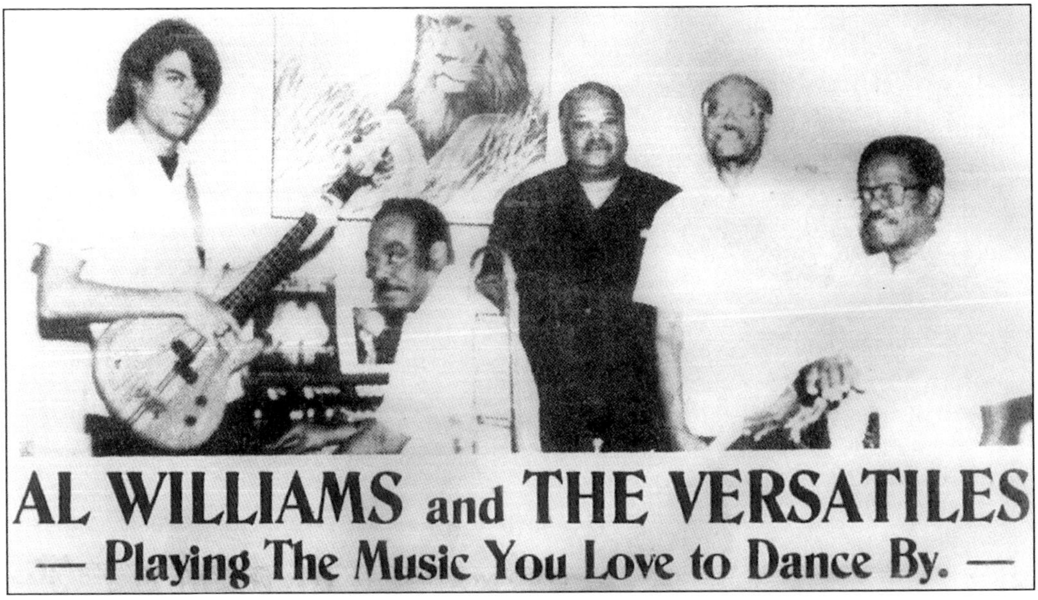

Above, Al Williams is joined by members of his band. From left to right are Guy Taylor, Warren McCray, Al Williams, unidentified, and Leroy Barton.

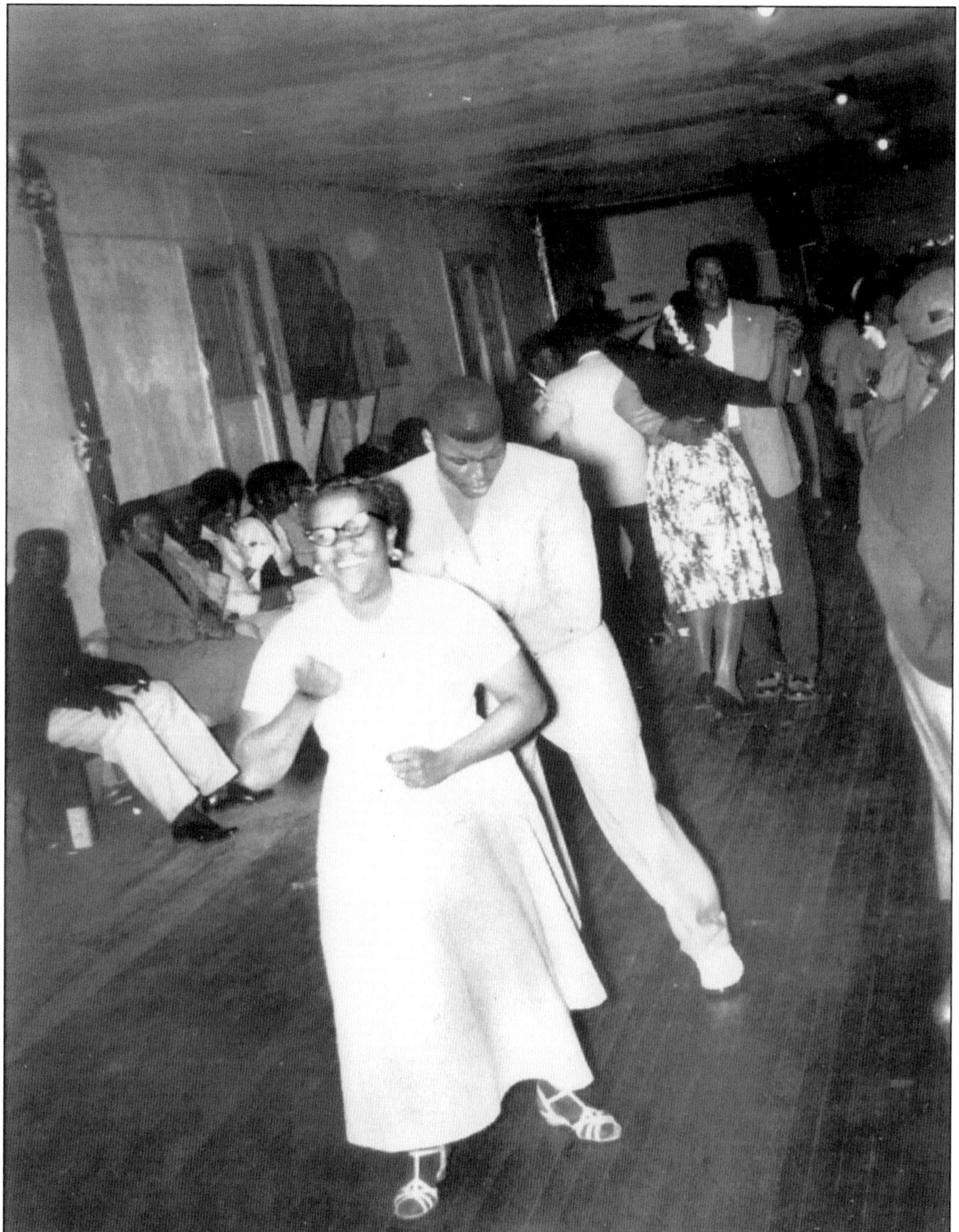

This picture brings the Manhattan to life. Dancers strut to the beat of the music. Mr. Paul Barco Sr. remembers this as his last dance at the Manhattan.

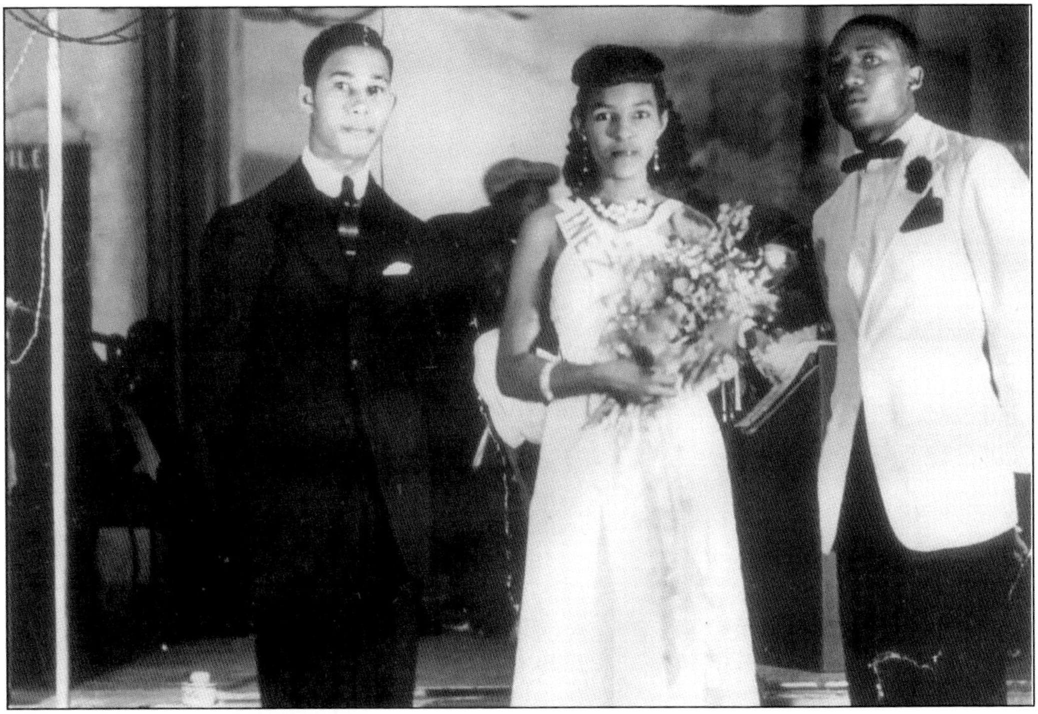

In this picture, Inez Dunlap is crowned queen. She is joined by Nathaniel Curington and E.J. Williams.

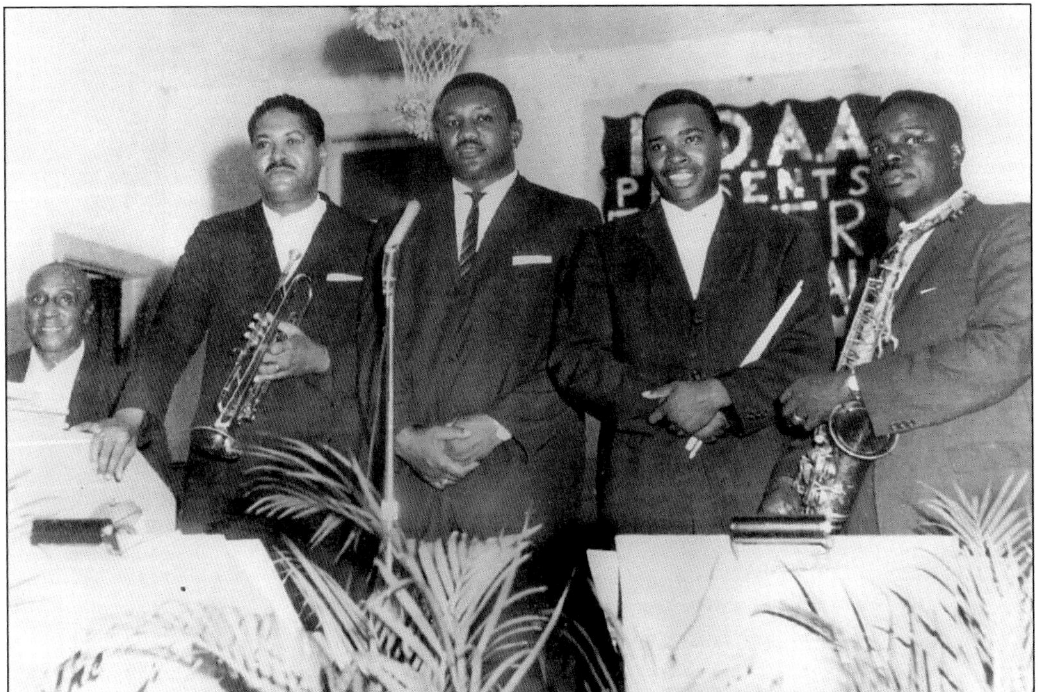

Shown above are Fess Clark, Al Williams, George Brown, Warren Rainey, and Leroy Barton.

Peggy Peterman (in the back on the left) enjoys a Valentine's Day gathering. Mrs. Peterman was for many years a reputable reporter for the *St. Petersburg Times*. She also founded the Black History Pageant Program to which she donates much time not only teaching young people about their heritage, but also providing them with an opportunity to showcase their talents. In 1985, the Ambassador Club, Inc. presented Mrs. Peterman with its Citizen of the Year Award.

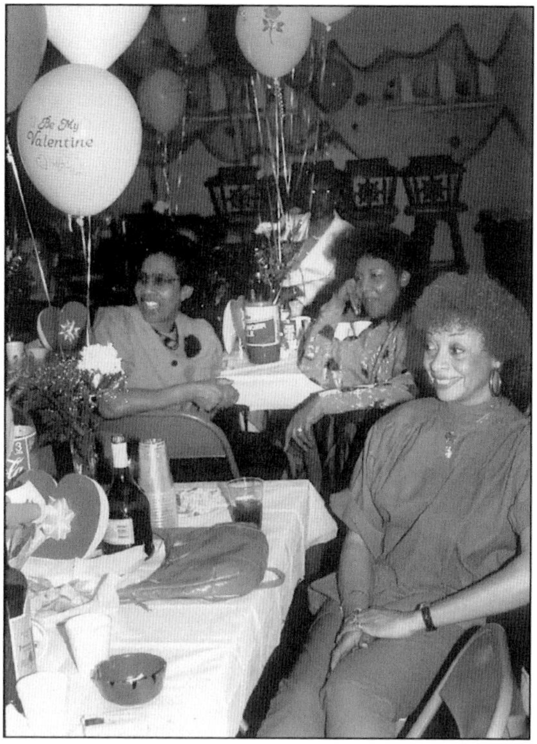

Below is a scene of a more formal affair. St. Petersburg Links Club members are joined by young debutantes at the Debutante Ball.

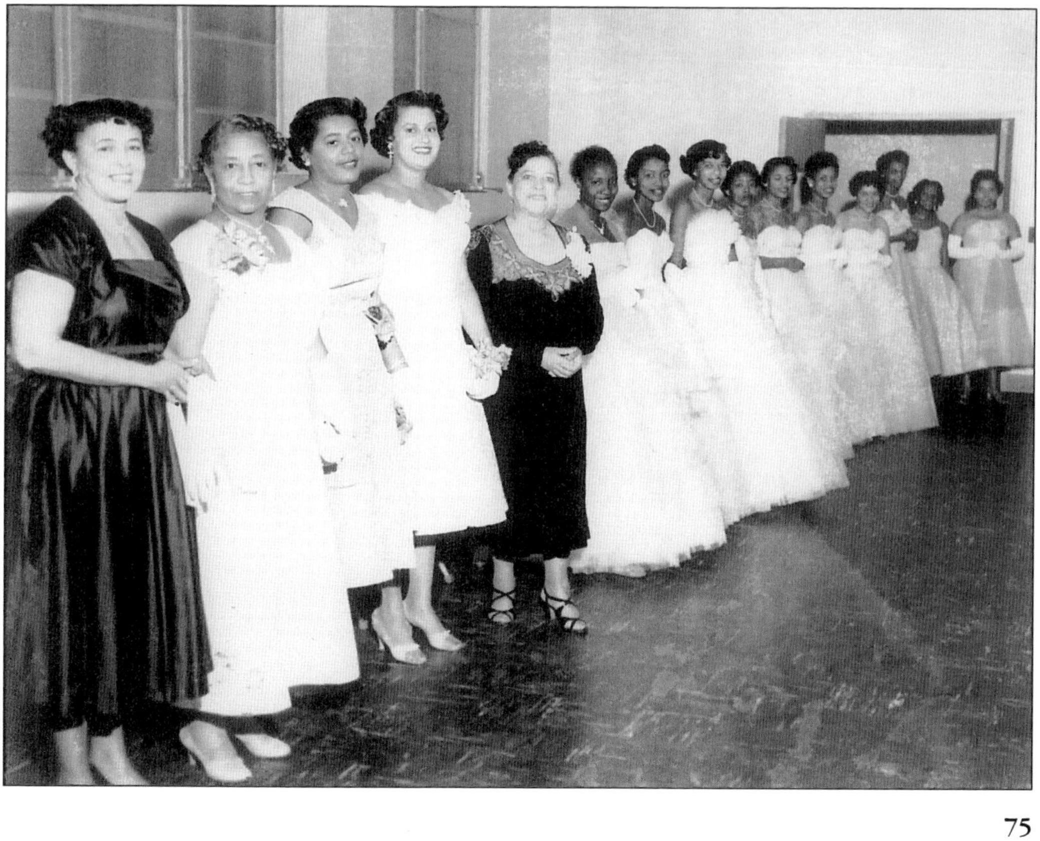

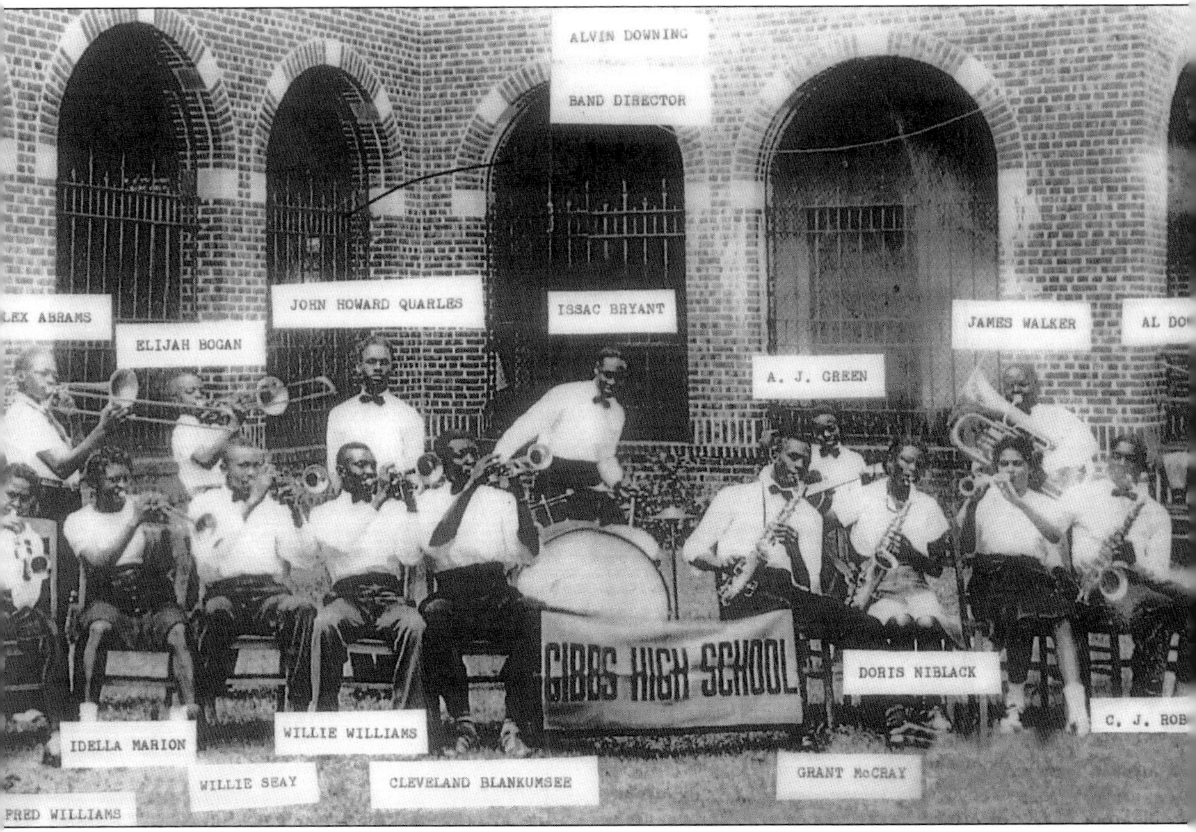

This picture shows the Gibbs High School band in action. Led by Al Downing, far right, the band is performing in the school courtyard during the 1939–1940 school year.

Seven

Clubs and Organizations

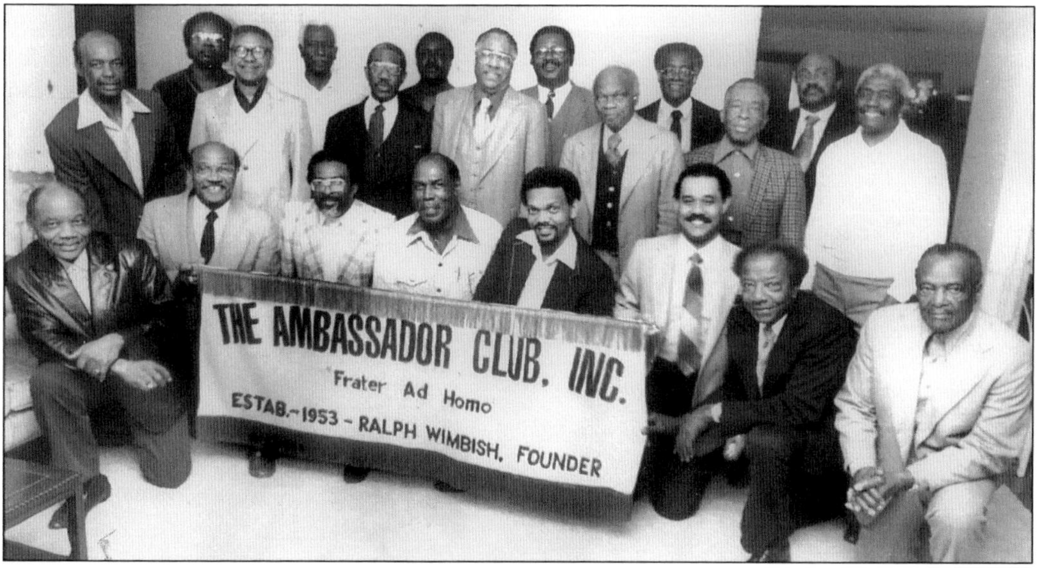

The Ambassador Club was established in 1953 by Dr. Ralph Wimbish when he decided that it was time that black citizens did something "within the system" to improve the rights of the whole community. He invited several black professionals and businessmen to assist him in this mission. The Ambassador Club was formed with the following charter members: Dr. O.T. Ayers, Samuel Blossom, Sidney Camble, George Grogan, John Hopkins, Ernest Ponder and Emanuel Stewart. The club made its formal debut to society on Sunday, January 17, 1954 at the Second Bethel Baptist Church. Judge Lawson Thomas, the only black judge at the time, was the keynote speaker. The club made history by entering a float with black women in the Festival of States Parade on April 2, 1954. The chairman and four members of the Ambassador Club were the nucleus of the Module 16 Project, the beginning of the Enoch Davis Center. Pictured above are club members displaying a banner depicting their name and motto, Frater Ad Homo, which translates "Brother of Mankind."

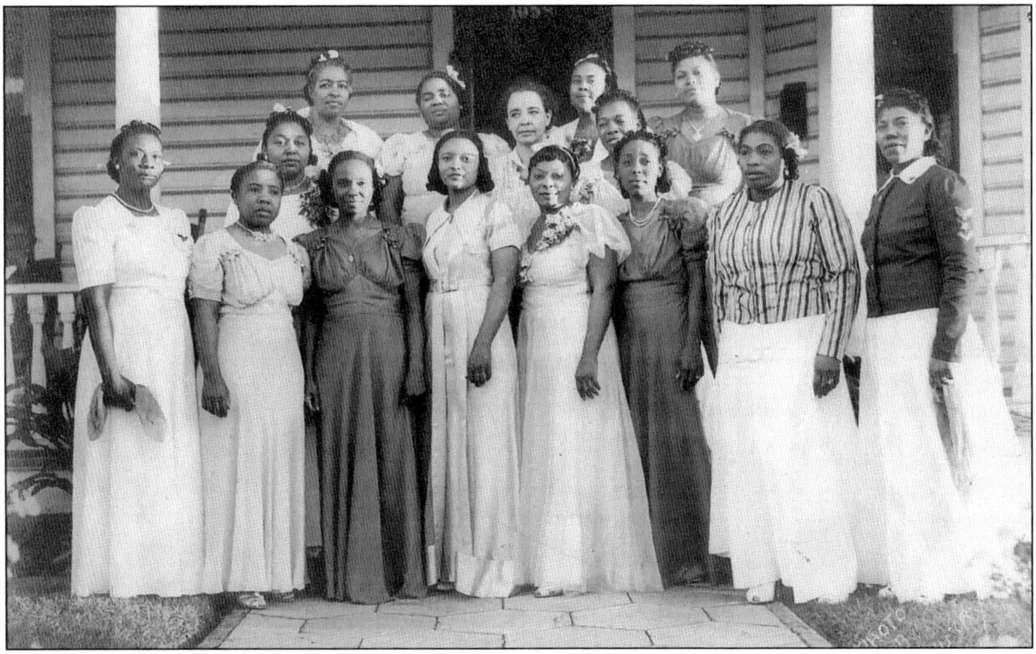

The City Federation of Colored Women's Clubs was born out of segregation and built by people who were denied participation in white civic, service, and social organizations. One of the clubs was the Quest Federated Club, founded in 1934 by Veleta P. Nelson. Members provided early support to the Health Clinic for African Americans and Mercy Hospital. They also provided wheelchairs and helped equip the first Campbell Park Recreation Center. This picture appears on the front cover of the book.

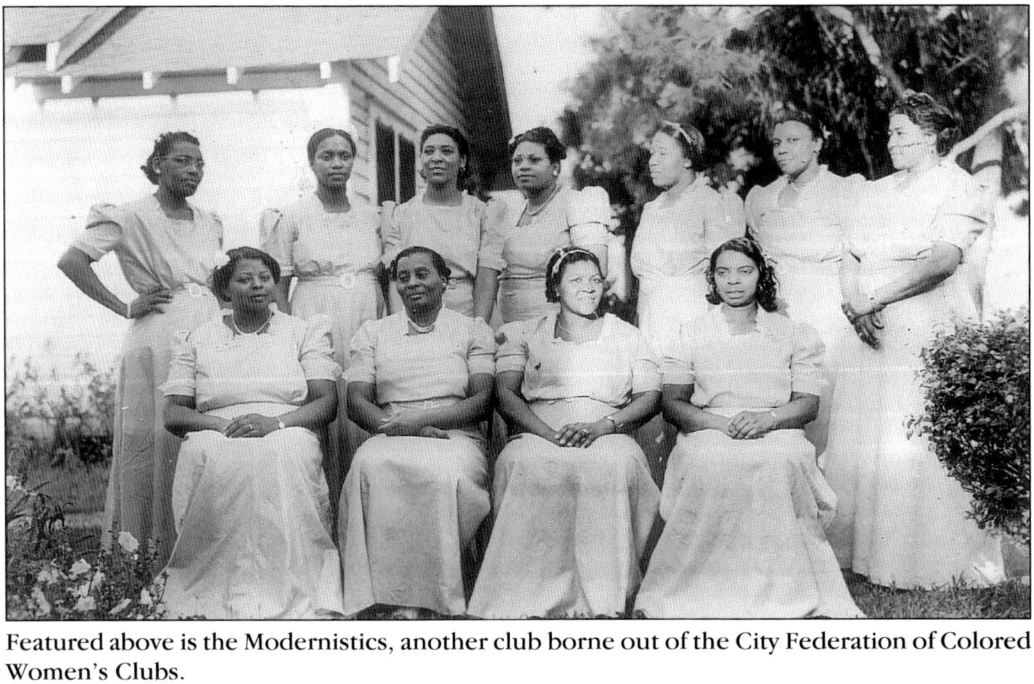

Featured above is the Modernistics, another club borne out of the City Federation of Colored Women's Clubs.

Featured here is Mrs. Fannie A. Ponder, the organizer and founder of the City Federation of Colored Women's Clubs. She also founded the St. Petersburg Metropolitan Council, an affiliate of the National Council of Negro Women.

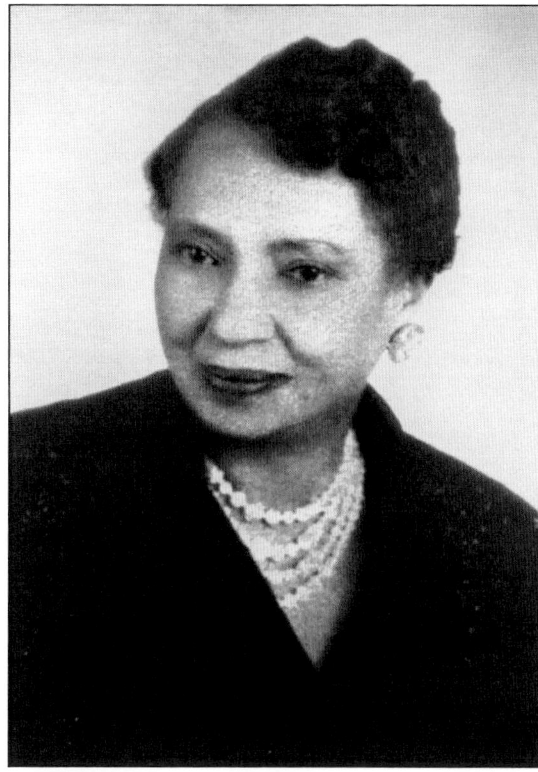

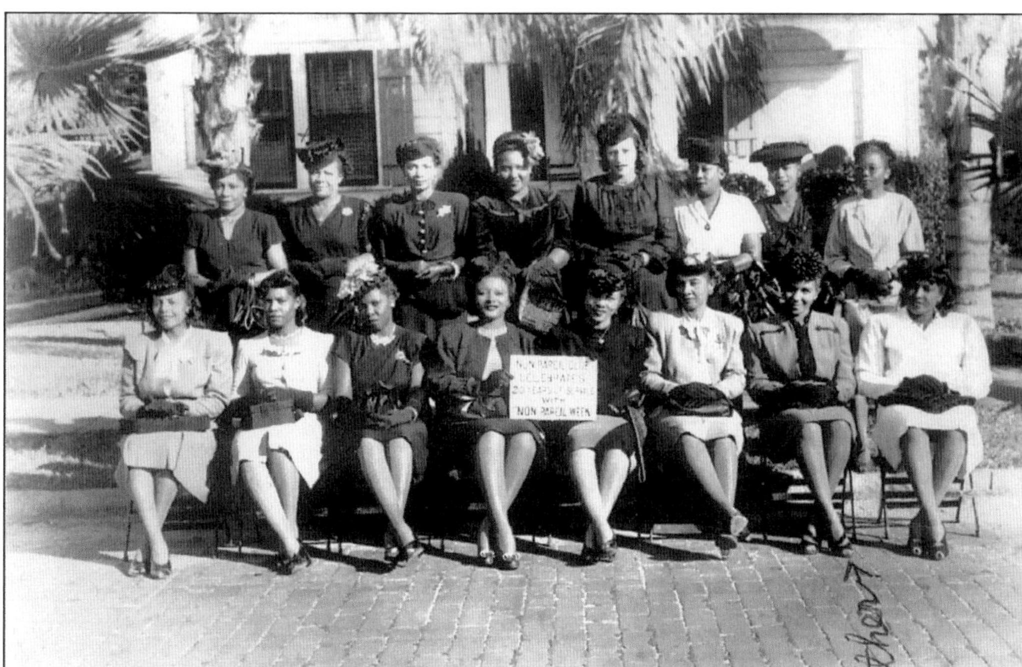

The Non Pareil club was organized in 1927 by Fannye Ponder. The club helped to establish the federation and the clubhouse.

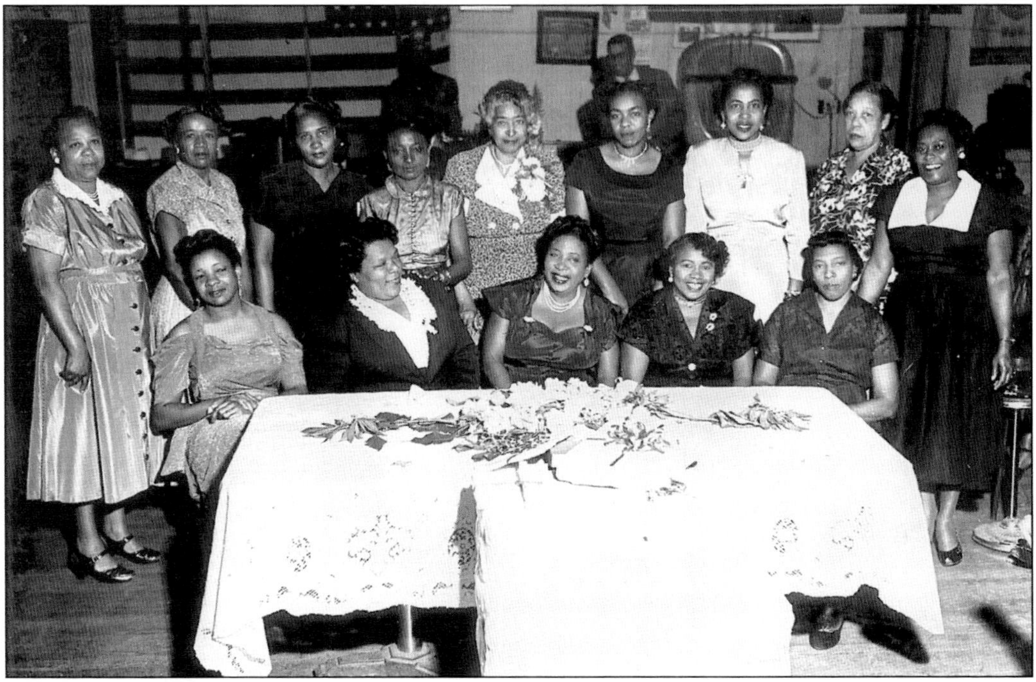

This organization was the Daughters of Elks Sunshine Temple #168. The group met in the late 1950s and early 1960s.

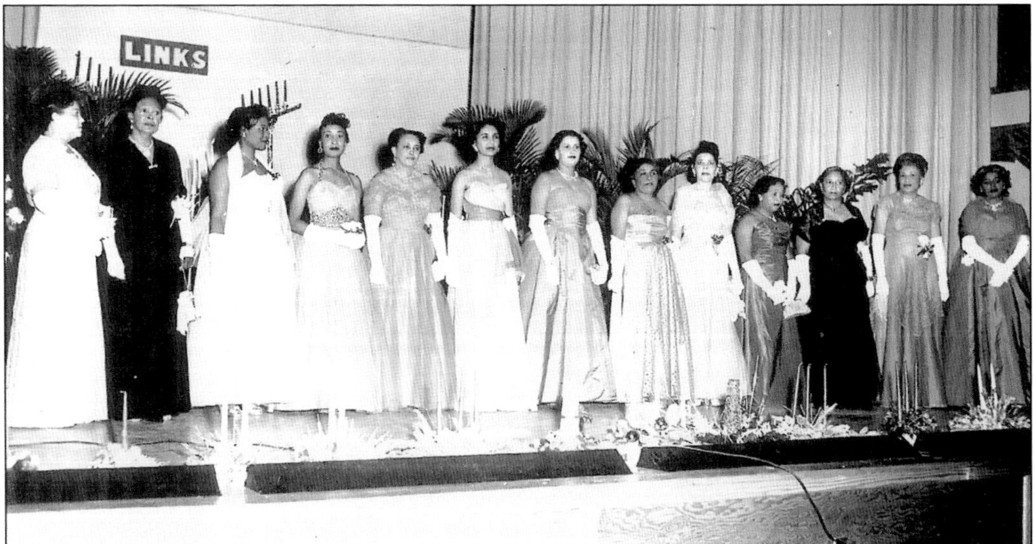

This photograph shows the Links Inc. Debutante in the 1950s. Pictured from left to right are Preston Pughlsey, Maggie Williams, Peggy Archie, Rose Archie, Eddie McCrae Williams, Anna Polk Walker, Helen Ayer, A. Leggett, Mary McRae, Jewell Archie, Johna Bell Andrews, Mary A. Polk, and Alice White. The national organization was first organized in 1946 in Philadelphia. The St. Petersburg-Tampa Chapter began in March 1951 at the home of Edward McRae in St. Petersburg. The first president was Helen Ayer. The organization presents debutante balls and holds fund-raising drives for scholarships.

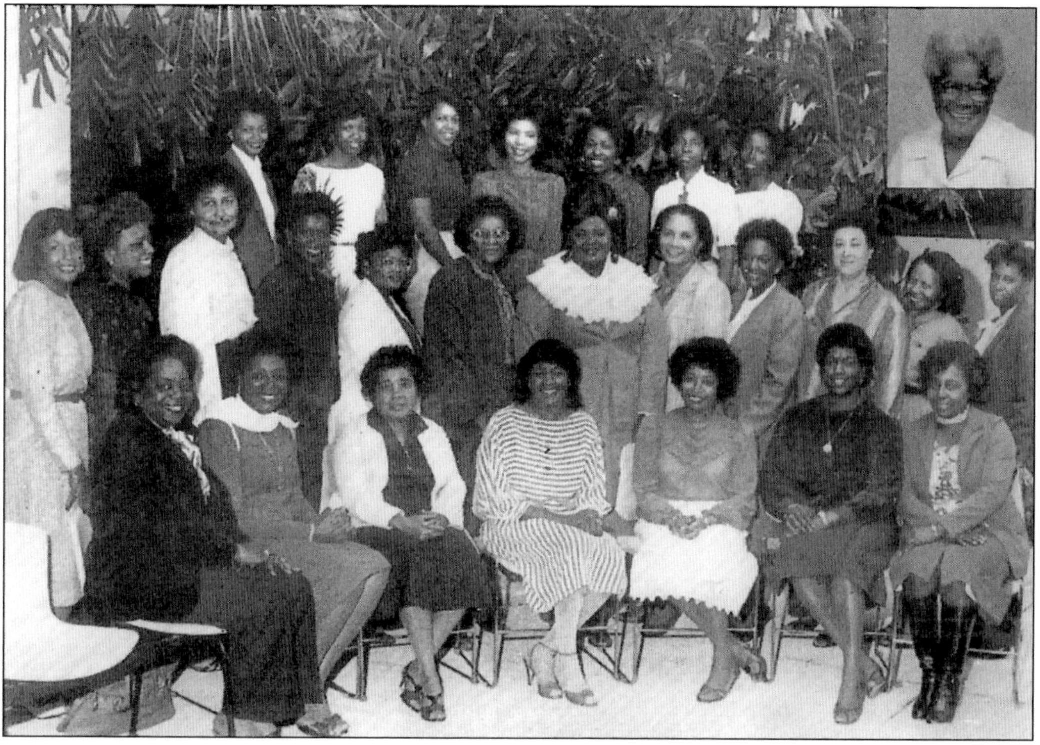

Pictured above is the St. Petersburg alumnae chapter of Delta Sigma Theta Sorority.

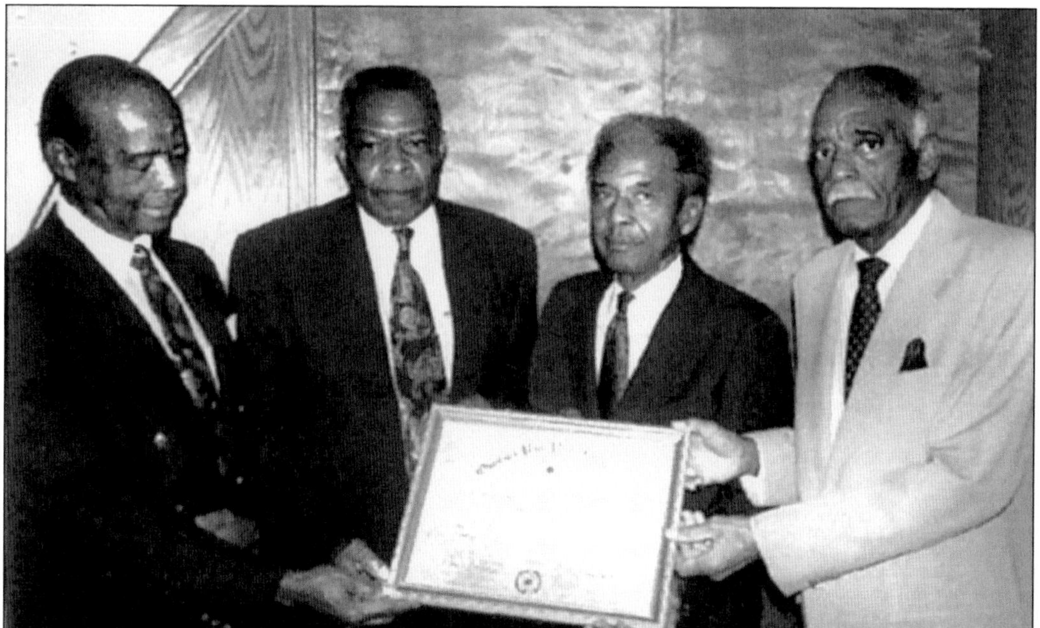

Pictured here are founding members of Eta Rho Chapter (St. Petersburg) of Omega Psi Phi Fraternity, Inc. From left to right, they are Mordecai Walker, James Jackson, Cyrus Everette, and James Chapman. Founders not pictured are Morris Milton and Willie Ervin Rouson.

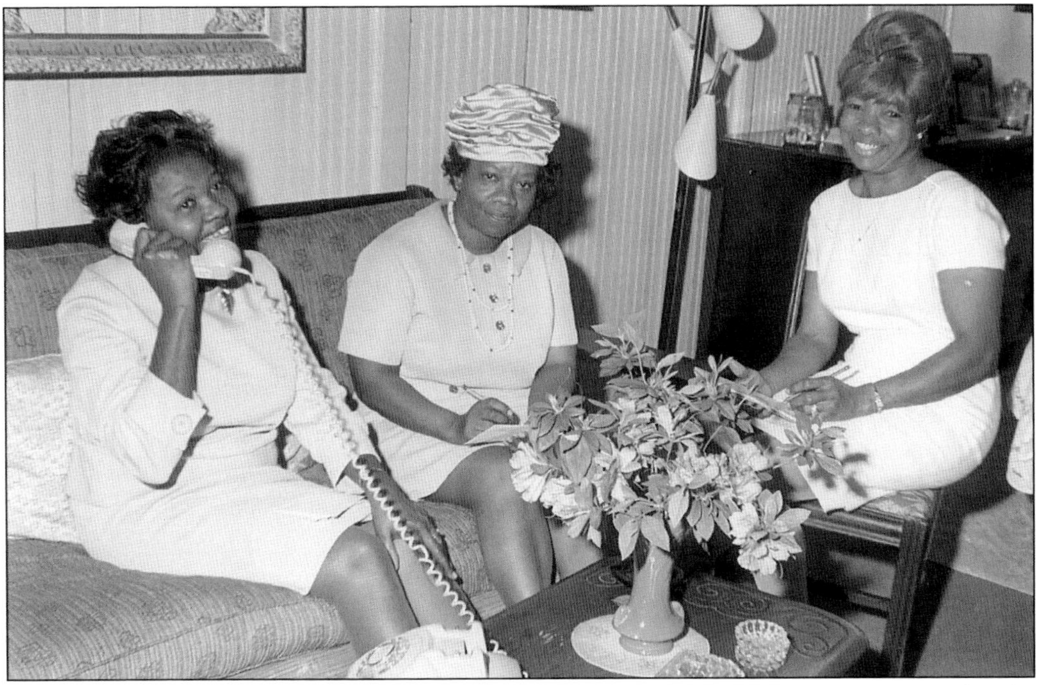

The Adrilla Cail Service Woman's League plans a tea in this 1971 photograph. Posing for the picture, from left to right, are Andrenia Shammon, co-chairman; Rosa Evans, vice president; and Vermell K. Johnson, president.

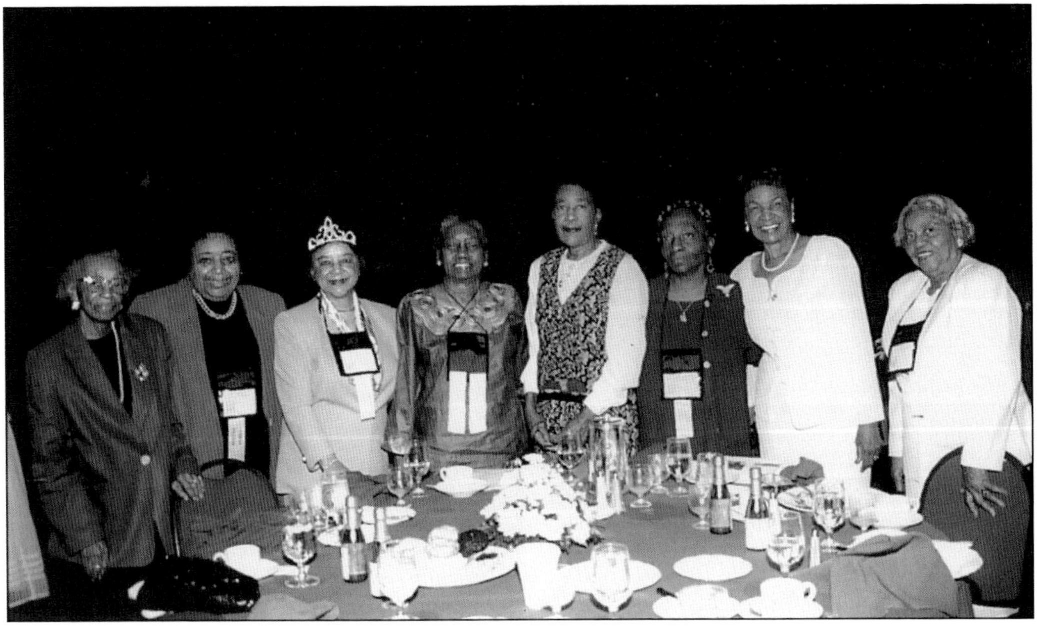

Pictured above are "Golden Sorors." These sorority members of Alpha Kappa Alpha have been members for 50 years or more. Pictured at the extreme left is Vivian Henry. Fifth from left is Inez Ford and to her right is Pauline Givens. This picture was taken in Orlando in 1999.

Eight

Trailblazers and Civic Leaders

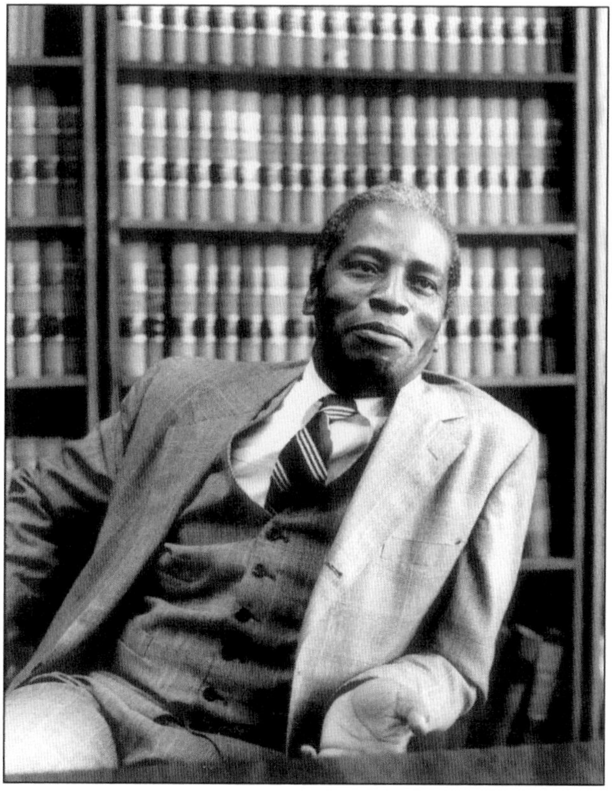

Judge James B. Sanderlin of St. Petersburg was the first African American to be elected to a countywide office in Pinellas County. He was elected as a county judge in November 1972. As a lawyer, he defended the sanitation workers who went on strike for higher wages in the 1960s. He also filed a petition on May 7, 1964, seeking an injunction against the school board from operating a state-imposed bi-racial school system in Pinellas County.

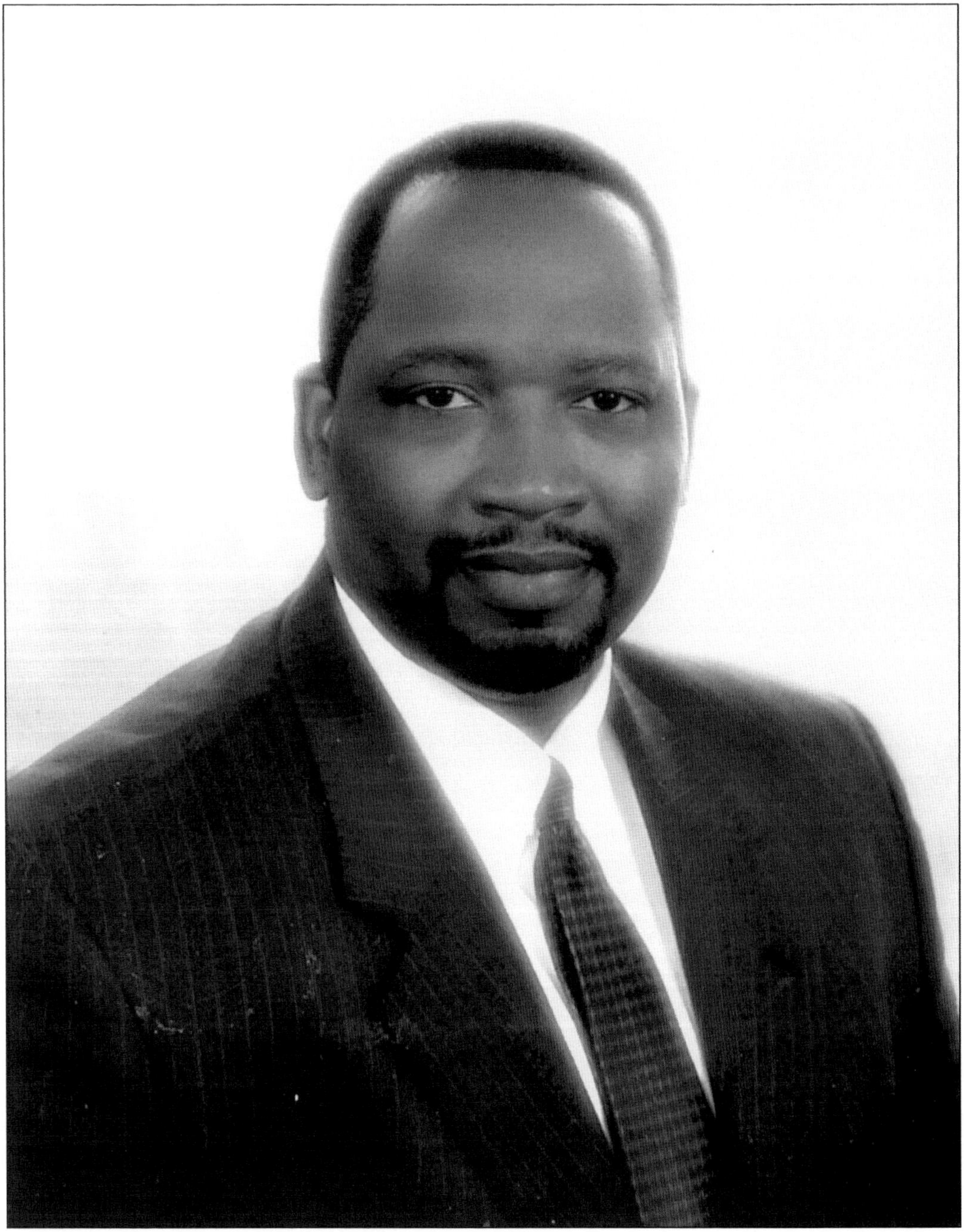

In November 2000, Kenneth T. Welch was elected to the board of county commissioners of Pinellas County. He became the first African American from St. Petersburg to be elected to the board. After graduating from Florida A&M University in 1987, he returned to St. Petersburg, married his high school sweetheart, and worked at Florida Power Corporation for more than 12 years as a senior account, IT analyst, and financial systems administrator. In 1998, he was appointed by Gov. Jeb Bush to the St. Petersburg Junior College board of trustees.

This is a photograph of C. Bette Wimbish. In March of 1960 she ran for the Pinellas County school board on a platform advocating school improvements that were not determined by racial considerations. Although she lost the election, she received much support and carried one all-white district. However, she was subjected to threatening phone calls and letters, and she had firebombs thrown at her house and crosses burned on her lawn. In 1969 she ran for city council and won.

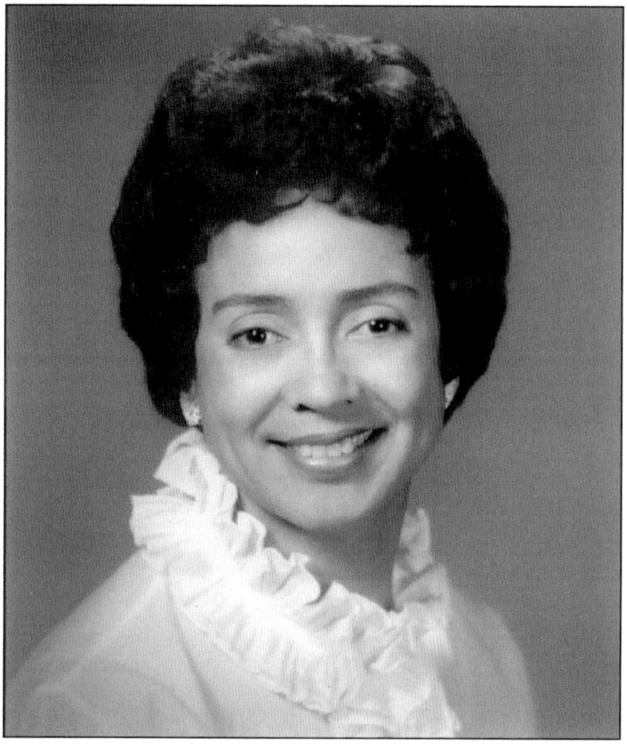

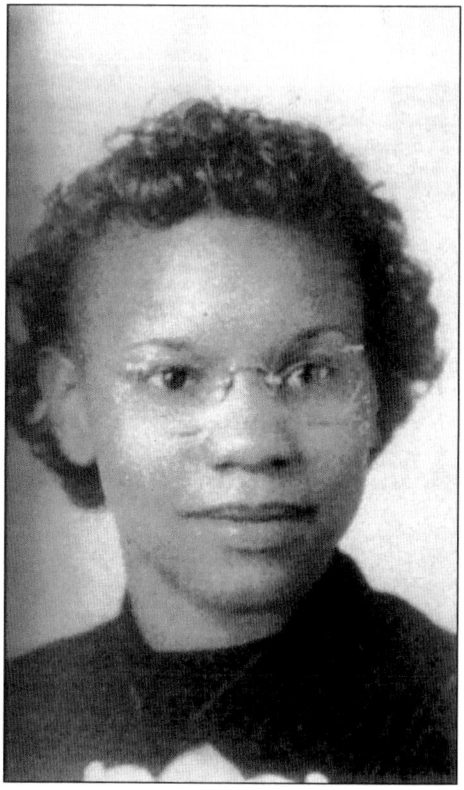

Pictured at left is Johnnie Ruth Clarke, who served as associate dean of academic affairs at St. Petersburg Junior College. In 1966, she became the first African-American woman to earn a doctorate at a Florida public university.

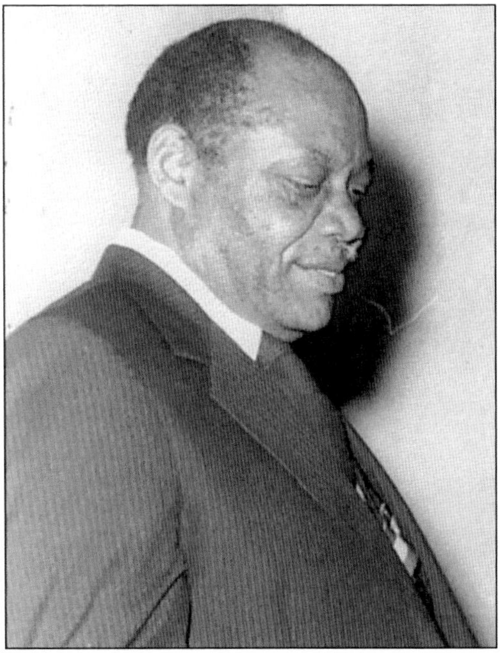

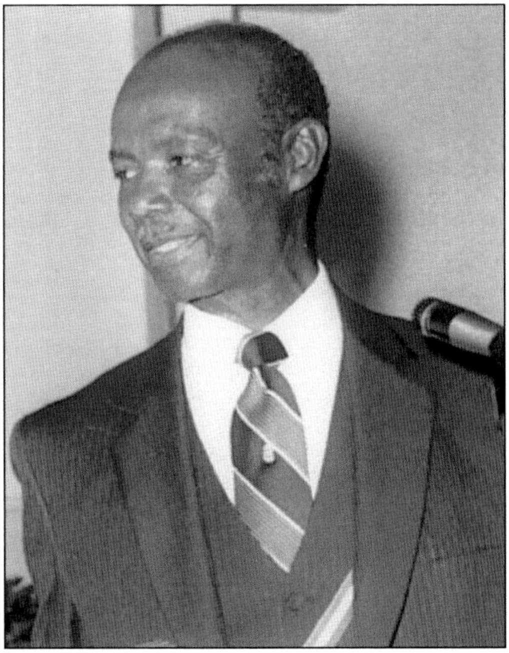

To the left is Dr. Robert Swain. In the mid-1950s he fought Jim Crow laws to build a six-unit apartment building at 1501 22nd Street South in St. Petersburg. For about six weeks each year, he rented apartments to African-American baseball players during spring training. To the right is Mordecai Walker, a former president of the Ambassador's Club, which provided numerous services to the community.

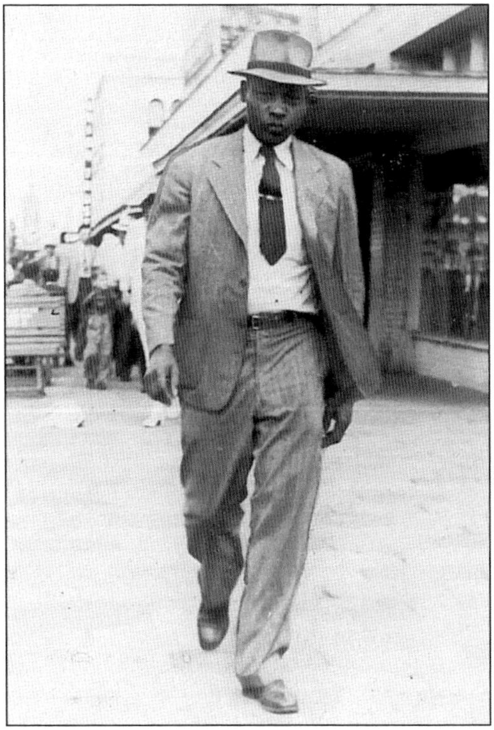

Pictured at left is F.A. Dunn, chairman of the local NAACP during the attempts to desegregate Spa Pool in the 1950s. A statement issued from his organization read, "We consider the act of city officials to close the beach as being arbitrary and unwarranted since there was no indication of violence or misconduct on the part of those who sought to use the facilities."

In picture at right, Fred G. Minnis receives a meritorious award. A local activist, he founded the community Democratic Club of St. Petersburg, an organization that developed political leadership for local blacks in the 1960s. He also served as co-chairman of the community alliance for two terms and his law firm landed many Civil Rights cases in the 1960s. From 1976 to 1978, Minnis served as national president of the Howard University Alumni Association.

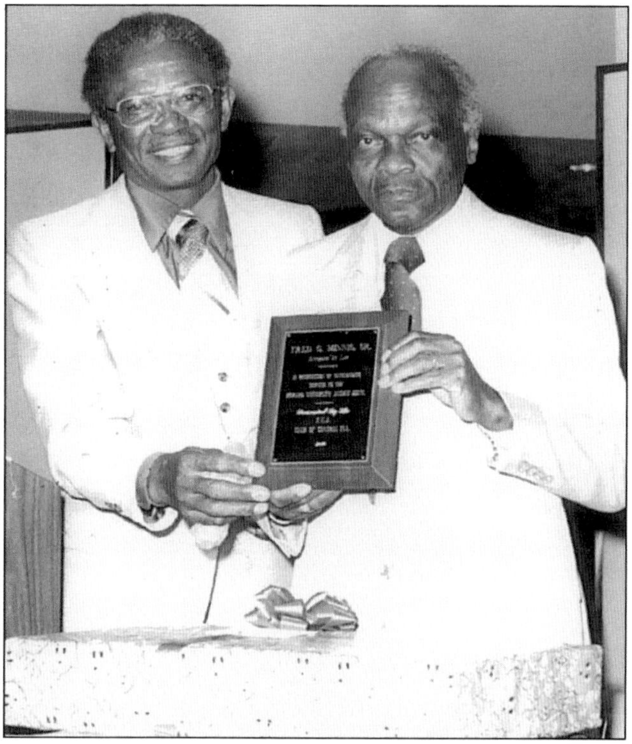

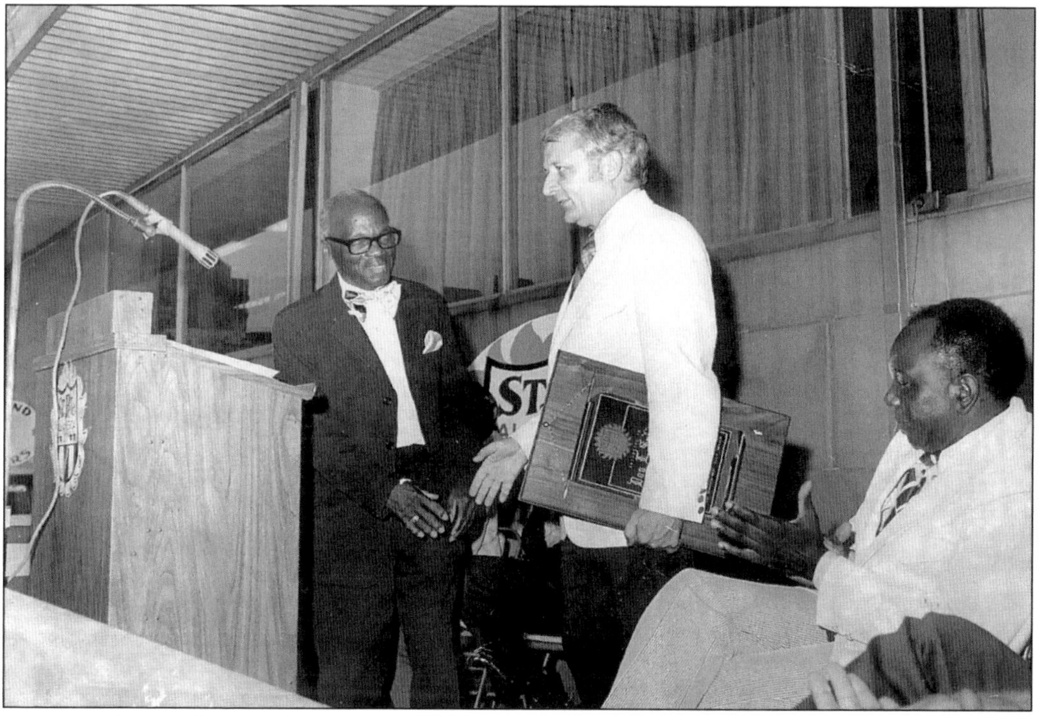

Pictured above, the gentleman on the right is Israel Heard, who was a plaintiff in a 1988 lawsuit for single district voting. To the far right is Fred Minnis. In the middle is Ron Spicer.

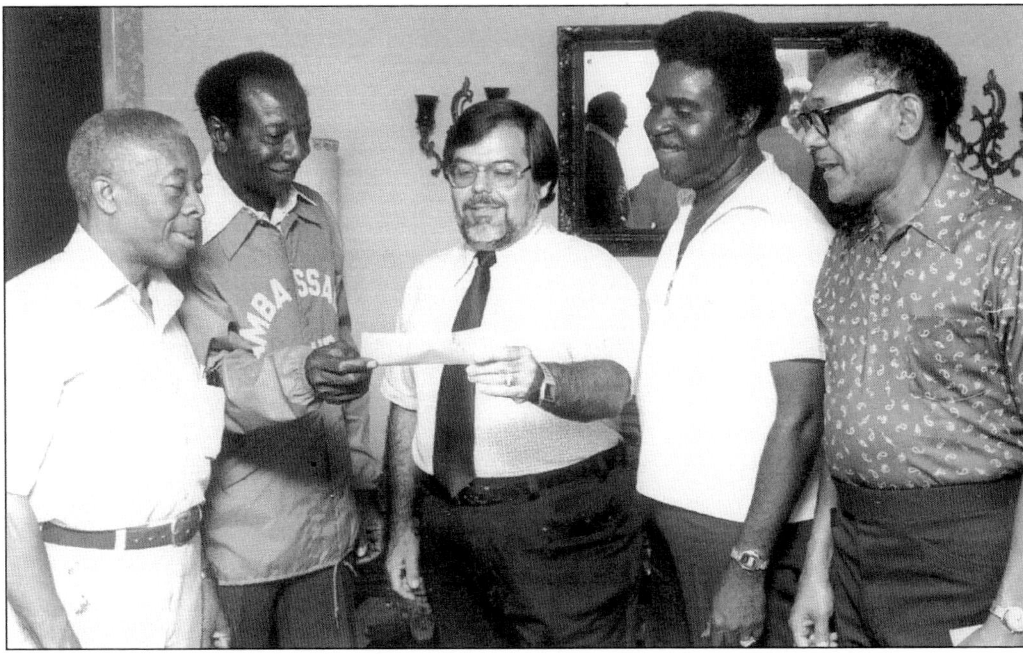

Ambassador Club members are presenting a check to the Juvenile Welfare Board in the 1980s. From left to right are L.D. Brown, Ralph James (son of Chester James), Louis McCoy, and Ernest Ponder.

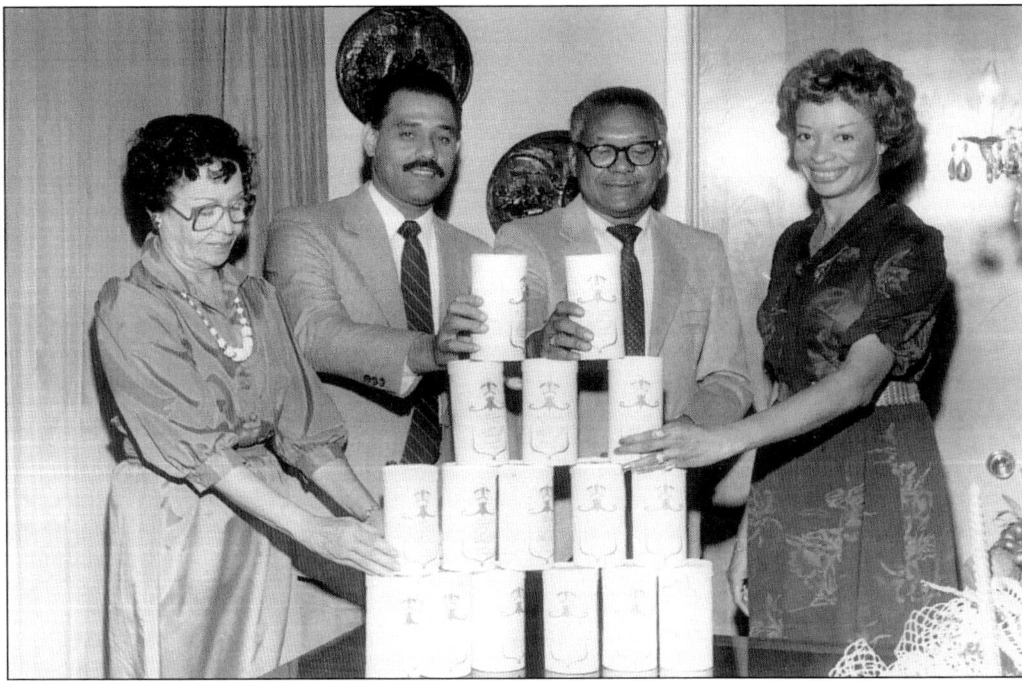

Above, donation cups for a food fund are being stacked. Ambassador Club members and some of the wives "Ambas" are involved in this project. Pictured from left to right are Clara Ponder, George Baker, Ernest Ponder, and Gwen Wade.

Cecil B. Keene served as principal of Gibbs High School from 1969 to 1971, was elected to the St. Petersburg city council, and was appointed to the State Board of Regents. Presently, he serves as a member of the Board of Trustees of St. Petersburg College (formerly St. Petersburg Junior College.)

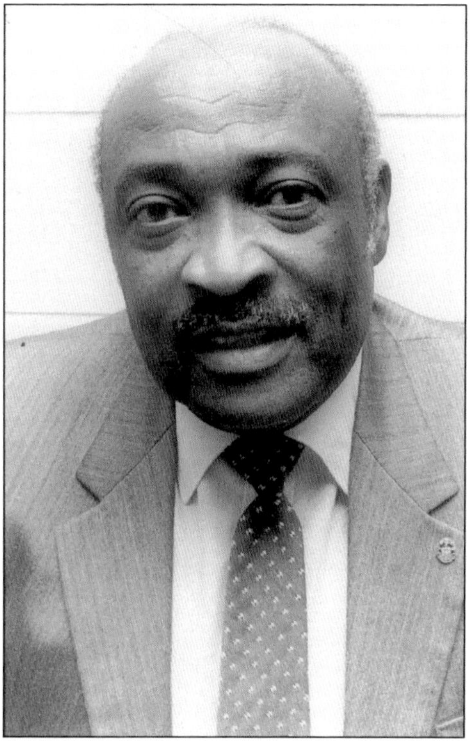

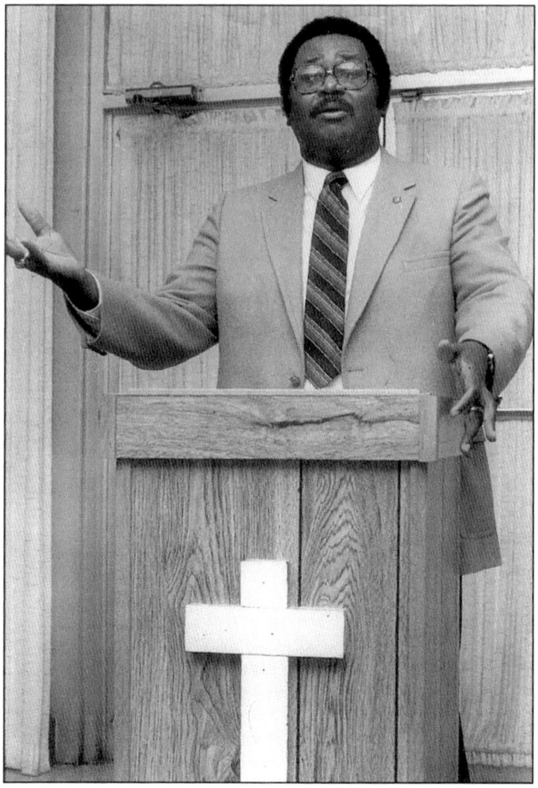

After serving several terms as the state legislator from St. Petersburg, in 1993, Douglas L. Jamerson (left) was appointed by Gov. Lawton Chiles as commissioner of education. He served in this position until 1995 and then served as secretary of labor from 1995 to 1998. A Pinellas County School was recently named in his honor.

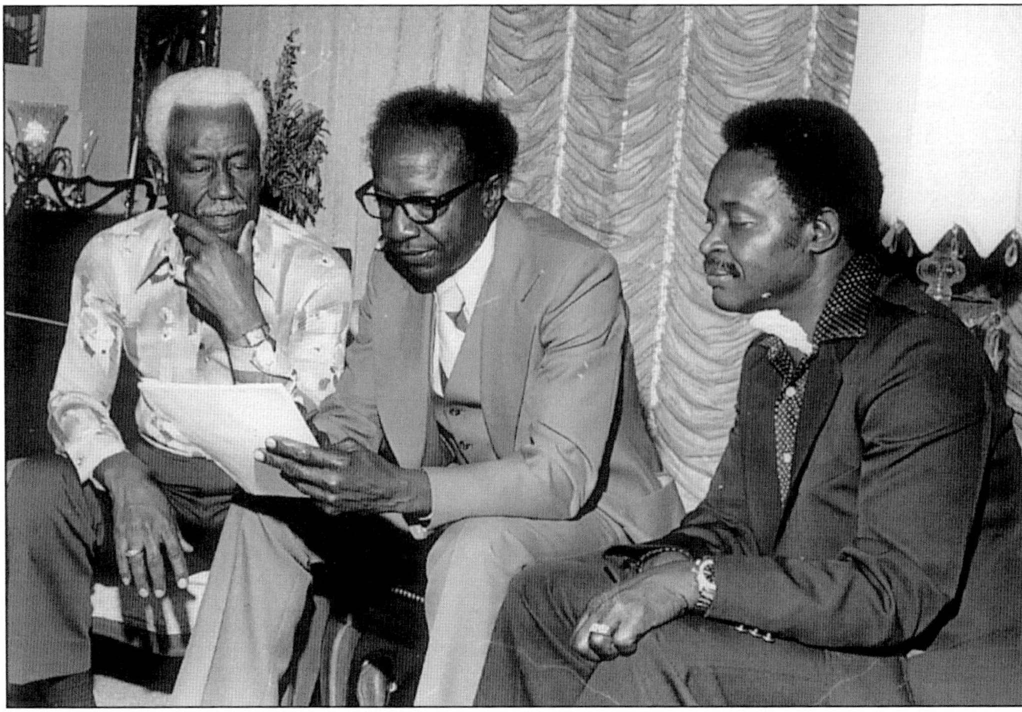

Pictured from left to right are Emmanuel Stewart, Ralph James, and Samuel Robinson. They are Ambassador Club Members who appear to be preparing for an upcoming meeting or other event.

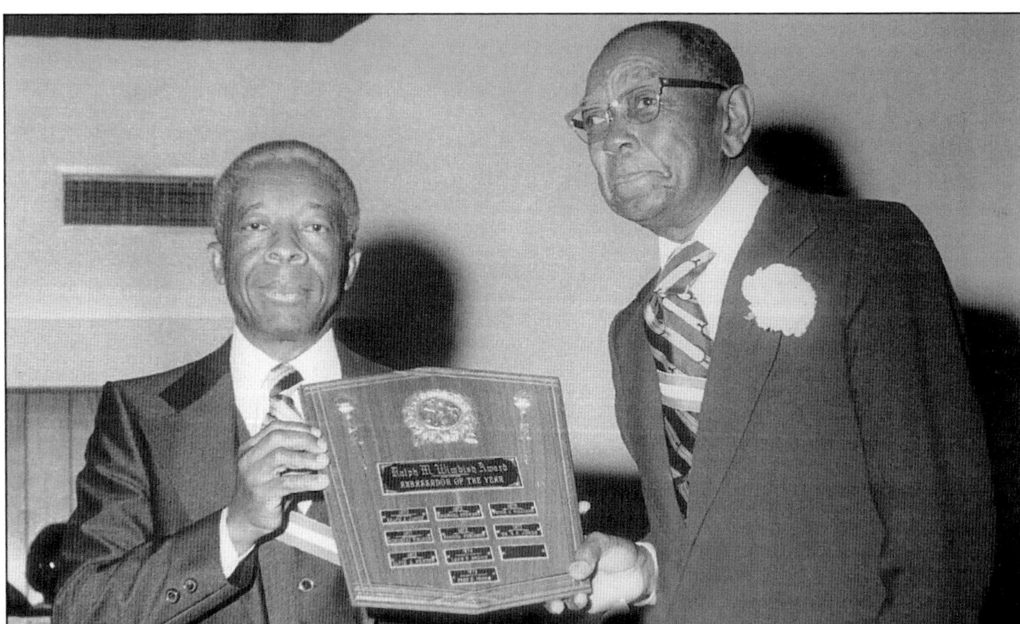

Above, the Ralph Wimbish Award for Ambassador of the Year is being presented to B.F. Jones by L.D. Brown.

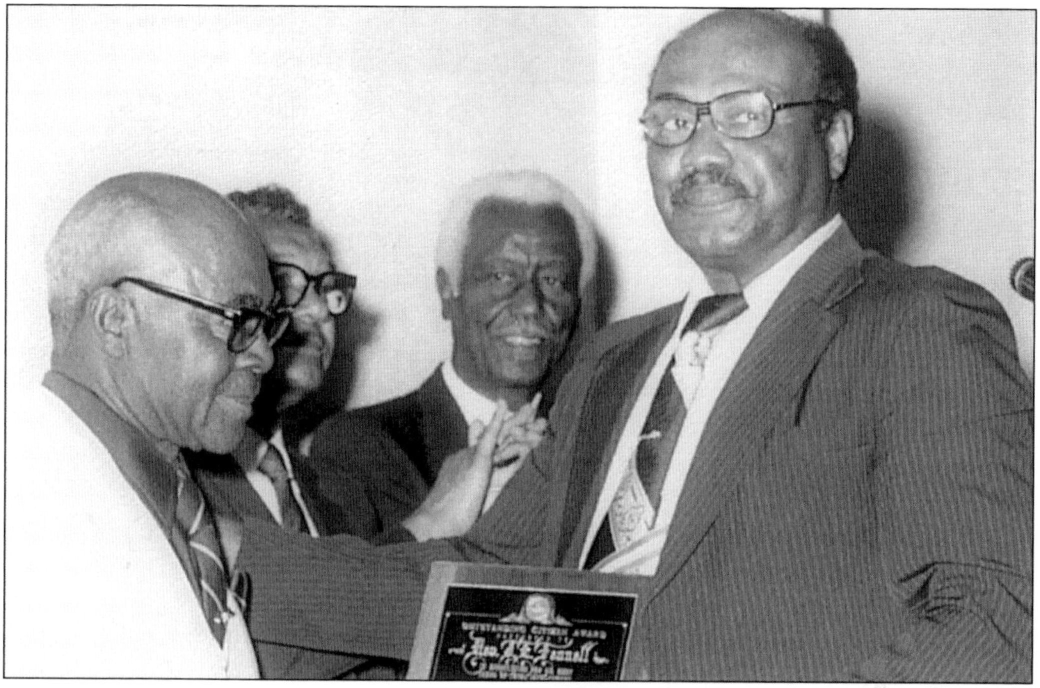

Reverend Fennell is being presented an Outstanding Citizen Award by Ambassador Club Member Henry Jones. Emanuel Stewart appears in the background.

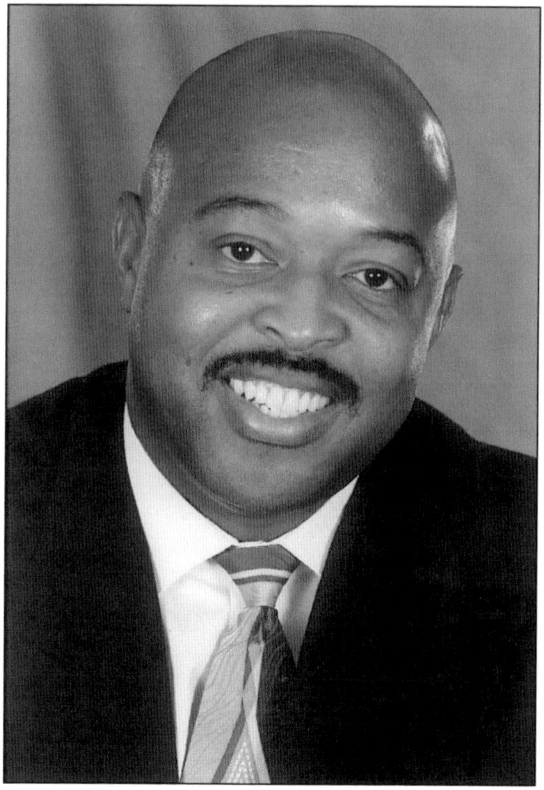

Dr. Goliath Davis was the first African American to be appointed to the position of chief of police for St. Petersburg, He currently serves as deputy mayor.

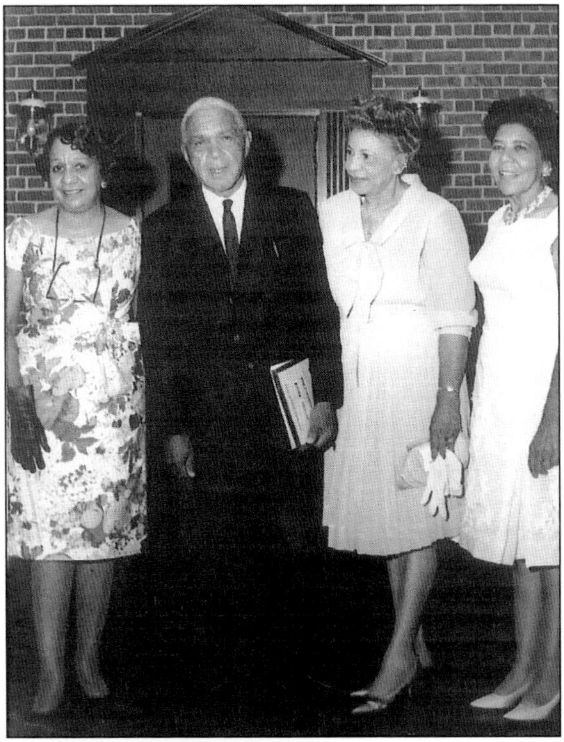

Dr. Andrew Polk, former principal of Gibbs High School (1946–1952), celebrates his retirement from Florida A&M University in this 1960s photograph. He is joined by (from left to right) Mrs. George W. Gore, wife of the college president; his wife, Mrs. Mary A. Polk; and Mrs. Mary McCrae.

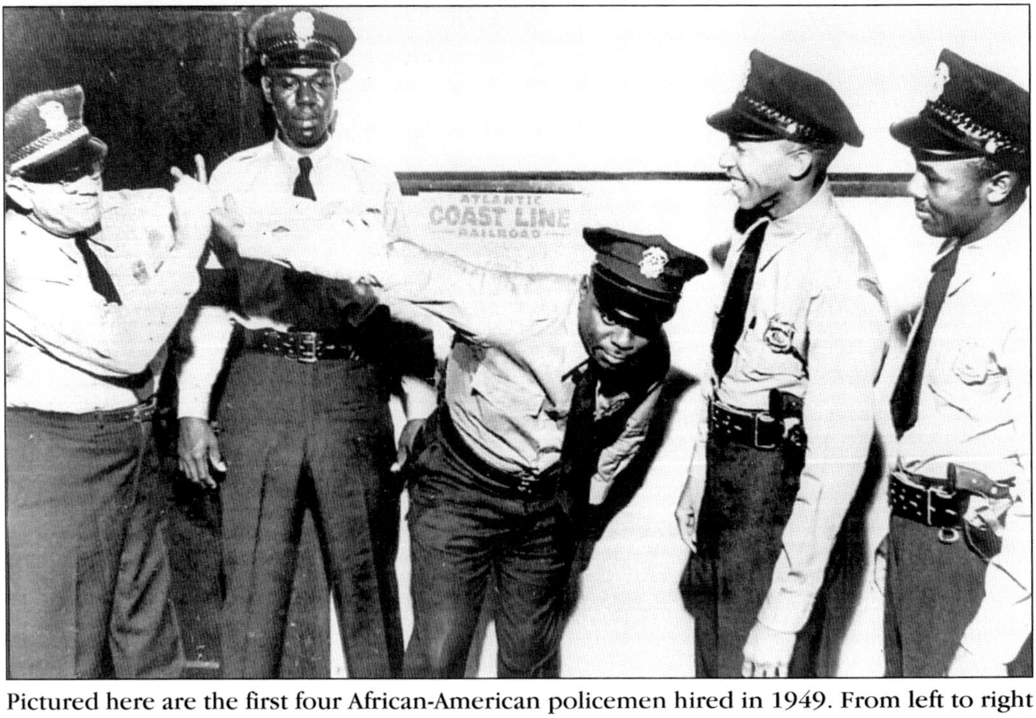

Pictured here are the first four African-American policemen hired in 1949. From left to right are Lt. Robinson, who supervised the recruits; Sam Jones, who became the department's first black sergeant; Titus Robinson; Willie Seay; and Louis Burrows.

Ike Williams, a prominent St. Petersburg attorney, also served as attorney for his church, Bethel Community Baptist. In a program honoring J.P. Moses, Ike Williams cited Moses's statement to a Clearwater judge in 1960 that a segregated courtroom was not conducive to justice. According to Mr. Williams in an article written by Joe Oglesby for the *St. Petersburg Times*, "J.P., not only took the leadership in integrating the courts, he was a primary force in registration drives at a time when it took courage just to register."

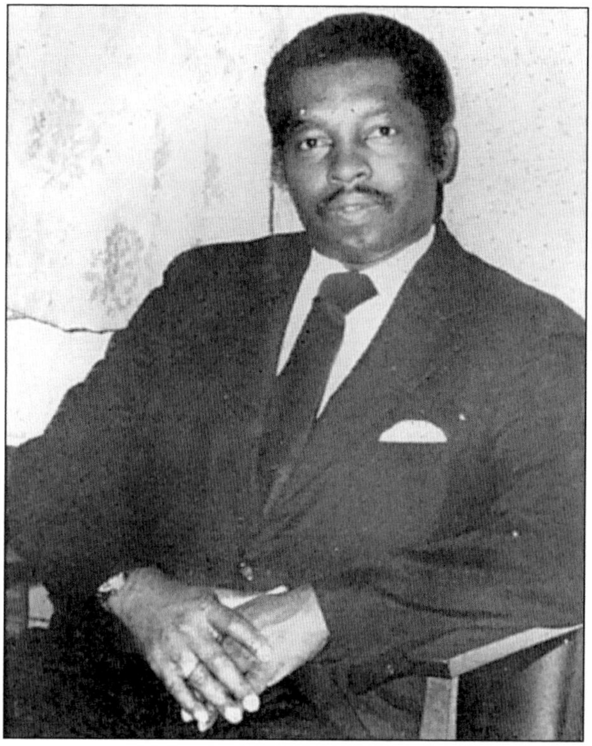

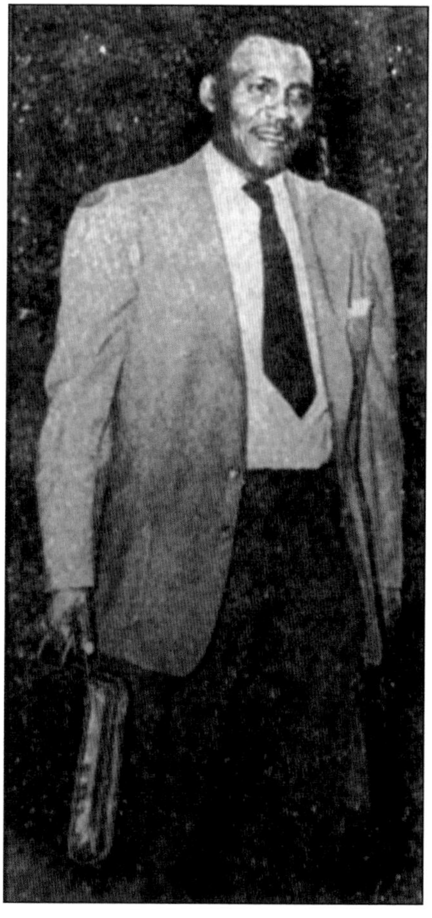

Jasper P. Moses was a local businessman who fought to integrate the Municipal Spa Beach and pool. He built Moses Enterprises, which included a dry cleaning and pressing business, sundry store, and a snack stand at Wildwood Park. Many credited him with convincing the county to build a gymnasium for Gibbs High School and providing school buses free of charge for African-American children. They had been charged 20 cents a day to ride the buses. In the 1940s, Jasper Philip Moses became St. Petersburg's first black bondsman.

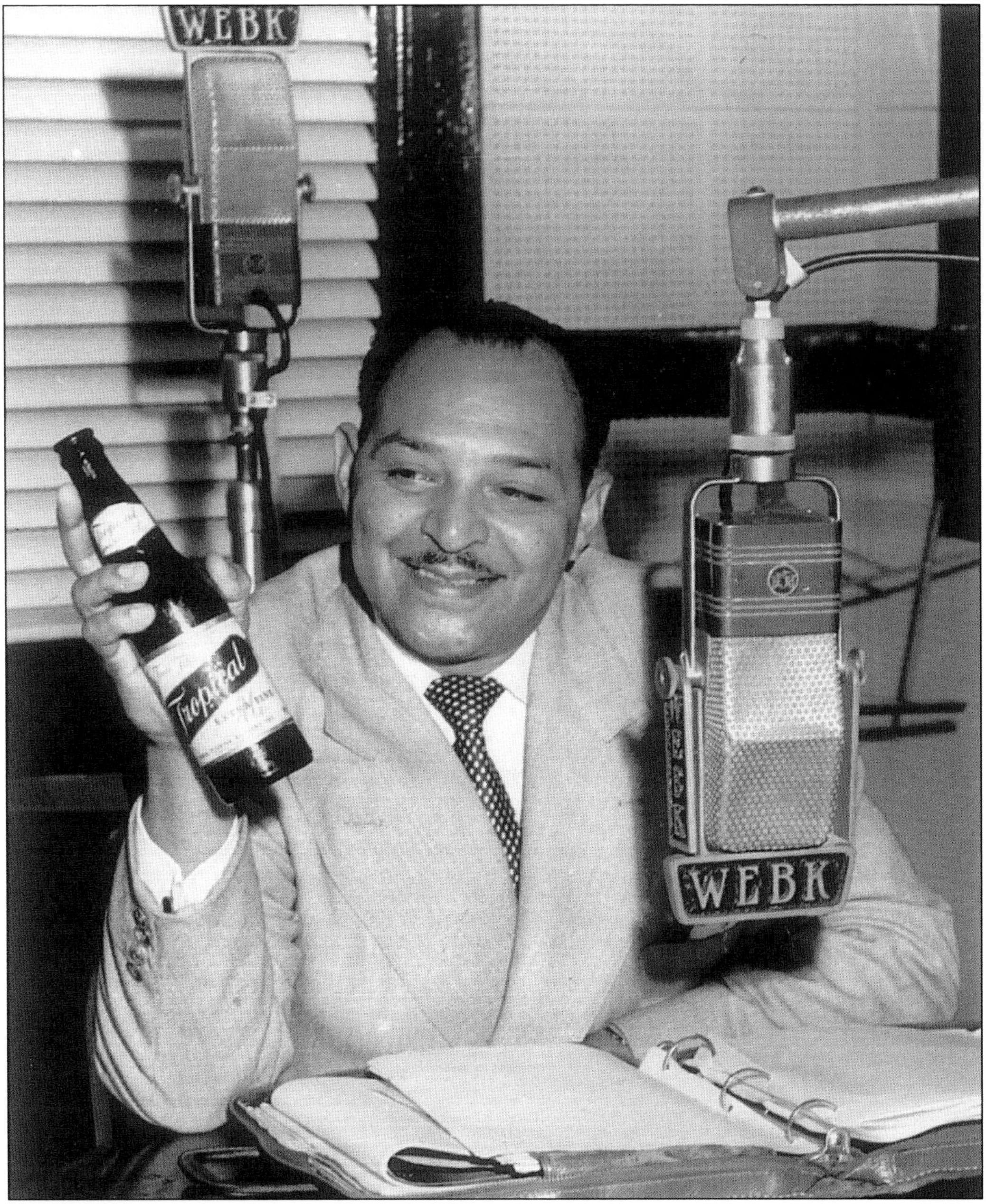

Norman E. Jones Sr. (1901–1990) was a photographer, publicist, and journalist. He was the Florida editor for the *Pittsburg Courier* and edited Negro pages of the *St. Petersburg Times* and *Evening Independent*. He contributed a column called "Let's Talk Politics" to black newspapers throughout Florida beginning in 1956 and did so for nearly 20 years. Jones was also very active in politics during his entire life. He became a supporter of George Wallace in 1968 and was chairman of the National Black Citizens Committee for Wallace for President in 1972. In the picture above Norman Jones advertises a beverage during his radio show, "Down on Central."

Nine

The Civil Rights Movement

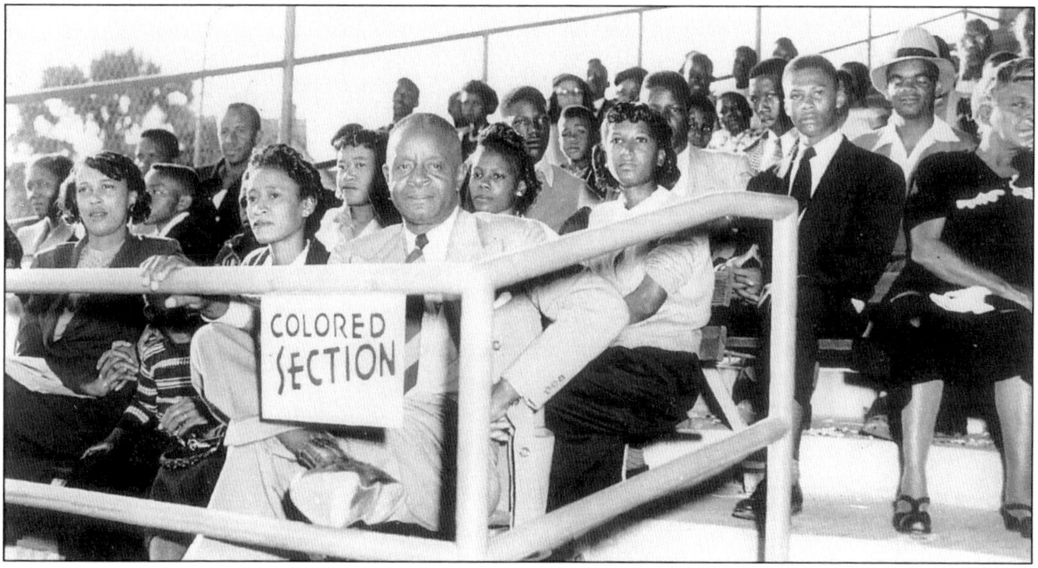

Even though many baseball players became national heroes during the Jim Crow era, their middle-class distinction and heroism did not gain them the freedom to live or shop wherever they desired. The baseball officials often ignored the problem by saying that the players were content with their living quarters and accommodations. It was not until the injustices in St. Petersburg were exposed and other surrounding areas joined the bandwagon that the officials felt they should remedy the situation. They undoubtedly were also concerned about the economical ramifications. The scene above was typical of what African-American fans had to endure while attending the spring training games in Pinellas County. The photograph depicts segregated seating at Al Lang Field in St. Petersburg. Pictured in the front to the right are Prof. Shirley W. Curtis, former principal of Pinellas High School, and his wife Gretchen Curtis. Some have also questioned if this is actually a segregated section of a stadium in Clearwater.

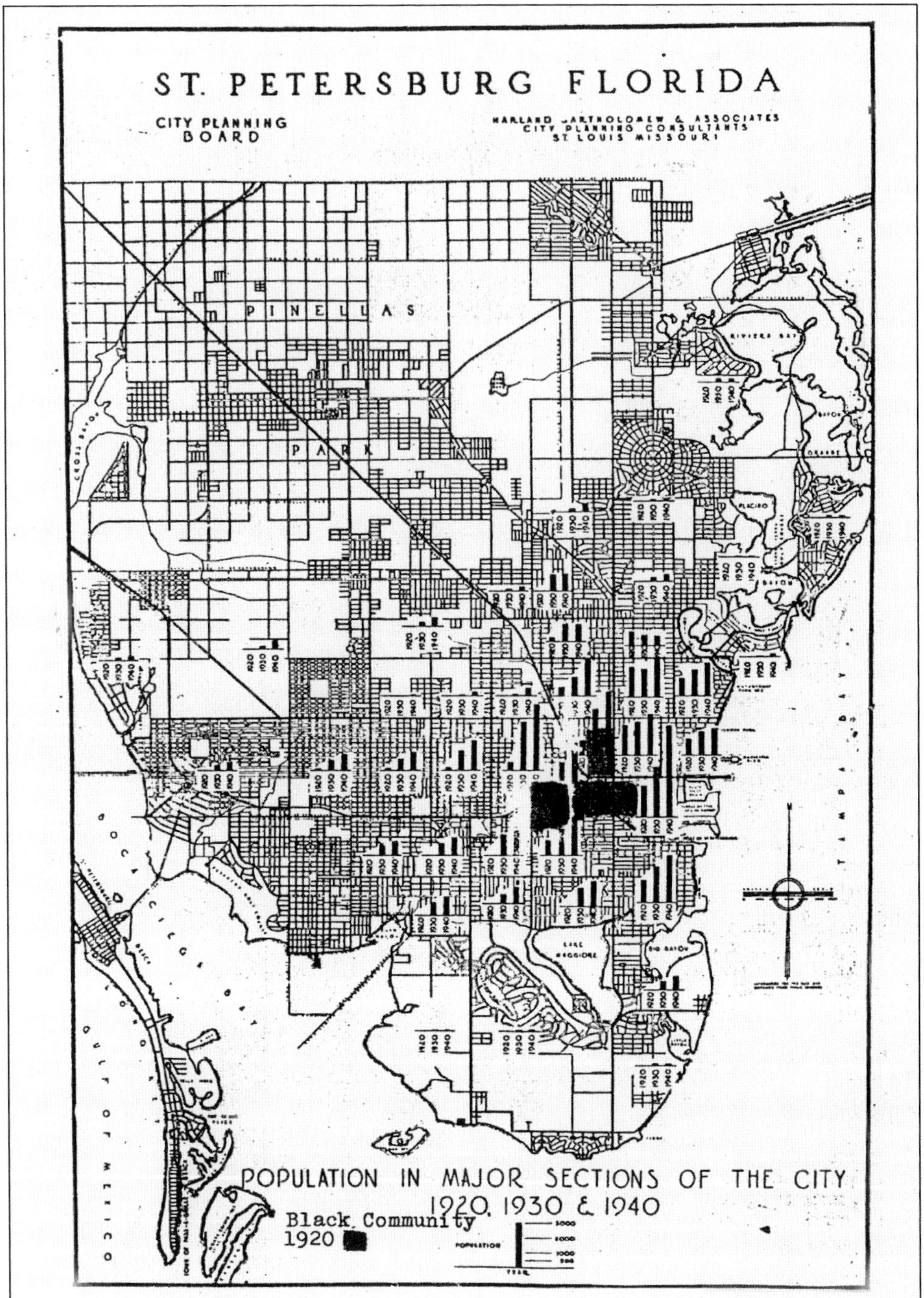

This map depicts the areas of St. Petersburg that were designated for African Americans. The darkened area to the left is "Methodist Town," located west of 9th Street and north of Central Avenue. The darkened area to the right is "Southside." The top darkened area was known as "Pepper Town" and was located along 4th Avenue South between 7th and 9th Streets, south of the railroad tracks (1st Avenue South).

CITY OF
ST. PETERSBURG
FLORIDA

DEPARTMENT OF LAW

CARROLL R. RUNYON,
CITY ATTORNEY
LEWIS T. WRAY,
ASST. CITY ATTORNEY
HARRY I. YOUNG,
ASST. CITY ATTORNEY

March 24,1936.

Hon. John S. Smith, Mayor,
St. Petersburg,
Florida.

Dear Sir:

The Committee appointed by you, composed of Col. McElgin, Raney H. Martin, and M.D. Wever, to recommend a district for the segregation of the colored people has worked hard to agree on lines, but have been unable to do so. However, the majority of the committee would recommend for the consideration of the Council the following district:

Commence at the intersection of 6th Ave. South and 17th St., follow 6th Ave. West to S. A. L. Railroad, follow right of way of railroad to 34th St. and South on 34th St. to 15th Avenue; East on 15th Avenue to 31st St., and on 31st St. N. to 12th Ave., East on 12th Ave. to 25th St. South on 25th St. to 13th Ave. S., E on 13th Ave to 22nd St. South on 22nd St. to 15th Ave. East on 15th Ave to 17th St., and North on 17th St. to intersection of 6th Ave., and 17th St. to place of beginning.

Respectfully submitted,

Raney H Martin
M. D. Wever
Chairman

3-24-36
Copies to be sent to each Councilman
5-1-36
Adopted
Sec 5-26-36

The letter above was written to Mayor John S. Smith on March 24, 1936, by the chairman of a committee designed to recommend a district for African-Americans to reside.

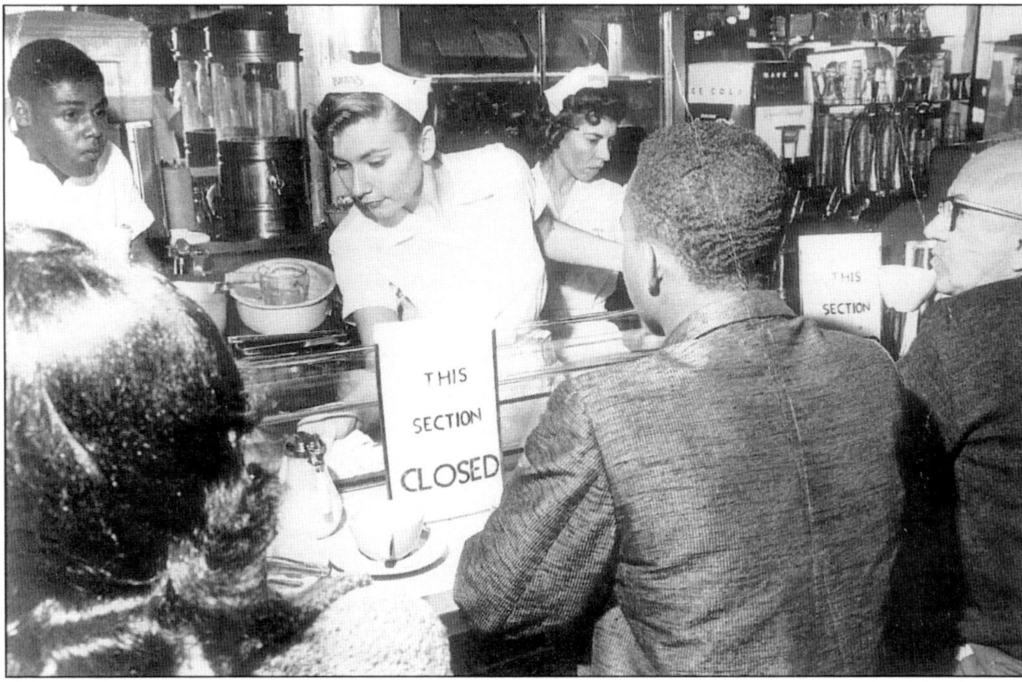

This *c*. 1960 scene depicts a lunch counter demonstration in Kress's Department Store. Demonstrators would take turns sitting until served; if not served, they would restrict the establishment from doing business.

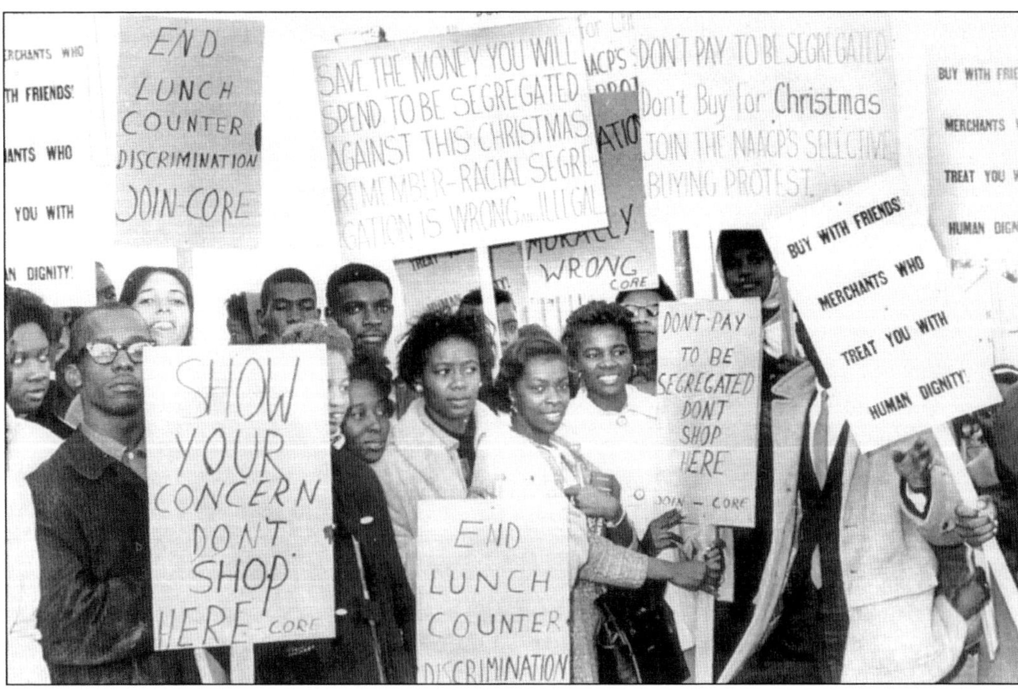

Above, students urge patrons to boycott businesses that discriminate. Note the sign: "Buy with friends: Merchants who treat you with human dignity."

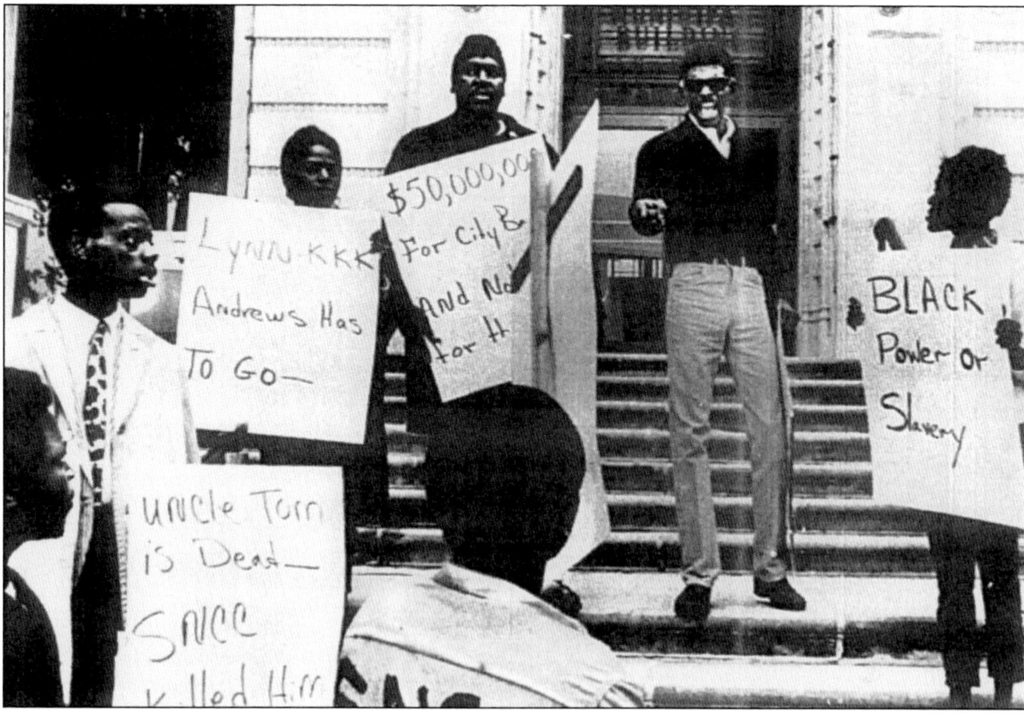

In 1966, Joseph Waller, vice chairman of the state's Student Nonviolent Coordinating Committee (SNCC), along with members of SNCC, marched to city hall in protest of a derogatory mural depicting black musicians performing for whites. The stereotypic mural had been displayed at City Hall since the 1940s. Waller and his group had asked the city council to remove the mural, but had received no response. The group therefore took matters in their own hands and tore the mural down, dragging it through the street. Waller was arrested and charged in municipal court and circuit court, but the conviction was overturned by the Supreme Court in a landmark case involving double jeopardy. Depicted in this scene is Joseph Waller vehemently expressing his disapproval of the derogatory image.

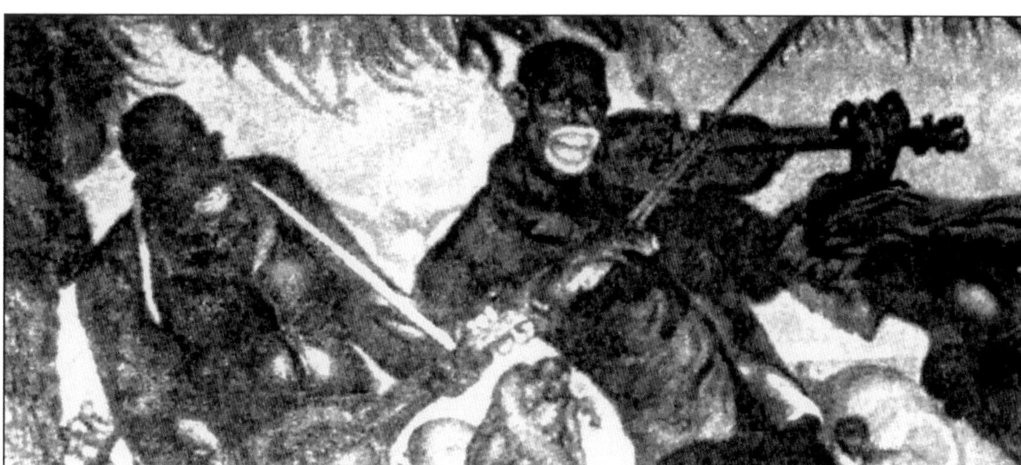

This is a picture of the mural that was removed from St. Petersburg City Hall.

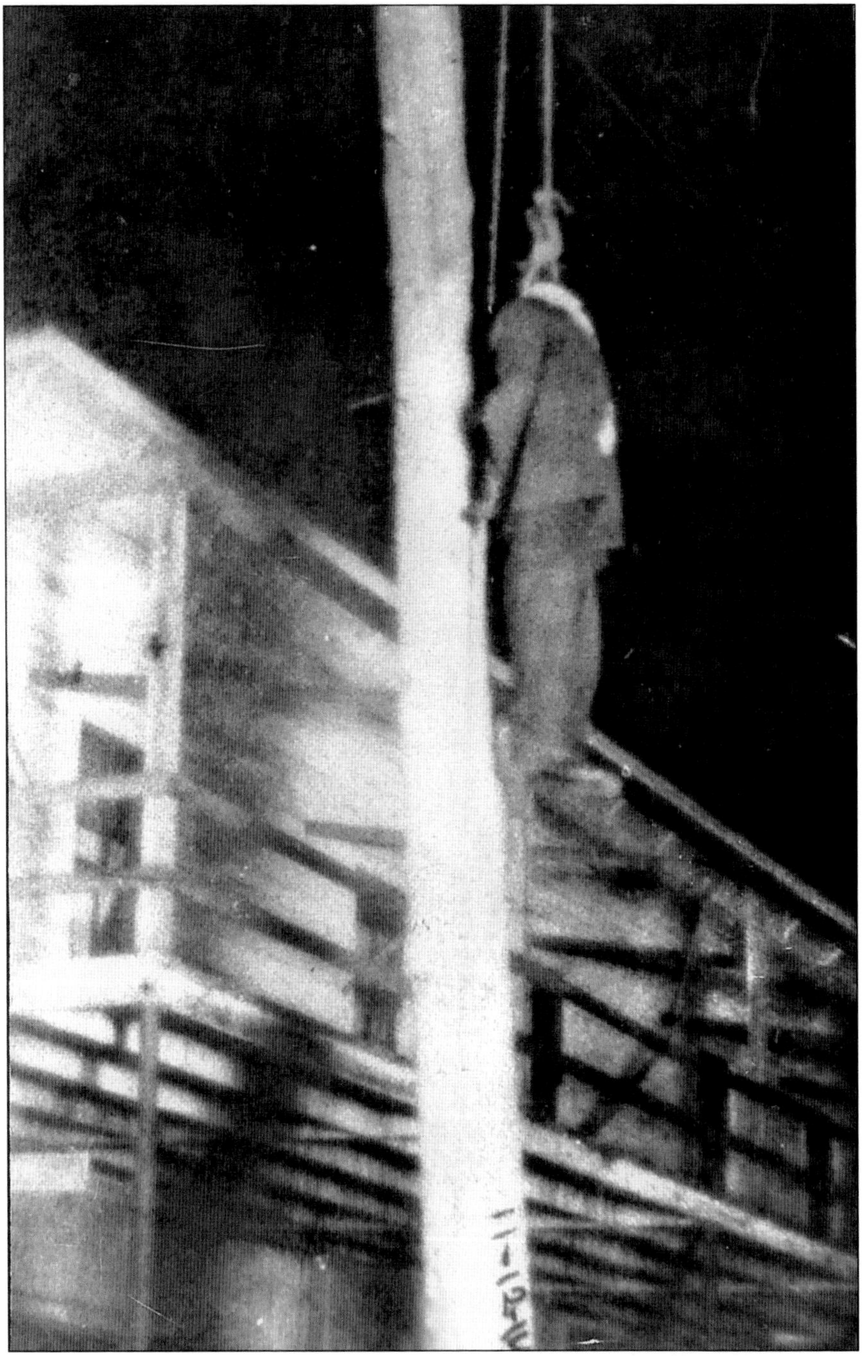

On November 12, 1914 John F. Evans was taken from the city jail by vigilantes after being accused of killing Edward F. Sherman and raping his wife. He was hanged from a telephone pole at the corner of 9th Street and 2nd Avenue South, and his dangling body was riddled with bullets fired by the lynching mob. The lynching caused hundreds of black residents to flee in fear of their lives, and it caused Florida governor Park Trammell to consider calling out troops to restore order in St. Petersburg.

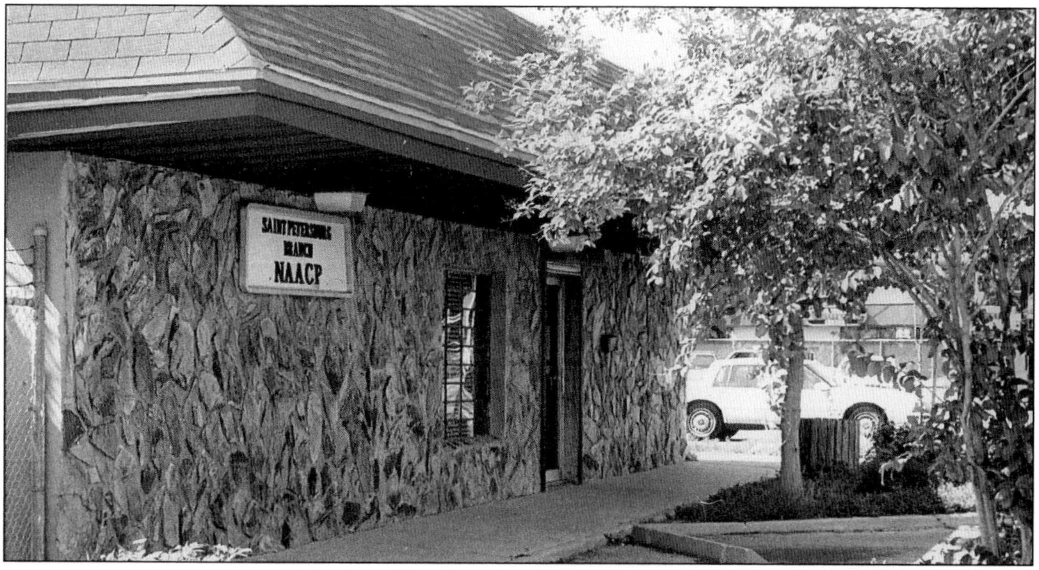

Pictured above is the local headquarters of the NAACP, located at 1501 16th Street South. The facility opened in 1987.

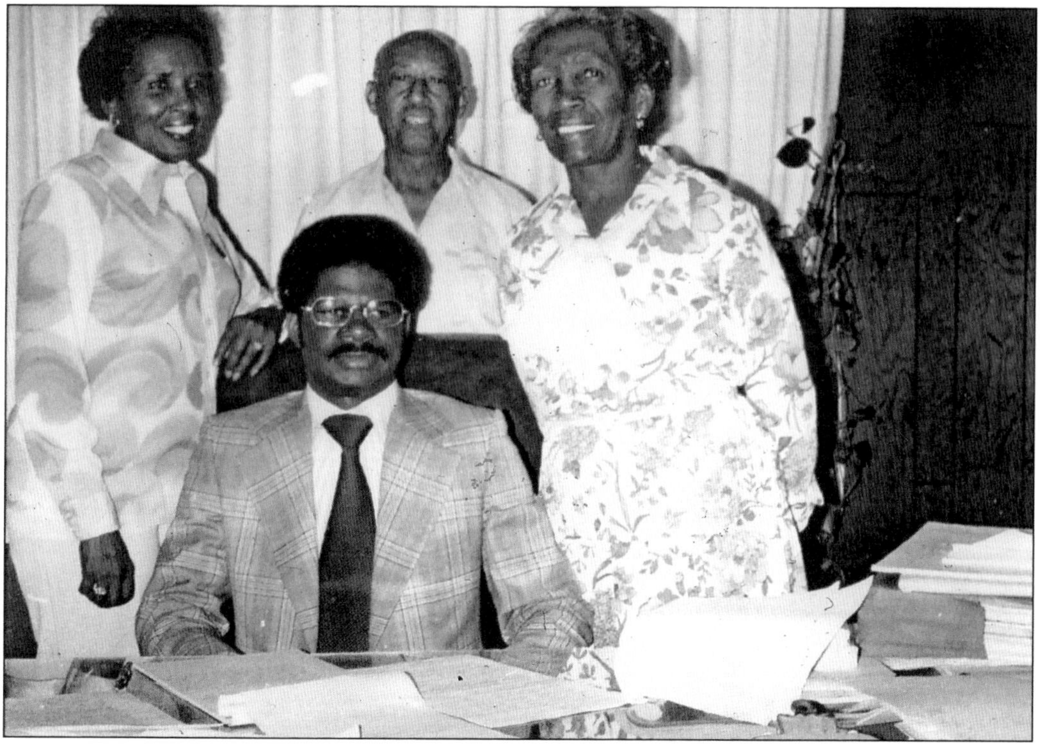

Attorney Morris Milton, former lawyer and NAACP President, sits behind his desk in the photo above. Surrounding him are members of the NAACP Executive Board. Milton represented four blacks in a 1975 federal lawsuit contending that St. Petersburg was discriminating against blacks in its hiring of police and fire employees. He was also counsel for the NAACP in a court fight against voter-registration practices in Pinellas County.

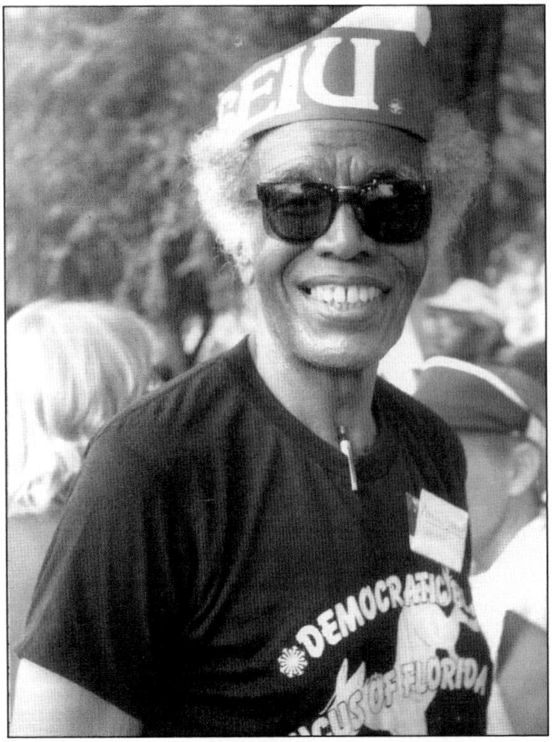

Perkins Shelton is pictured here at the second March on Washington in 1983. Shelton served as vice president of the Democratic Black Caucus of Florida.

Depicted below is a peaceful march in support of single member districts. The march occurred in the late 1970s.

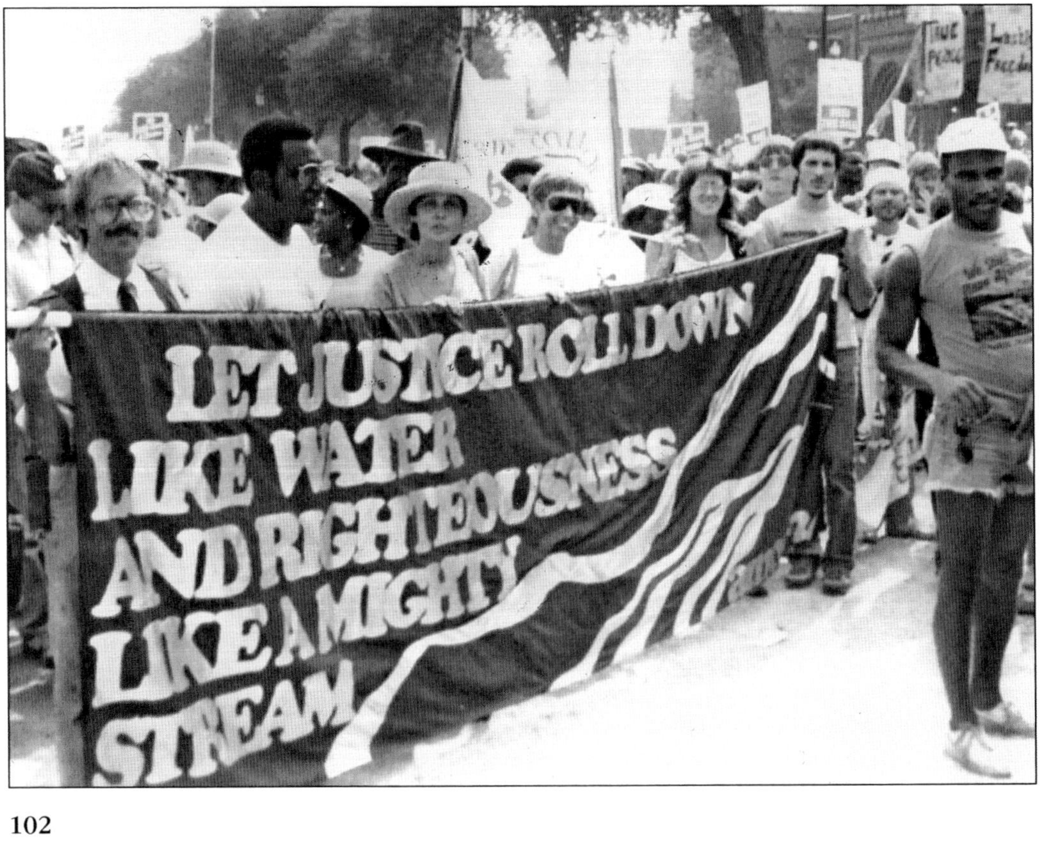

Hank Aaron campaigned for Jimmy Carter in St. Petersburg in 1976. The rally took place at Faith Memorial Church on 18th Avenue. In this photo he takes time out to get "a shoe shine."

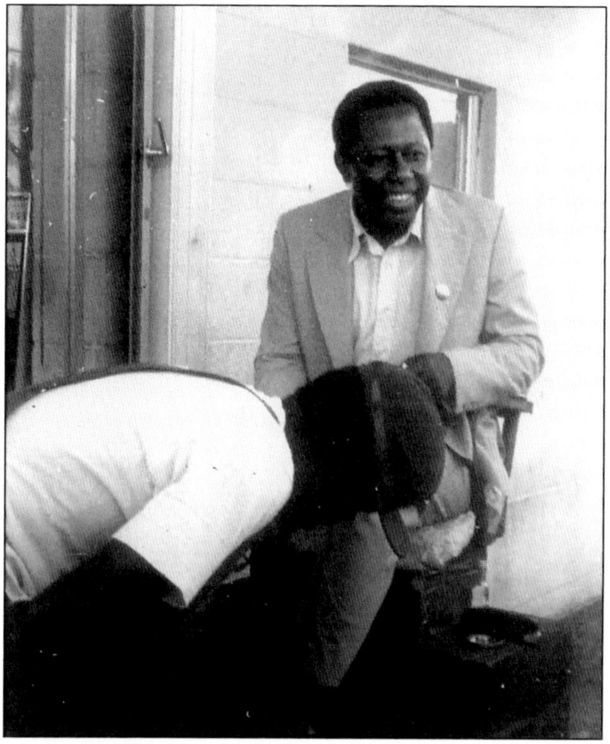

Ralph Abernathy, a national Civil Rights leader, poses with local NAACP member Sharon Baldwin in this photo taken in the late 1970s.

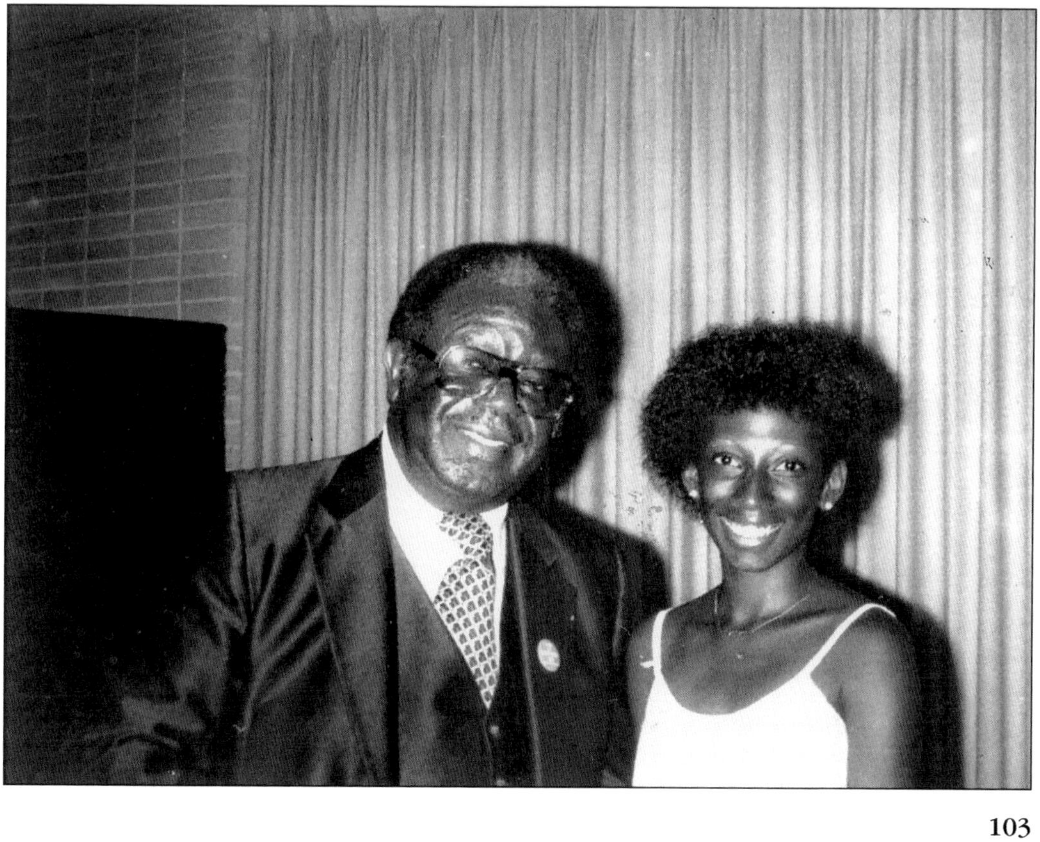

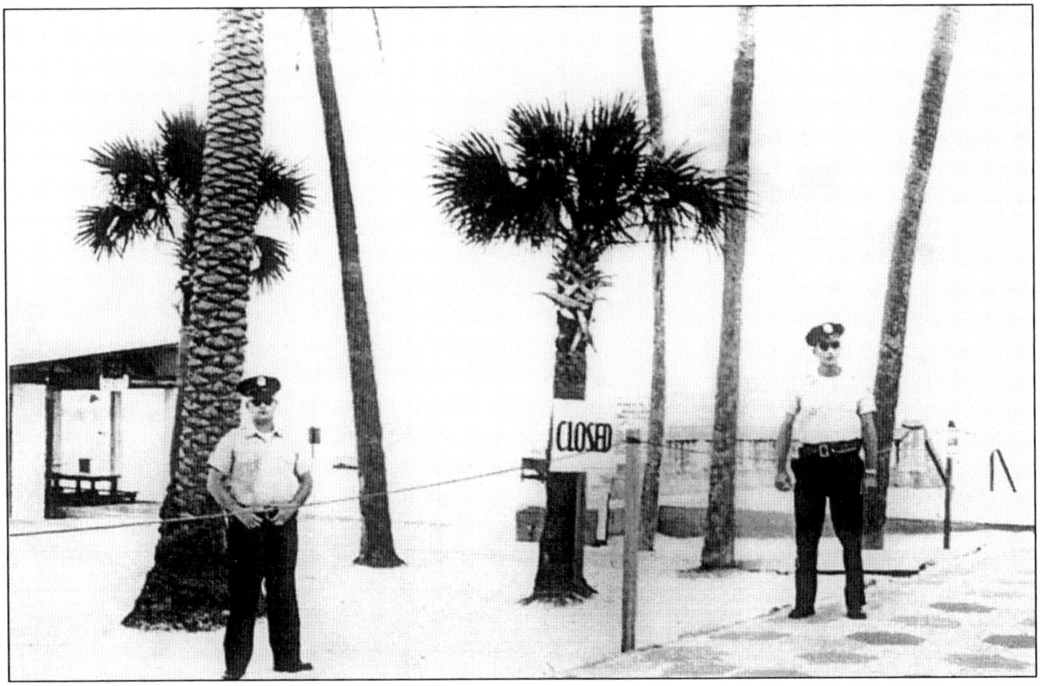

Police officers stand guard after the beach is closed because blacks swam there.

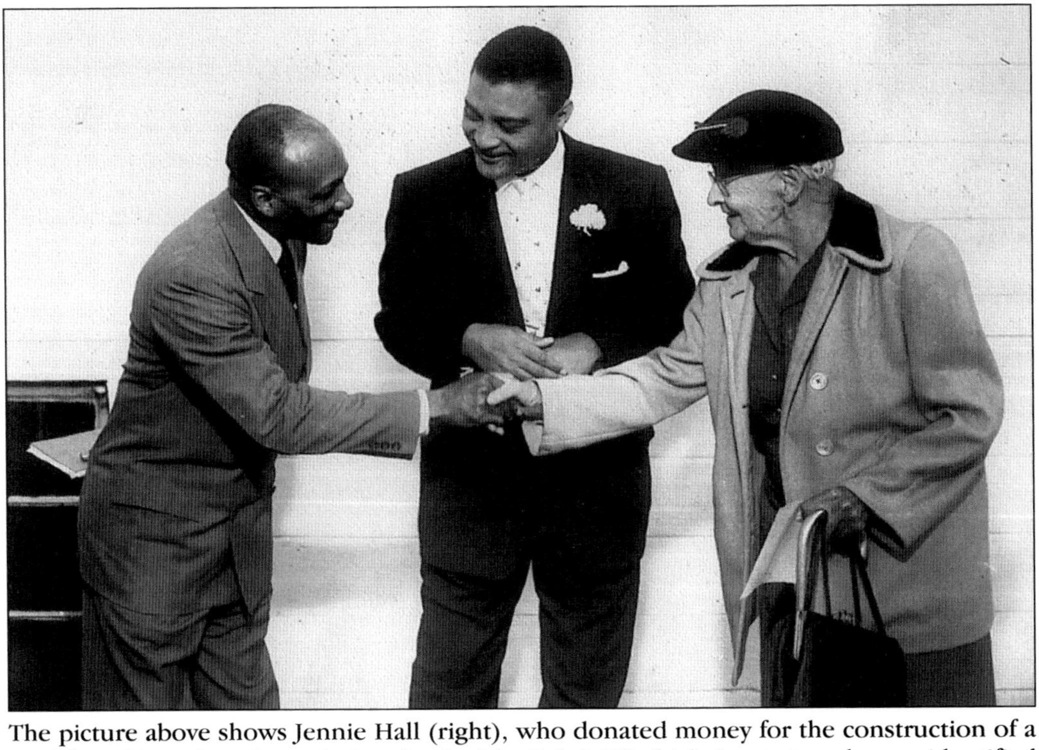

The picture above shows Jennie Hall (right), who donated money for the construction of a pool for African Americans, being thanked by Ralph Wimbish (center) and an unidentified gentleman to the left.

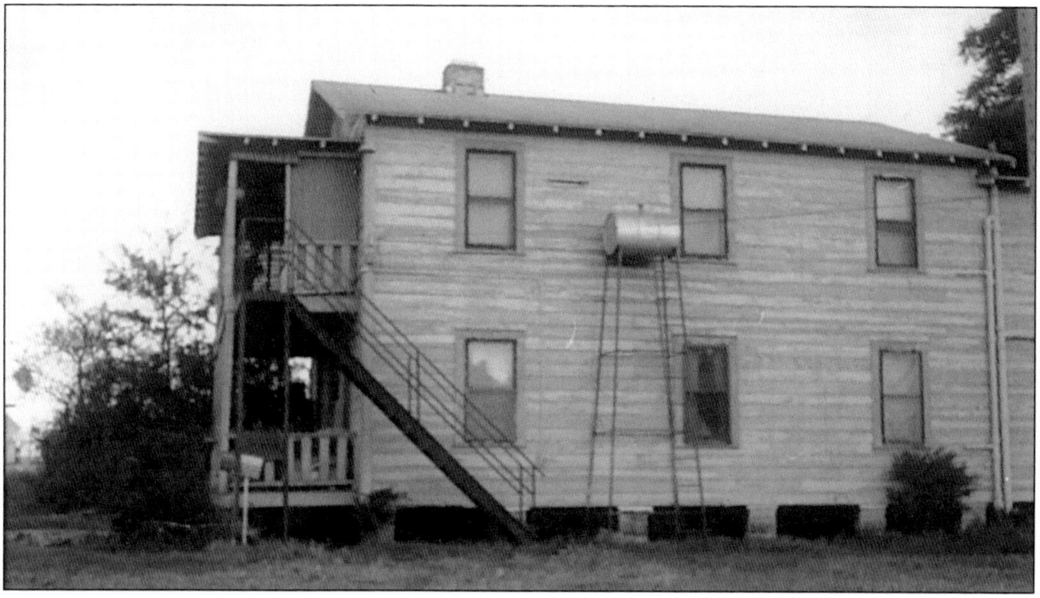

The rooming house above was located in the gas plant area. The picture was taken in the 1950s.

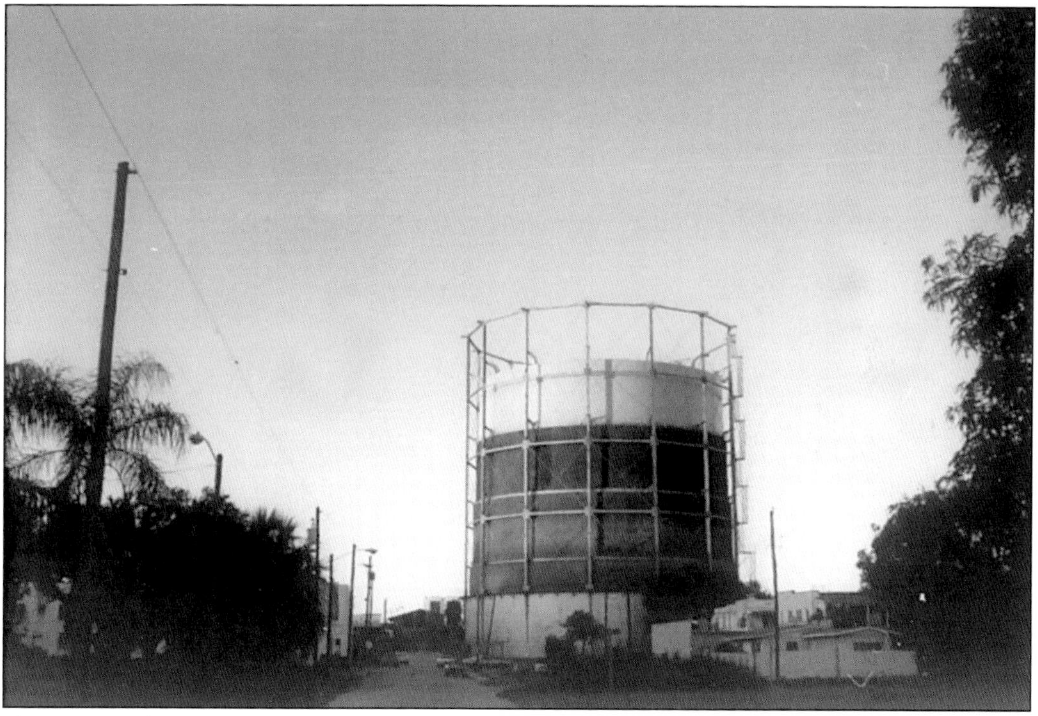

This gas tank once sat where Tropicana Field is today. Many African-American families, churches, and businesses were uprooted and moved to other areas in the city. The St. Petersburg City Council declared that the area, bounded by 9th and 16th Streets South, and 1st Avenue South and Interstate 275, was a slum and was eligible for community block development. Later, an industrial park was proposed for the area.

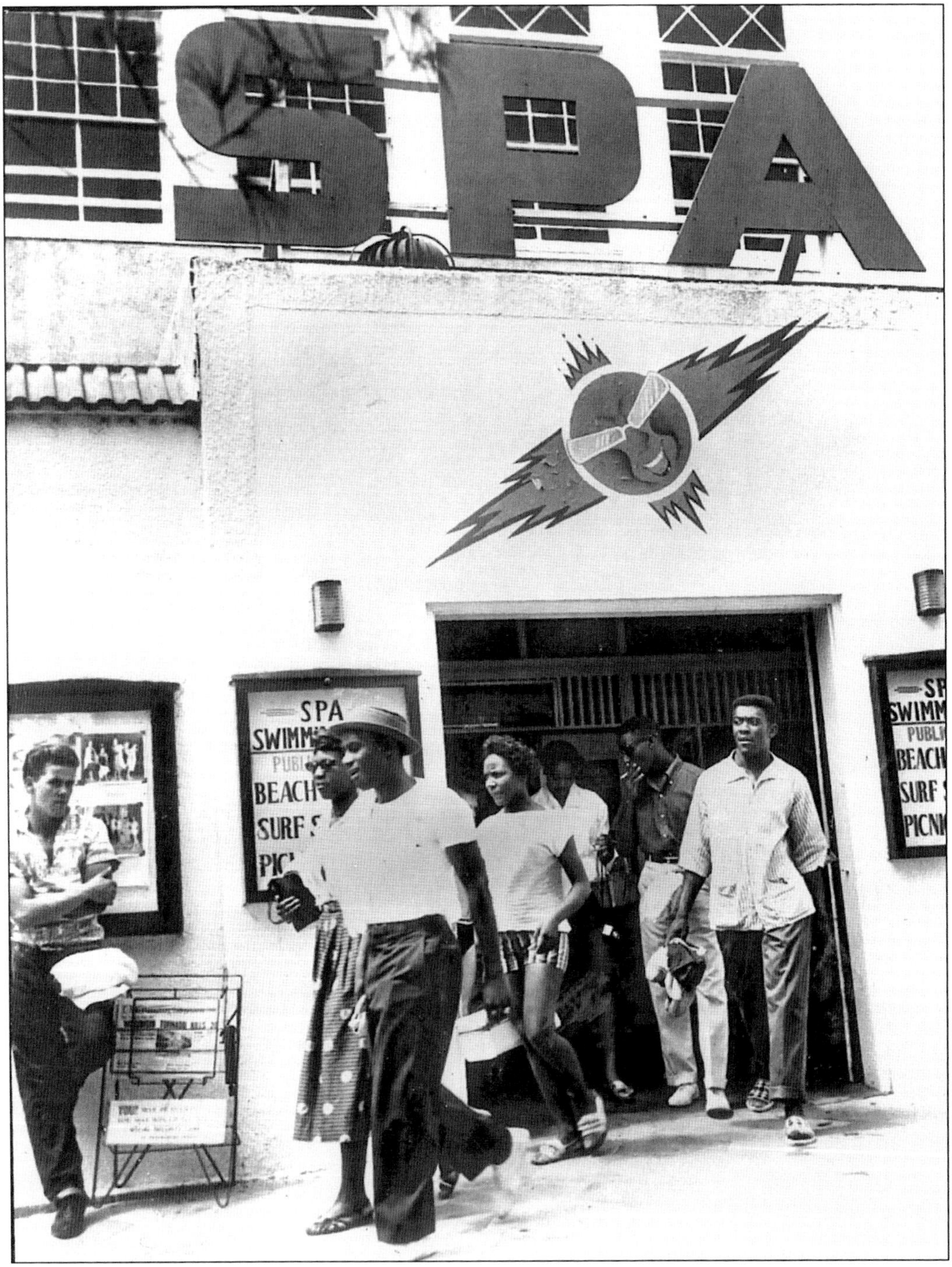

The Spa Pool is open in black residents in January 1959. F.A. Dubb, chairman of the local NAACP, had made several attempts to desegregate the pool in the 1950s.

Ten

FAMILY UNITY

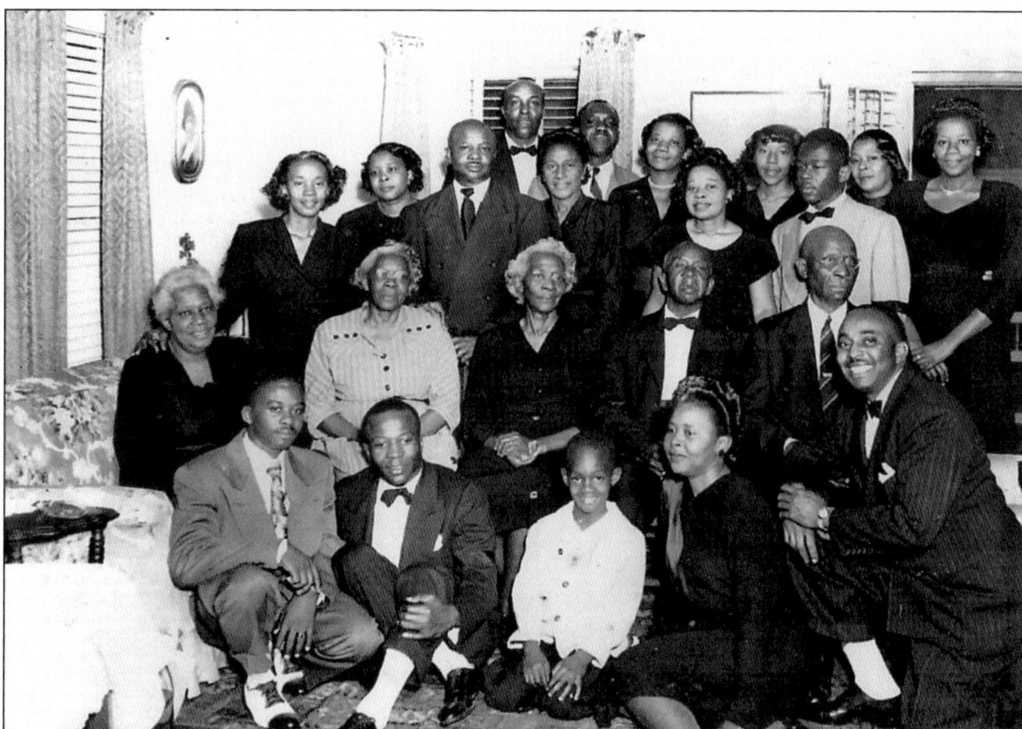

The immediate and extended black families have always provided a wholesome atmosphere for fun and laughter when things on the outside seemed bleak and dismal. There were and continue to be activities like church outings, Sunday dinners, barbecues, fish fries, and just visiting the homes of friends. Children knew not to interrupt adult conversations and adults often used codes to send messages across the room—things children should not hear. And this adage was very important: "The family that prays together stays together." The picture above shows relatives of William "Buddy" West, spanning at least three generations.

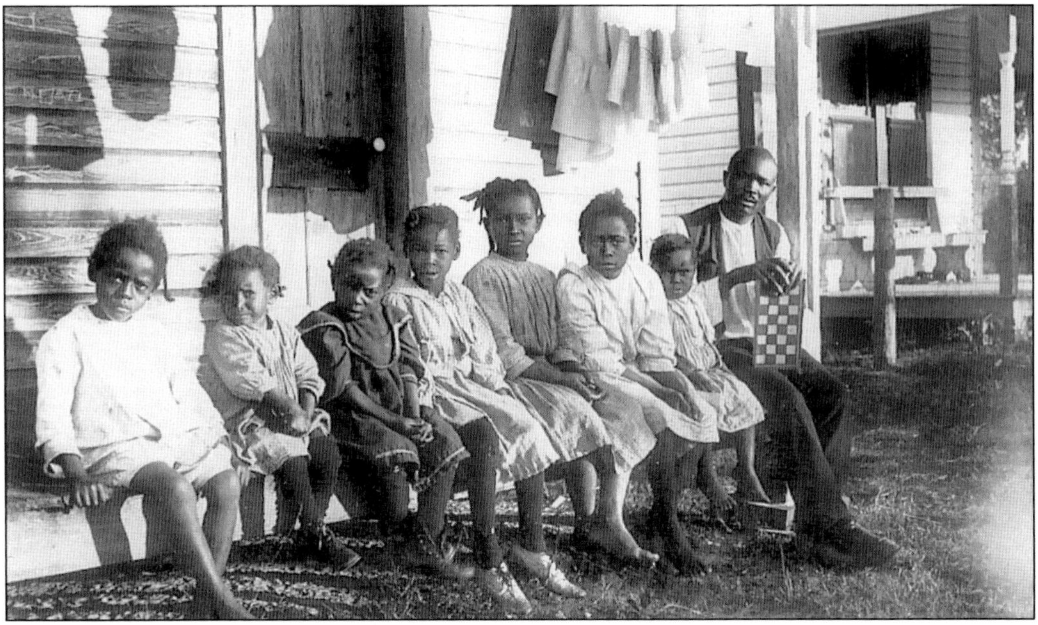

This family from the early 1900s consists of several small children and a father. Note the checkerboard he holds in his hand. A game of checkers was a common way to pass the time during this period.

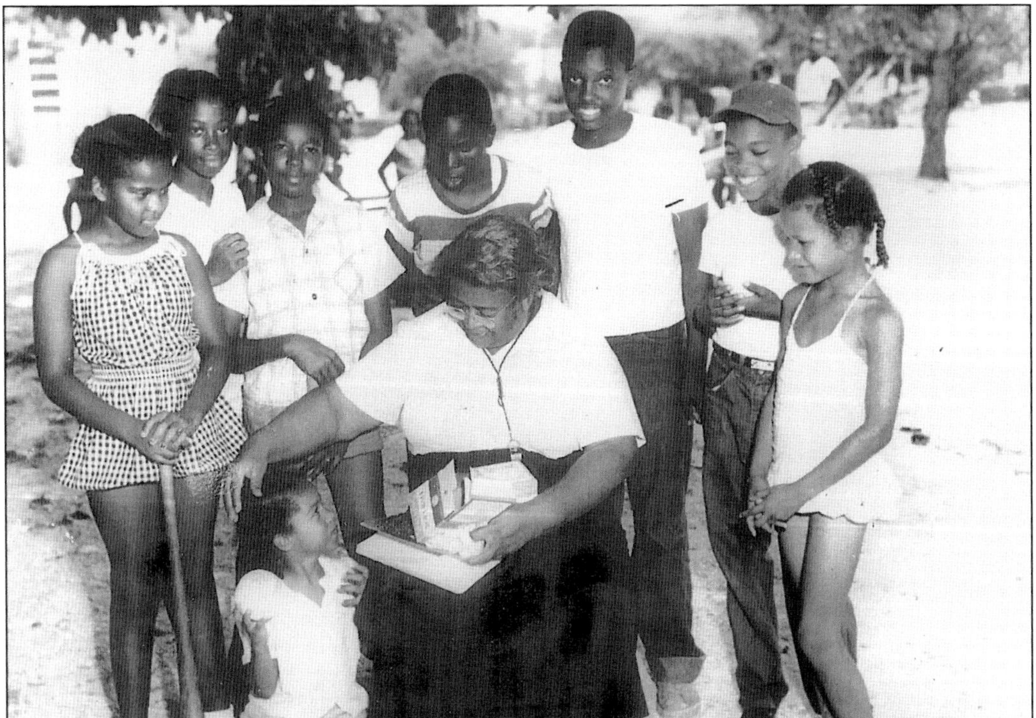

The mother of Mr. Joseph Albury Jr. is surrounded by happy children. Mrs. Albury was a schoolteacher.

Sisters and brothers are dressed in beautiful attire for church or a social event. Pictured from left to right are Joseph Albury Jr., Ruth Albury Southland, Melissa Spencer Summers, and Samuel Albury.

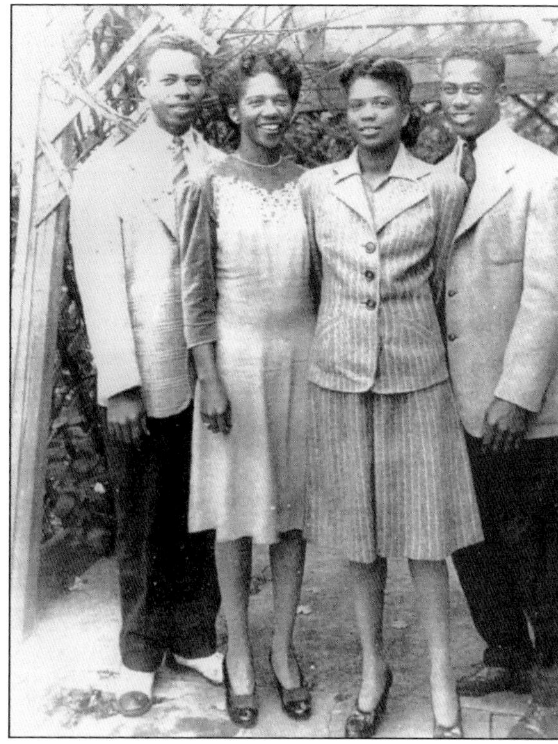

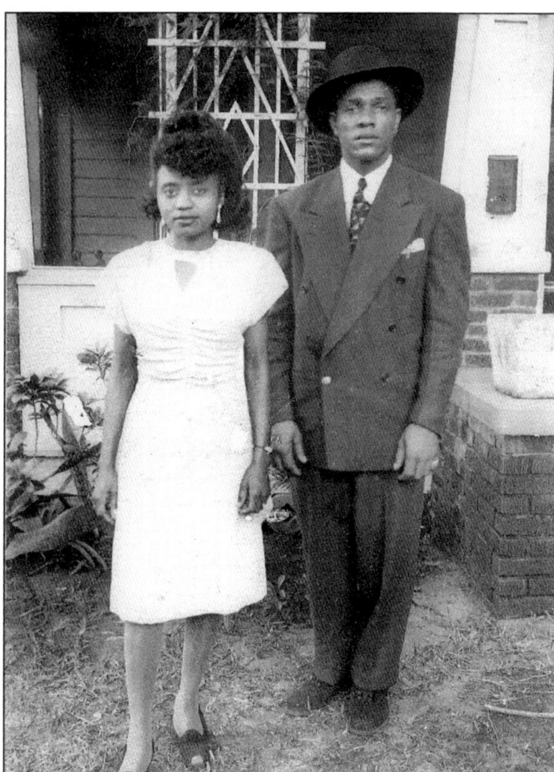

Mr. and Mrs. Robert James look charming together, him sporting a double-breasted suit and her a cream-colored dress.

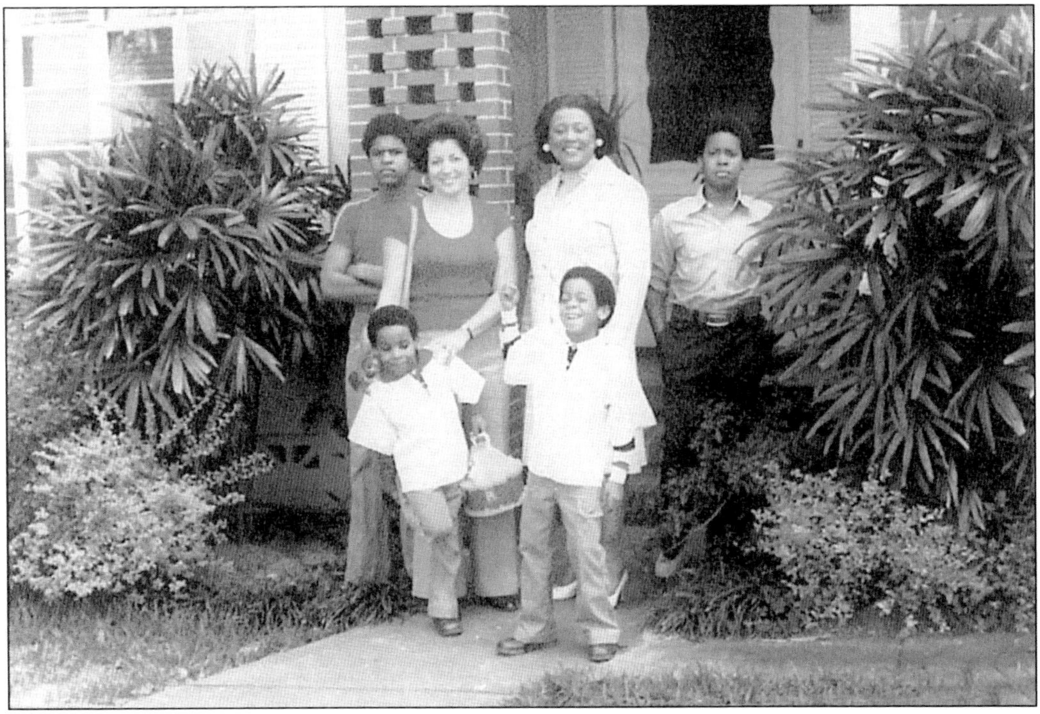

Mrs. Pat Taliafaro, second from right, poses with a family friend, Mrs. Francis Thomas. Her four sons are also in the picture.

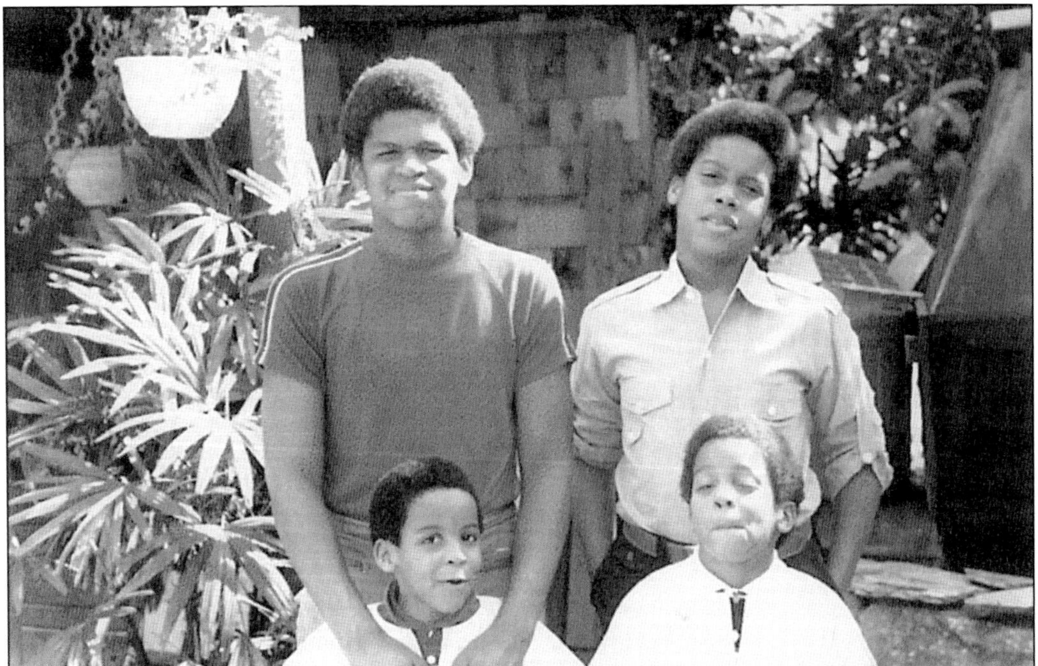

This bottom photograph depicts the four sons of Mrs. Pat Taliafaro The two younger sons appear to be striking amusing poses for the camera.

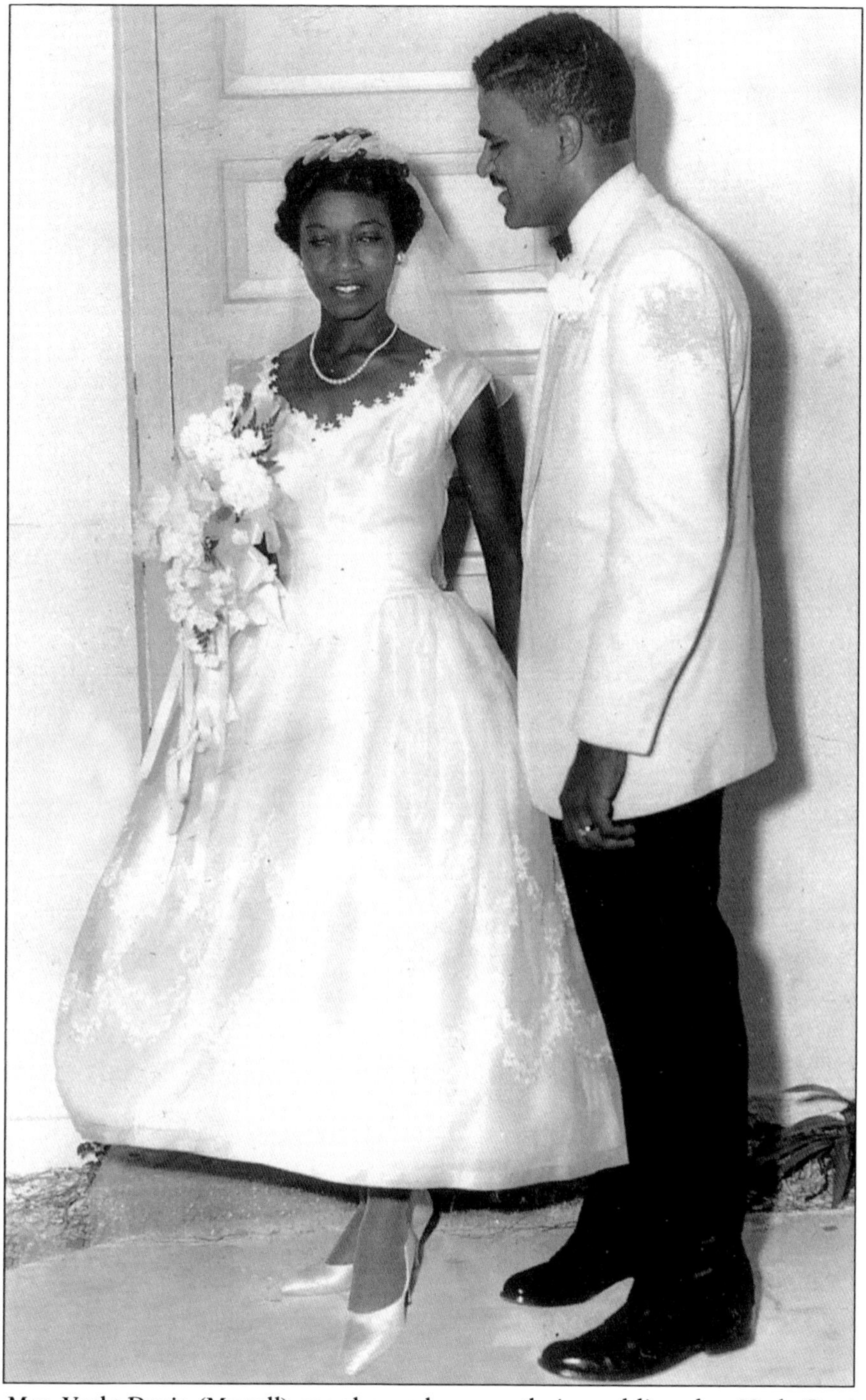

Mr. and Mrs. Vryle Davis (Mozell) are shown here on their wedding day. Vryle Davis was the principal of St. Petersburg High School, a former all-white school. He later became an area superintendent for the school system. Mozell Davis was a supervisor for special education in the school system. Both are now retirees who volunteer for numerous projects in the community.

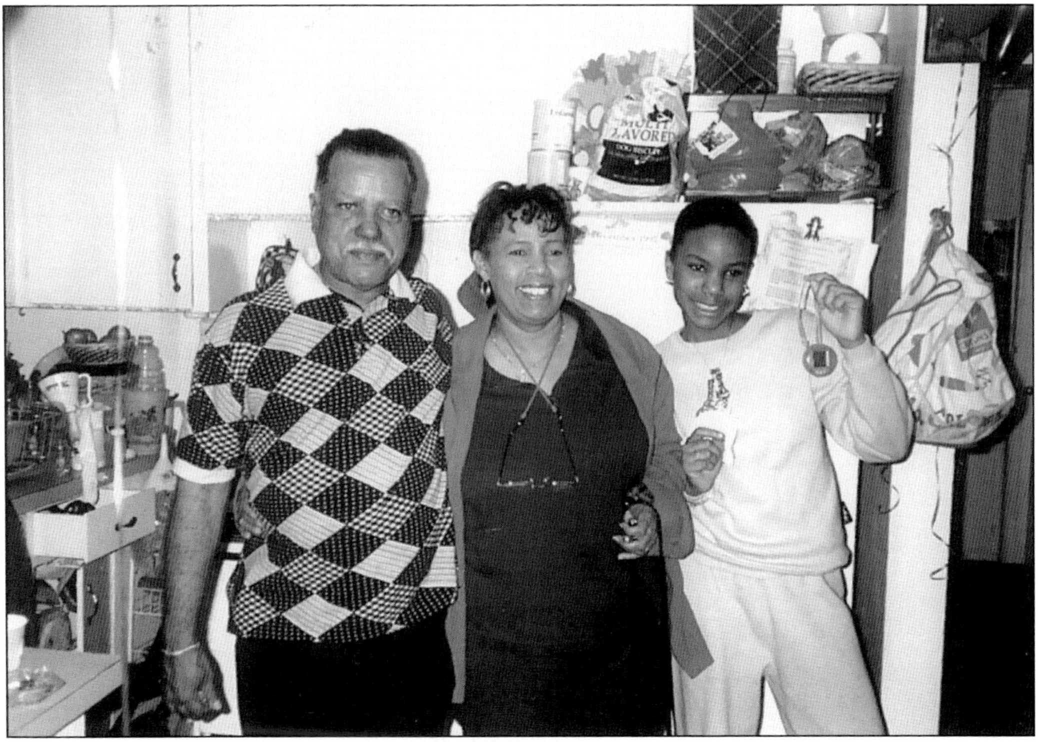

Shown here is Joseph Albury III, his wife Enid and daughter Joelle.

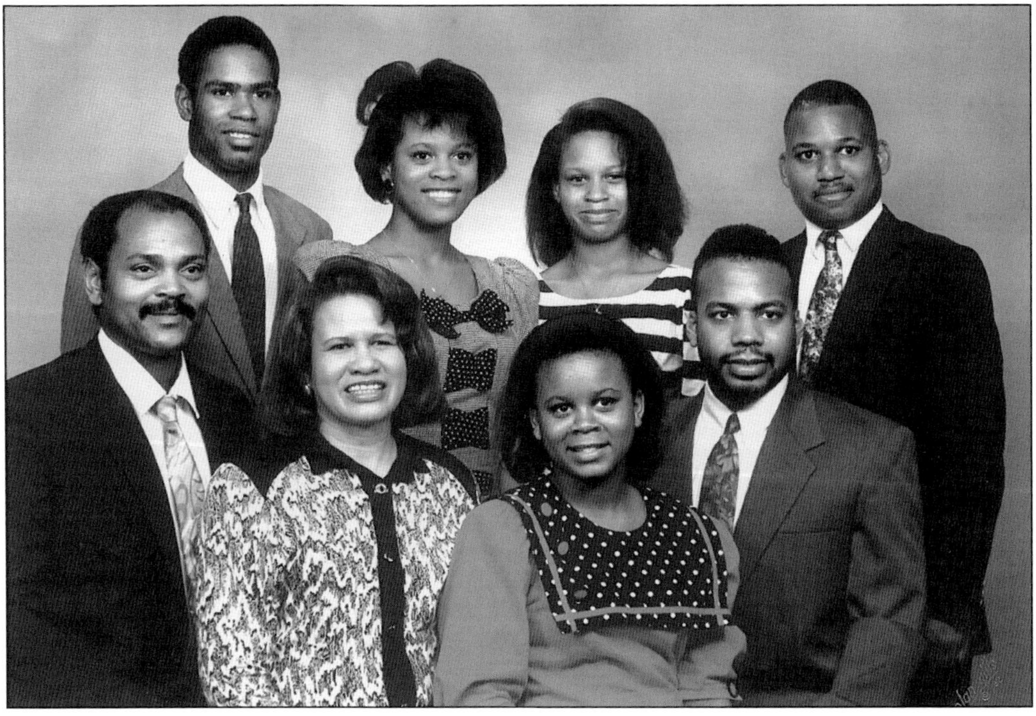

Pictured above is a family portrait of Mr. Jackie Waller, his wife Nancy, and their children.

Two brothers, Buster and Steve Cooper, are both very fashionably dressed and about to play music together in this portrait dating to the late 1950s or early 1960s.

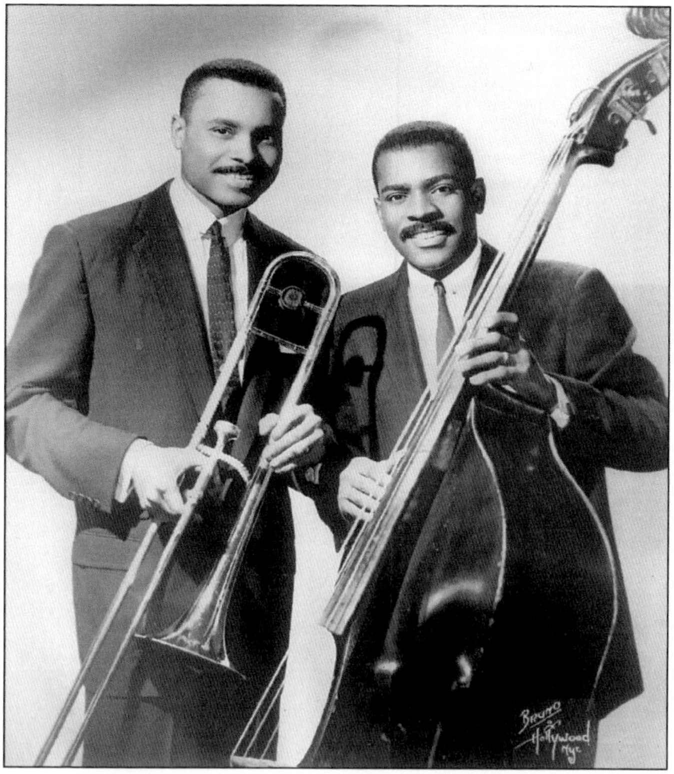

Brothers Joseph Albury III and James Albury, sons of Mr. Joseph Albury Jr., both opted to serve their country in the Air Force.

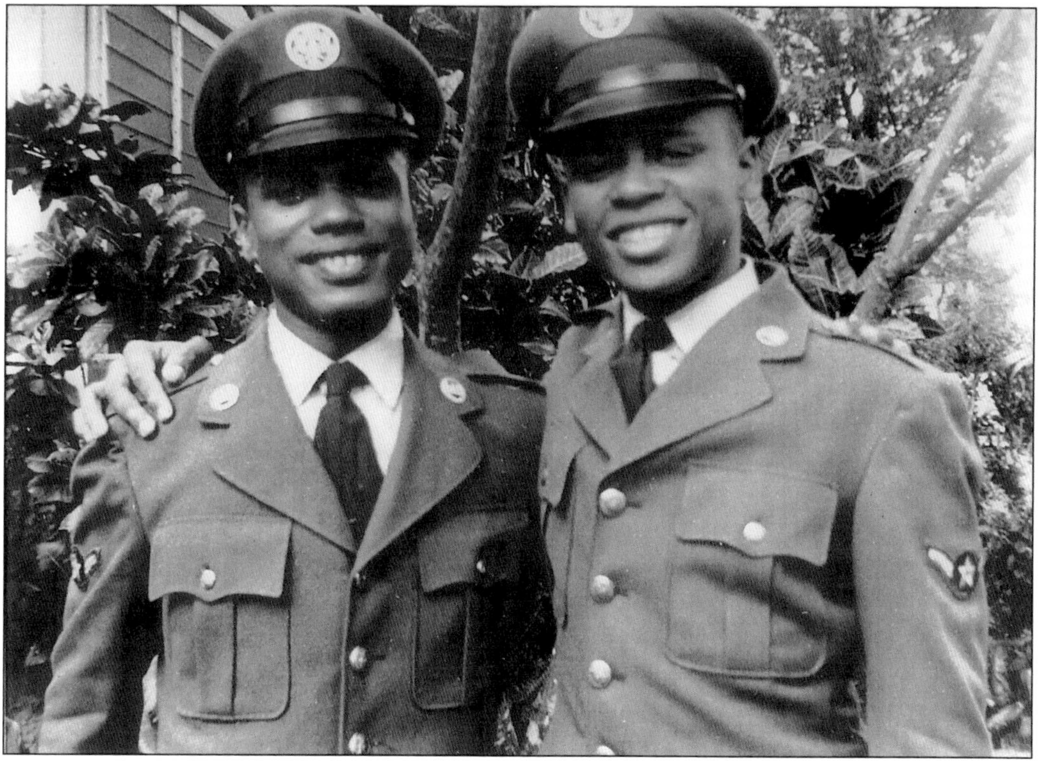

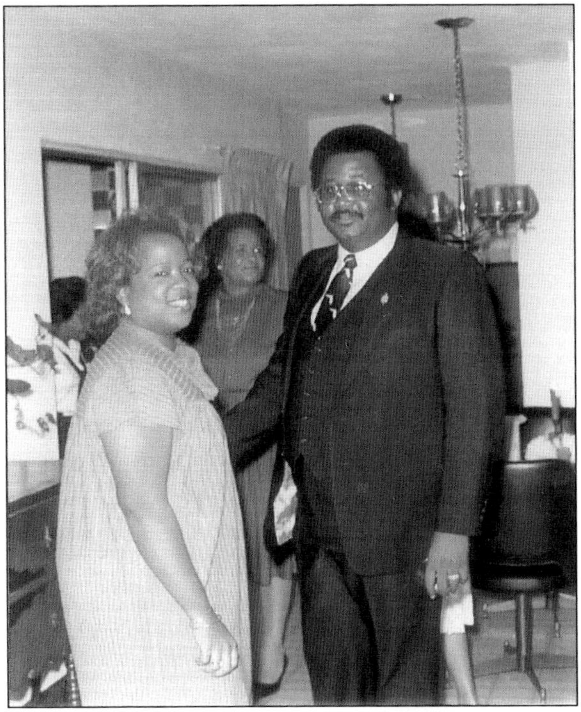

Mr. and Mrs. Douglas Jamerson pose for the camera while friends observe in the background.

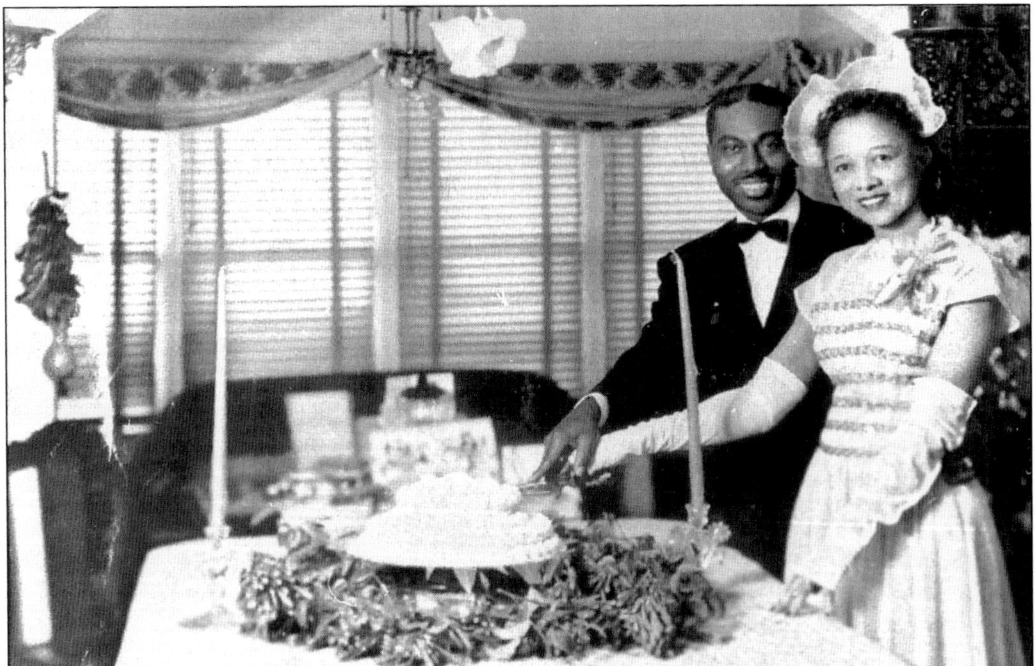

Mr. and Mrs. Titus Newkirk's 1947 wedding reception was hosted by Dr. and Mrs. James M. Ponder. The Ponders lived on 5th Avenue South between 12th and 16th Streets in an area where a number of black families lived in beautiful homes.

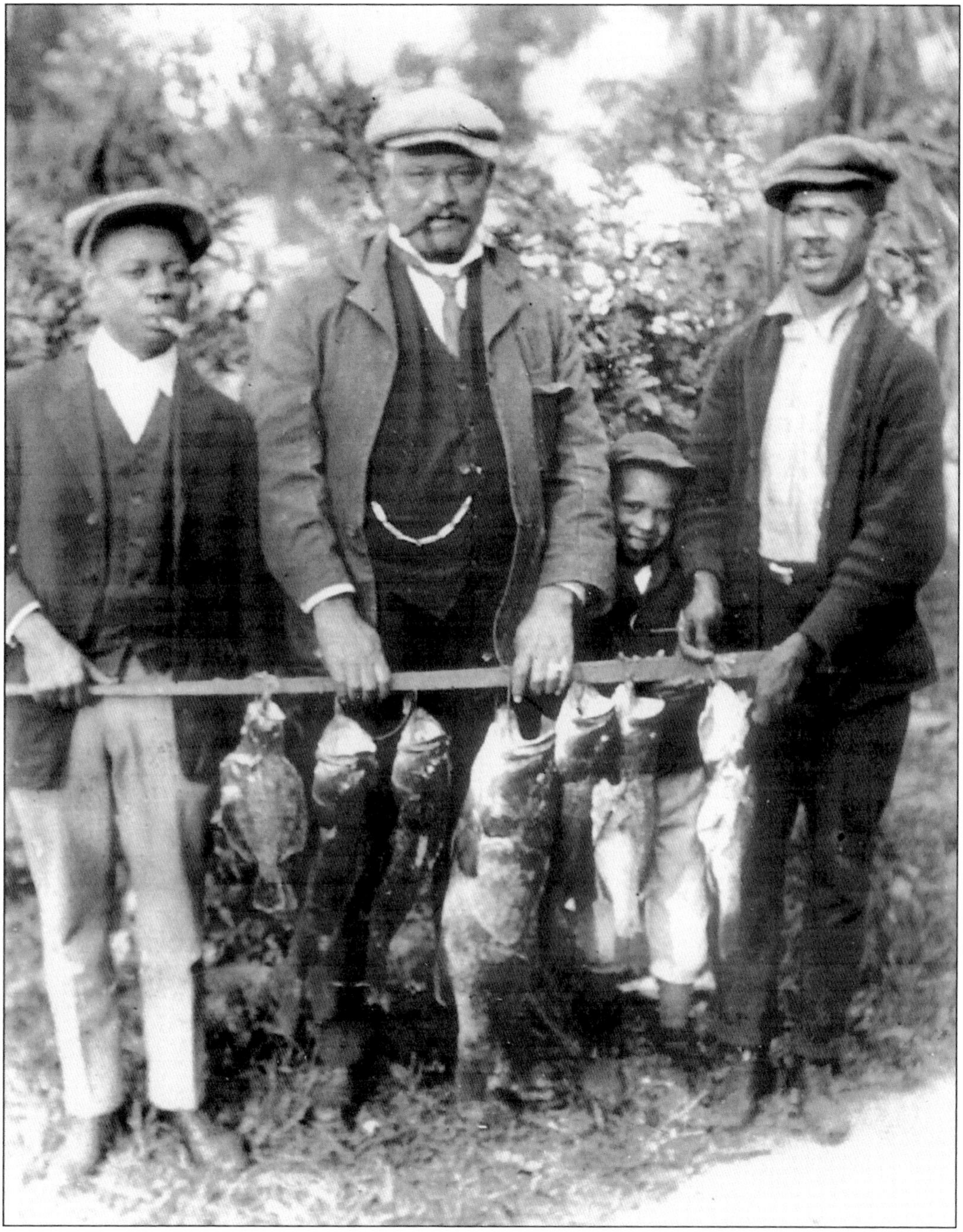

Here are a father, son, uncle, and family friend back from a local fishing trip. From left to right are Dr. Carter, Sam Moore (uncle of Joseph Jr.), Joseph Jr. (peeping through on the far right) and the father Joseph Albury Sr.

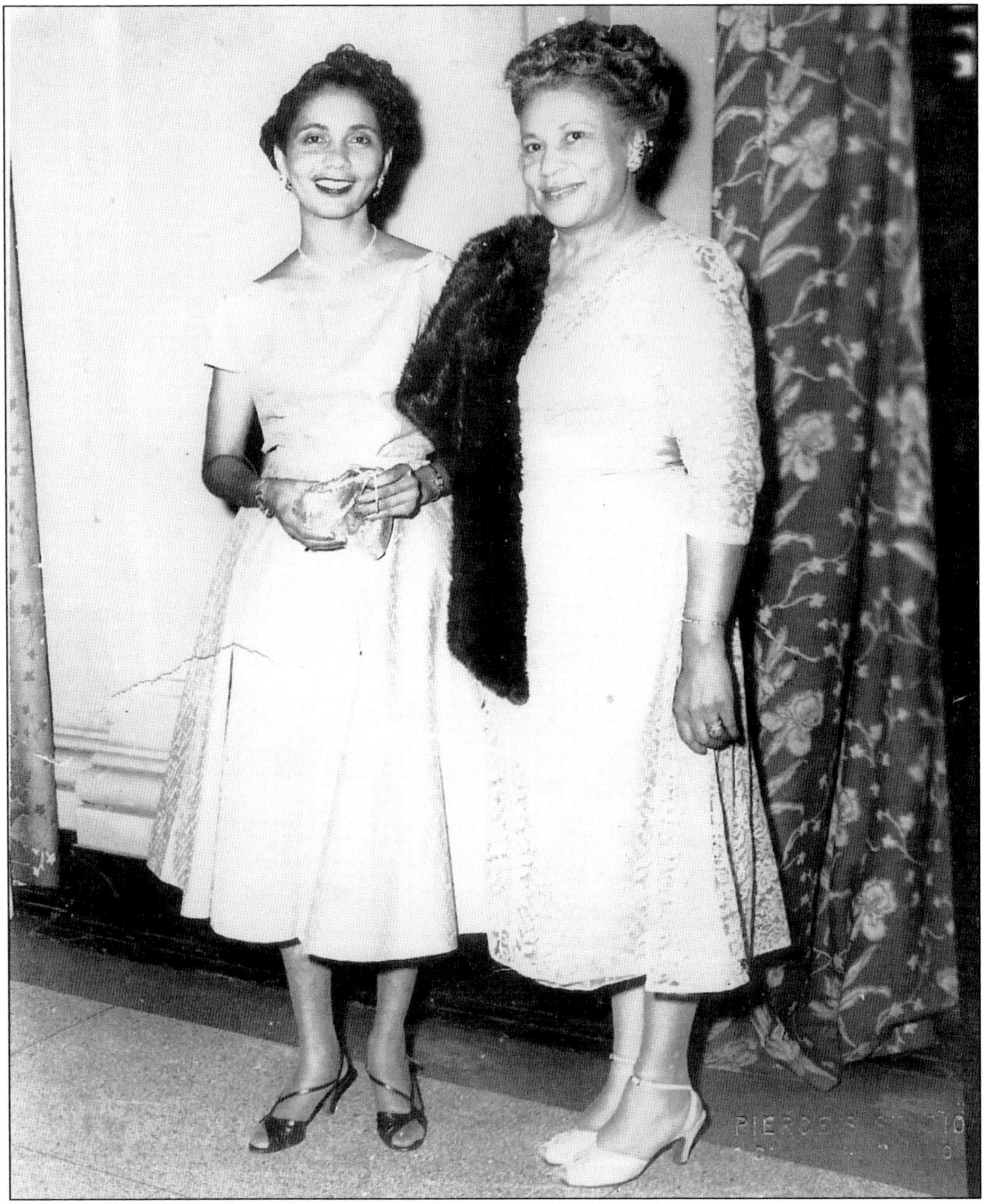

Mrs. Anna Polk Walker and her mother, Mrs. Mary Polk, attend the Links Inc. National Convention in Columbus, Ohio. The mother and daughter were both educators, they both married educators, and both were members of Links Inc.

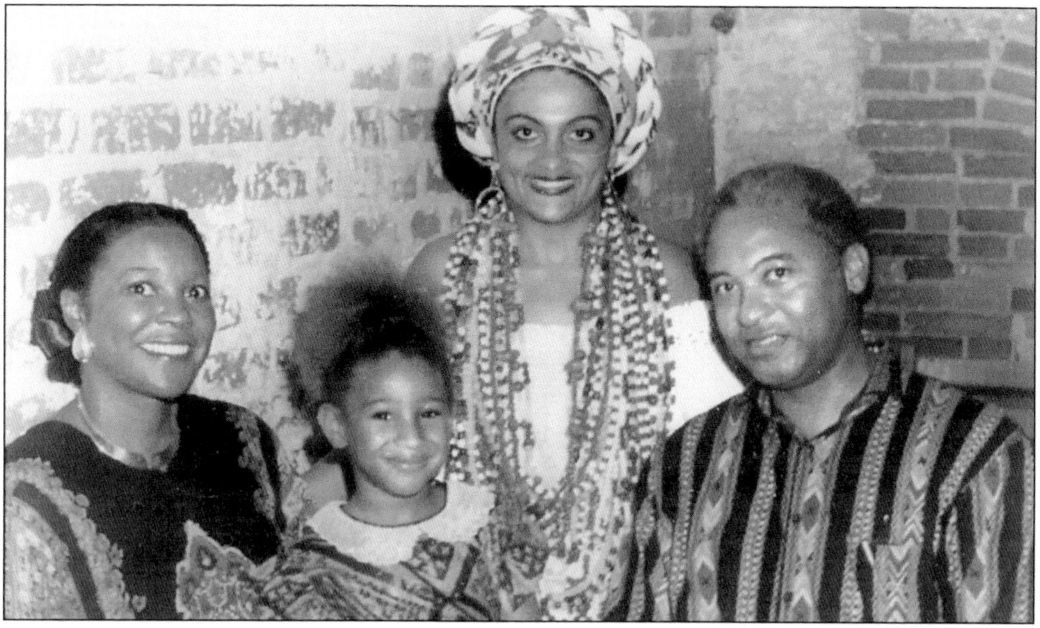

The Cotman Family enjoys an African Heritage Tour in Brazil. The mother, daughter, and father are joined by a performer. Dr. Cotman is a radiologist at Bayfront Medical Center. His wife was a former Miss FAMU (Florida Agricultural and Mechanical University.)

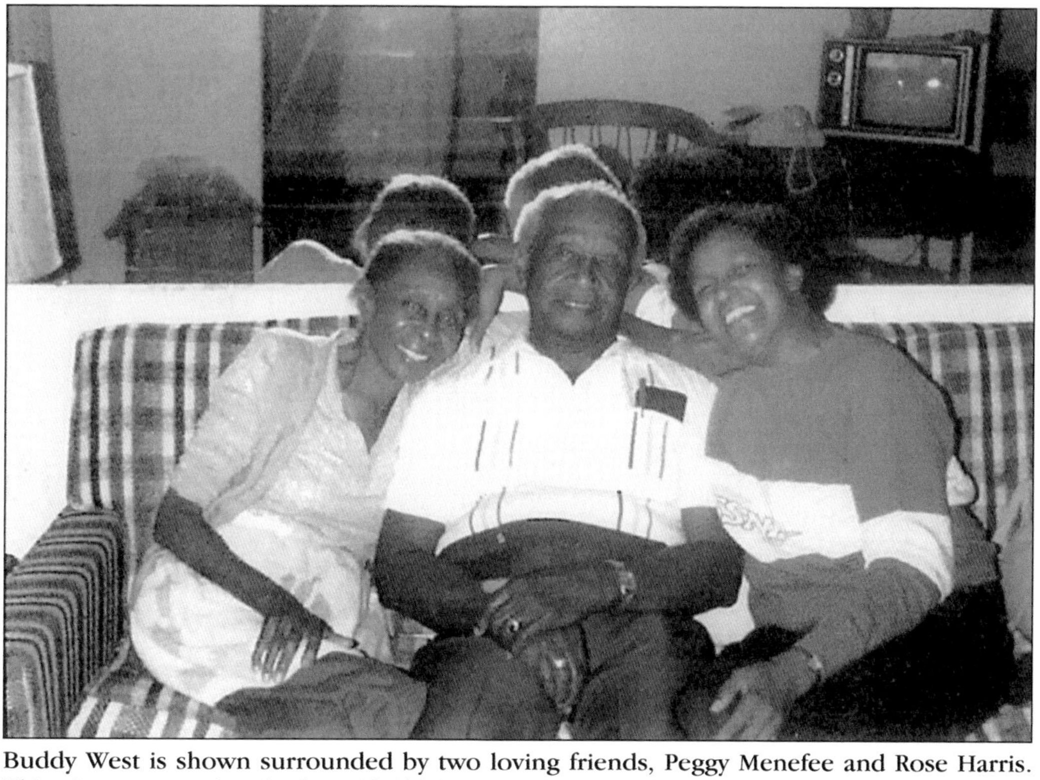

Buddy West is shown surrounded by two loving friends, Peggy Menefee and Rose Harris. This picture was taken in the mid-1980s.

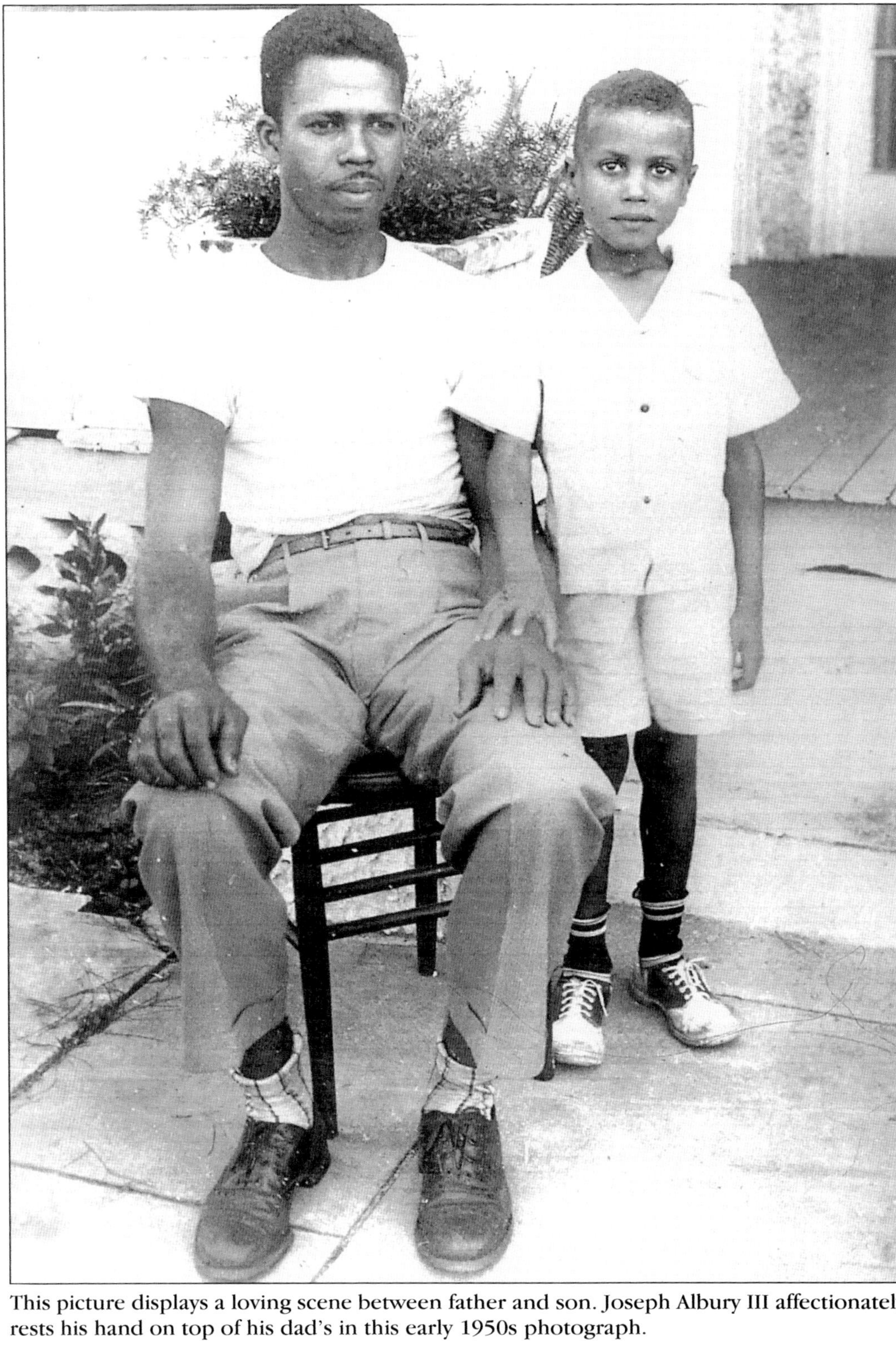

This picture displays a loving scene between father and son. Joseph Albury III affectionately rests his hand on top of his dad's in this early 1950s photograph.

Eleven

Little Darlings

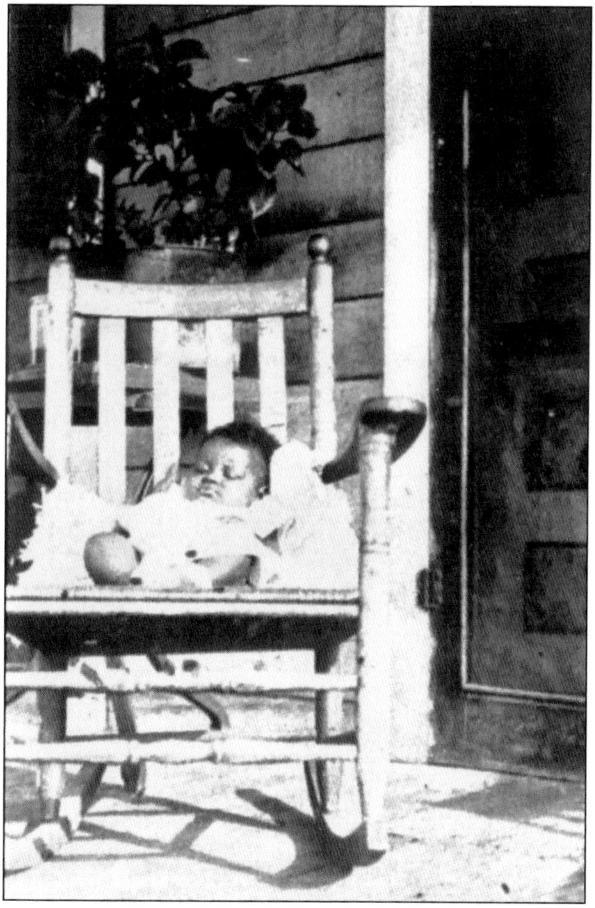

Little Freddie Dyles is fast asleep in a rocker in this 1930s photograph. This young one grew up to become a coach at Gibbs High School.

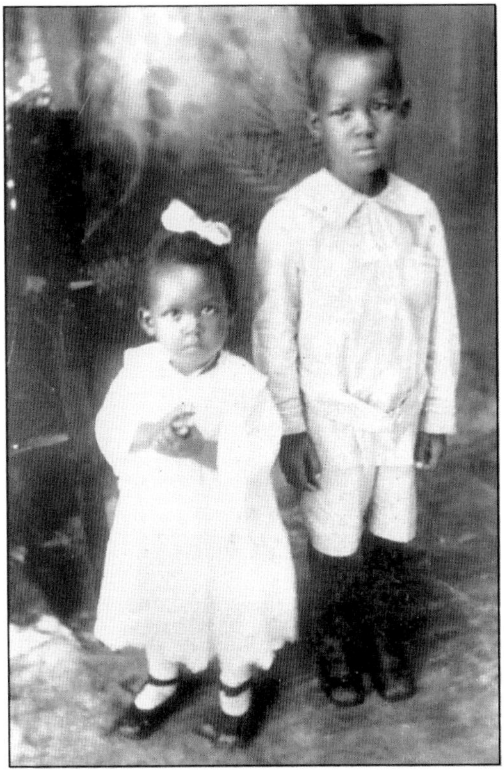

The picture at left was taken by Joseph Albury Sr., one of the first professional African-American photographers in St. Petersburg. Paul Barco Sr. is portrayed at an early age with his sister, Theda Mae. Paul Barco graduated from Gibbs High School in the mid-1930s.

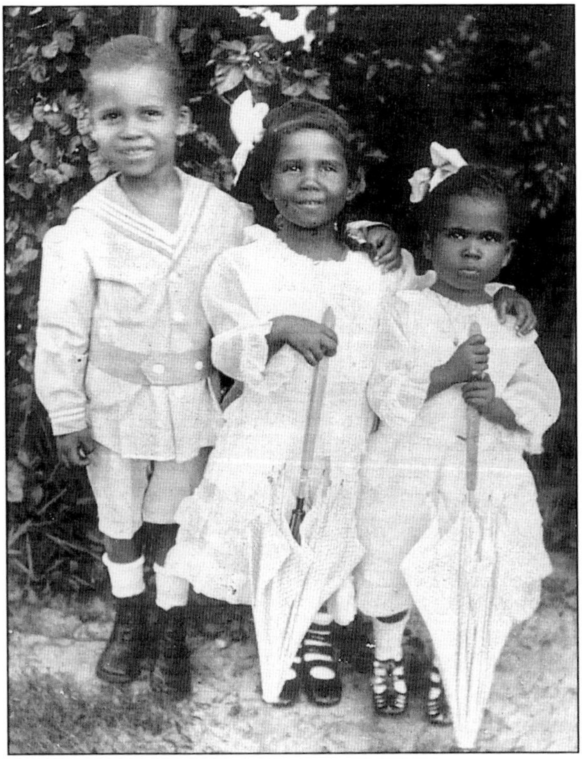

The picture at right was also taken by Joseph Albury Sr. Pictured from left to right are Joseph Albury Jr., Ruth Albury, and Spencer Albury. This photograph also appears on the back cover of the book.

To the right, Little Joe Albury Jr., at age three, sits comfortably in his chair with his legs crossed.

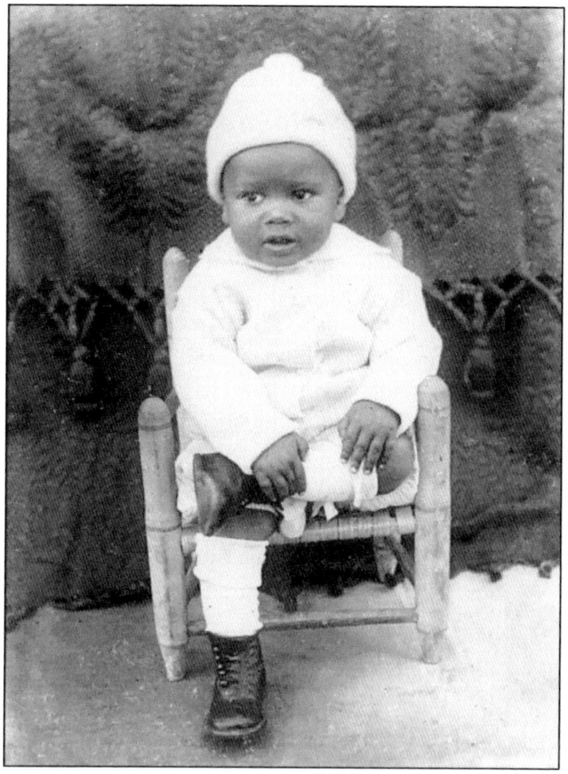

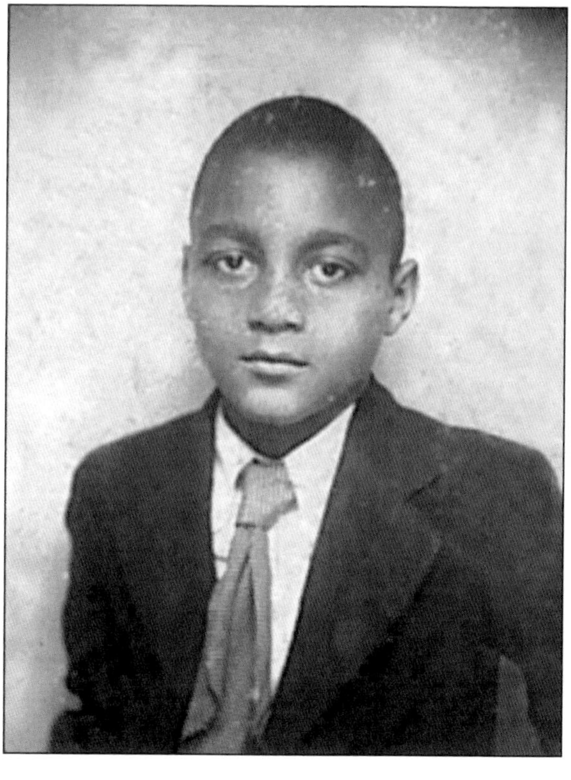

Ralph Wimbish, shown as a sixth grader at Davis Elementary, grew up to become a doctor and a major Civil Rights leader in St. Petersburg.

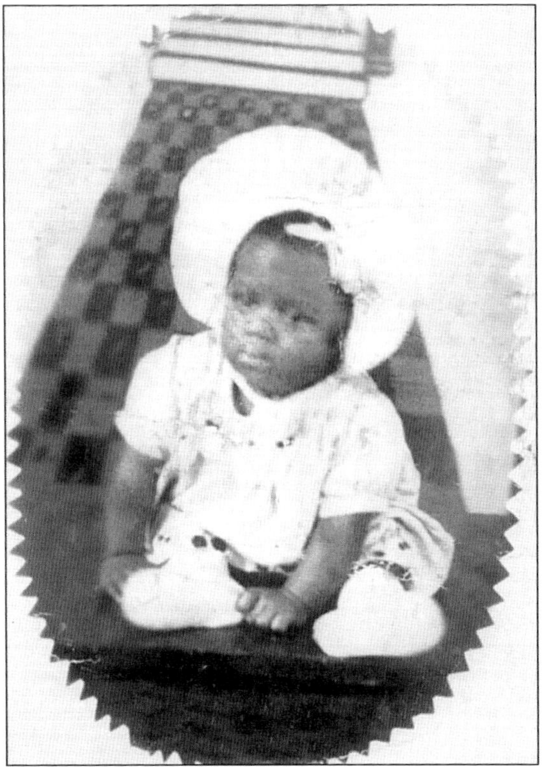

One-year-old Jacqueline Ware is outfitted in bonnet and booties in this 1948 photograph.

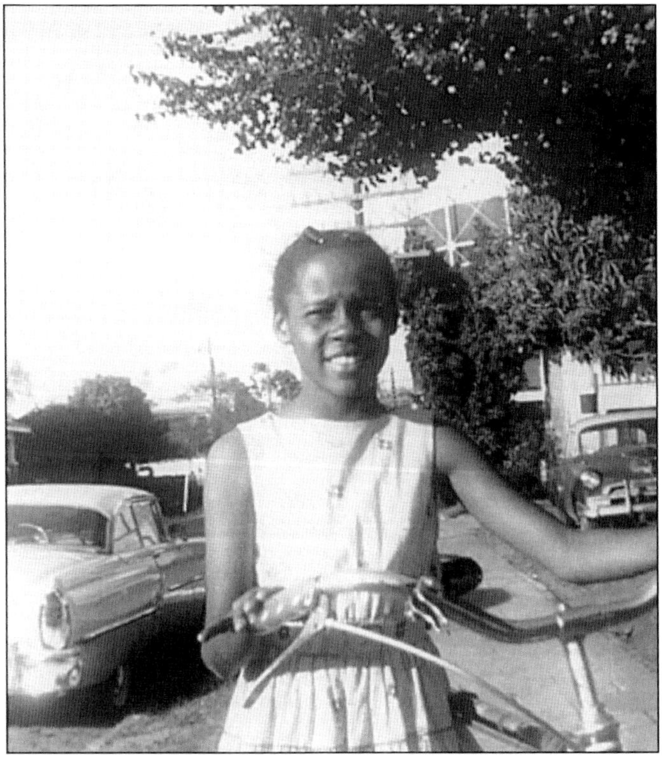

Katrina Herndon poses with her bicycle at the age of 10.

Little Nancy Albury sits with her legs crossed and a happy look on her face.

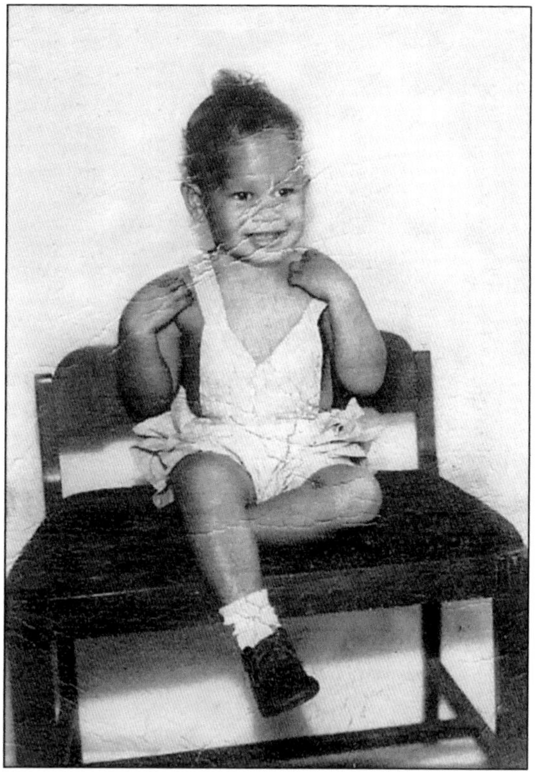

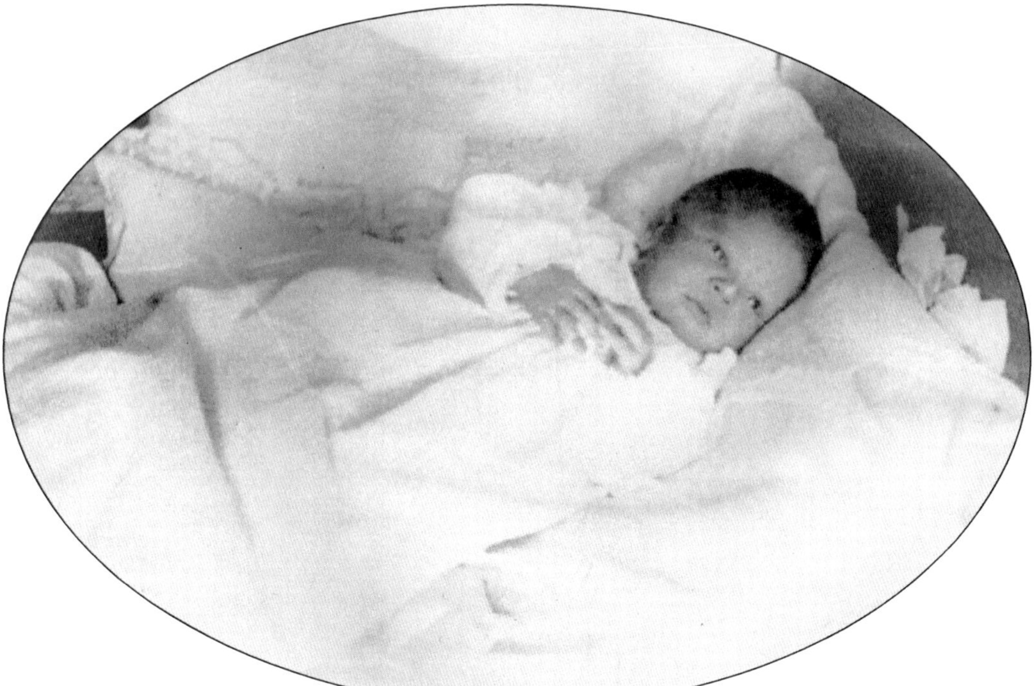

Six-day-old Joseph Albury Jr. looks most content and wide-awake in this early photograph.

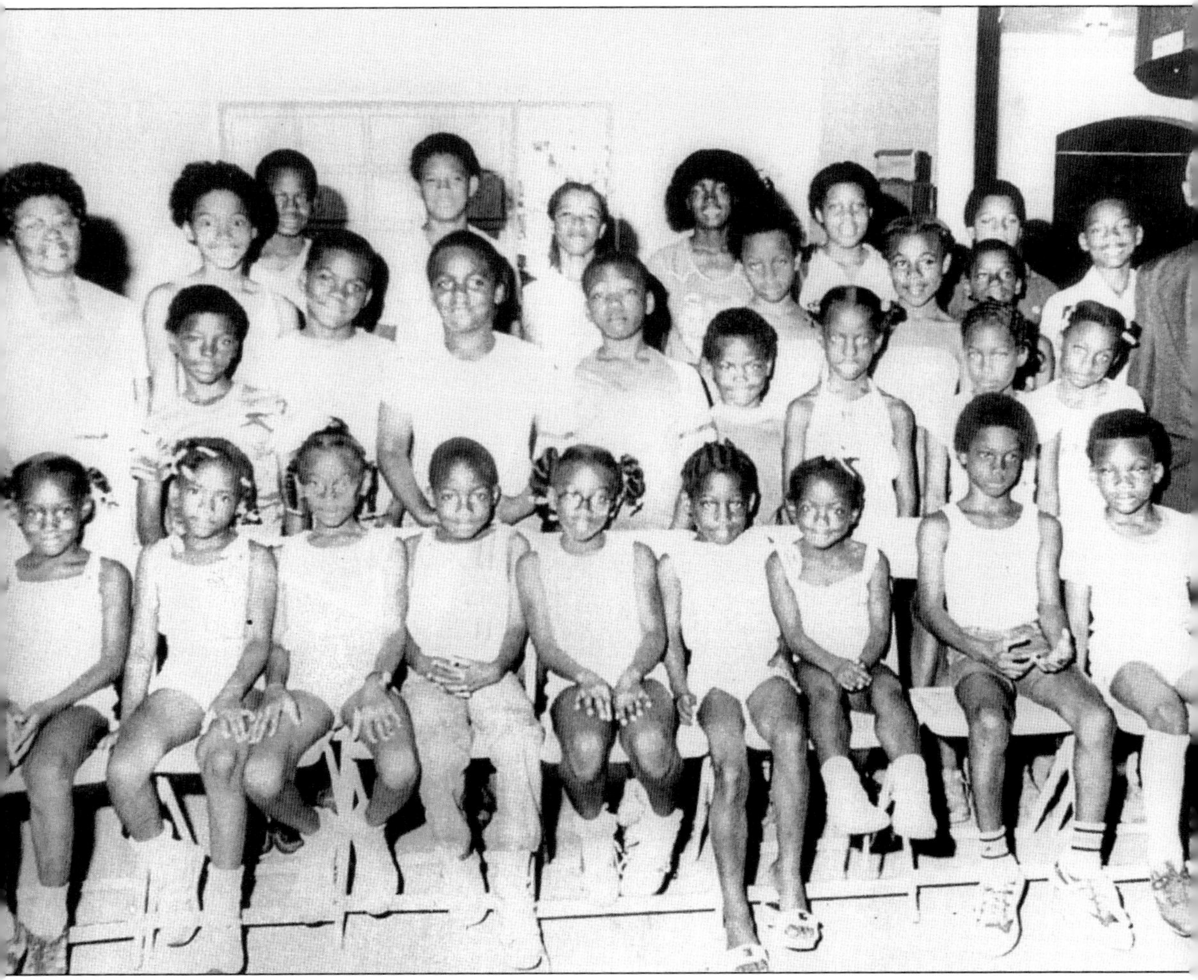

Rev. H. Mc Neal Harris of Bethel A.M.E. Church is surrounded by little darlings who appear to be dressed for recreational activity.

Faye Lumpkin Hines, age 6, wears a white bow in her hair. Faye was a student at Davis Elementary School during the 1950s.

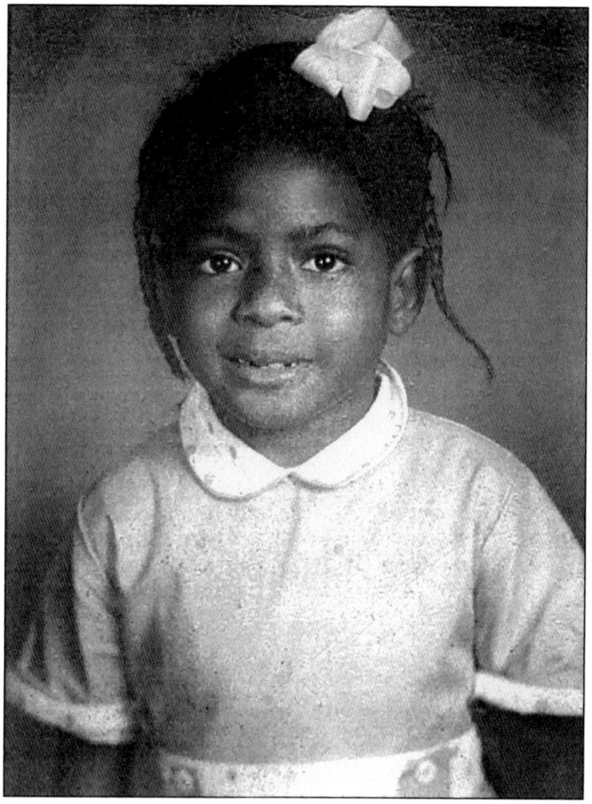

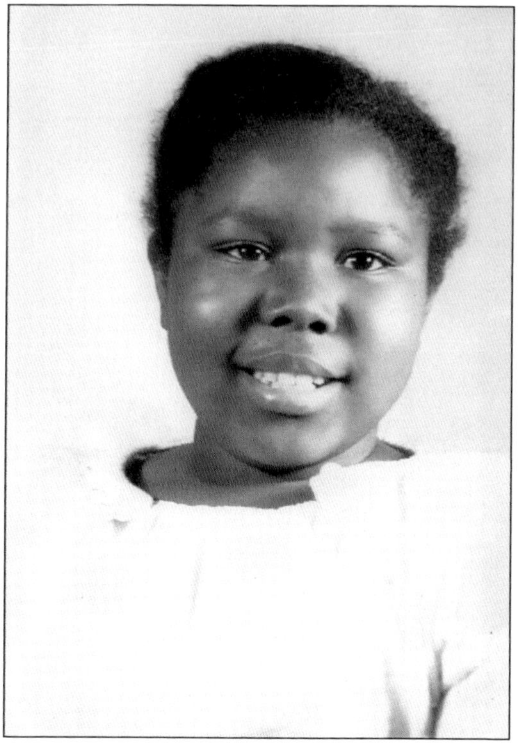

Phyllis Coachman, smiling brightly for the camera, was a student at Jordan Park Elementary School.

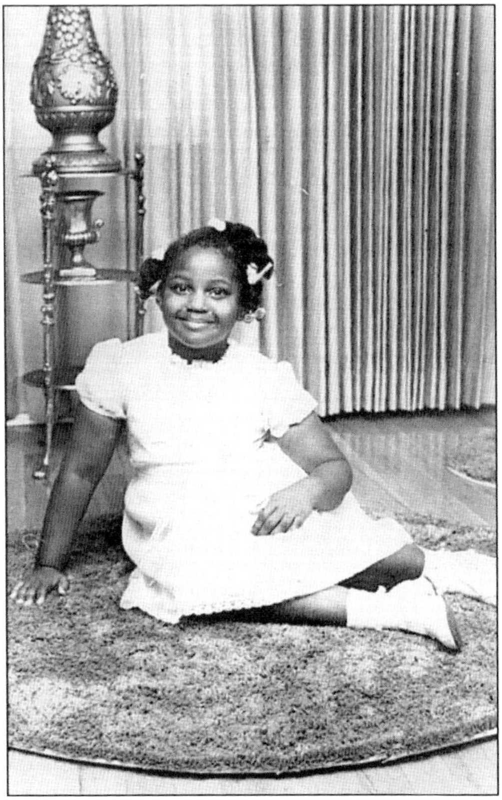

The photos on this page depict calendar children for the 1984 Zeta Upsilon Chapter of Alpha Kappa Alpha Sorority. Pictured to the left is Tricina Nicole Jenkins, daughter of Mr. Curtis Jenkins and granddaughter of Mrs. Pauline Russell. Tricina sits comfortably on a rug with a pleasant smile on her face.

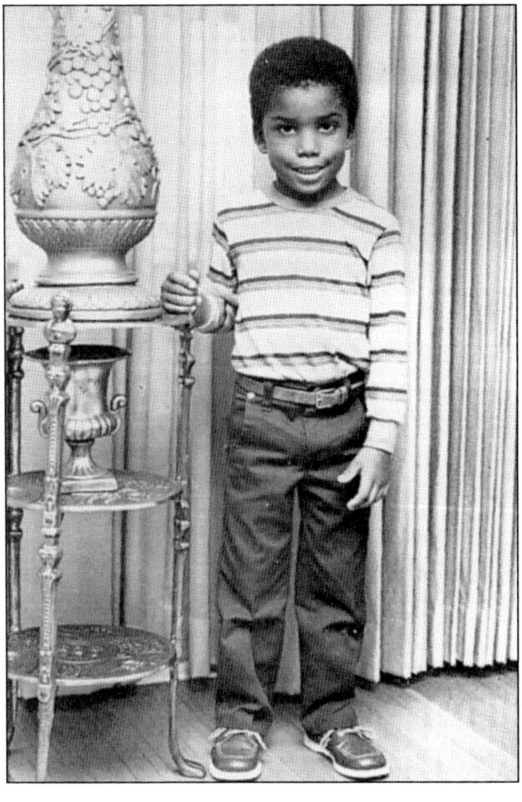

Pictured here is Ricardo Robinson Jr. son of Ms. Ellen Robinson. Ricardo appears to have a firm grip on the stand.

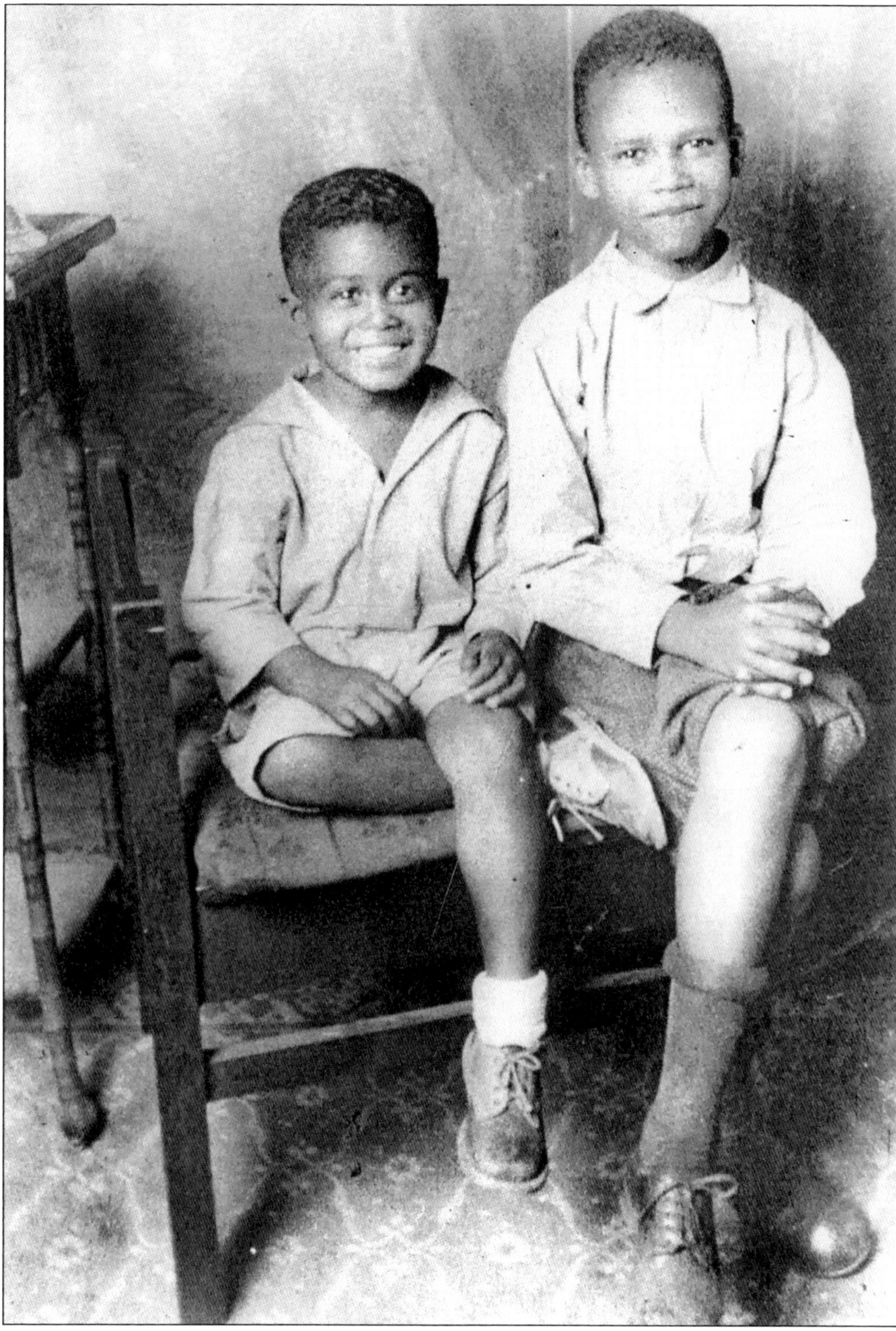

Leo and Joe Albury both sit with legs crossed and handsome smiles. Perhaps they were coached by their dad, the professional photographer.

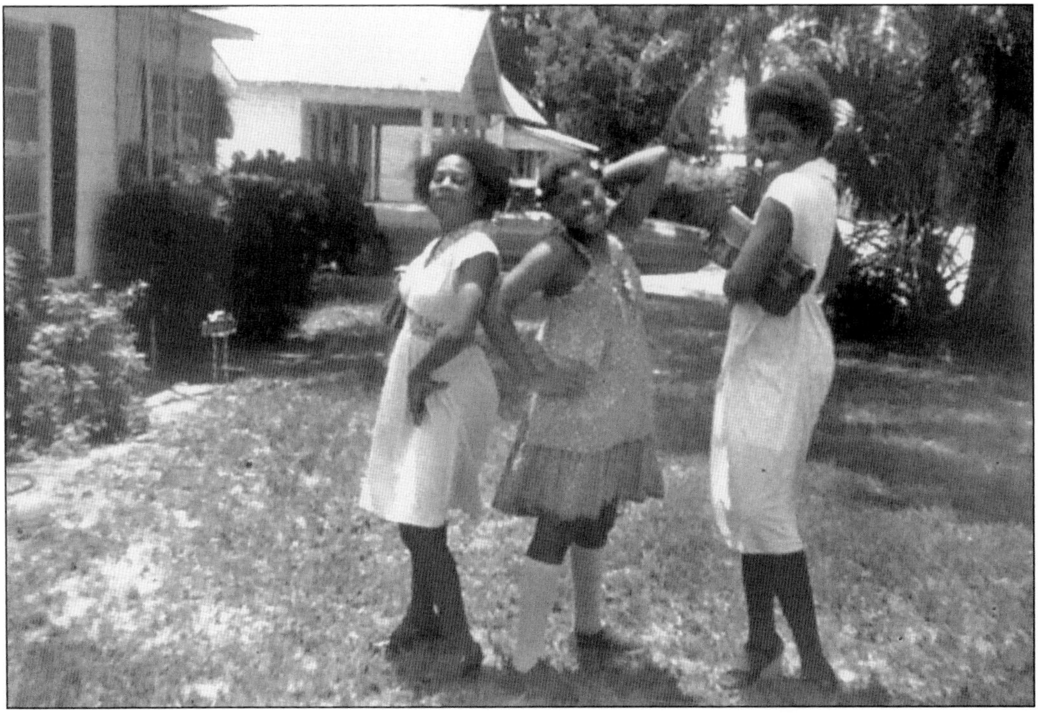

The "little darlings" on this page are relatives of the author. The first photograph depicts her sister, Deborah Wilson, daughter Tarsha, and stepdaughter Noliwe, all striking interesting poses for the camera.

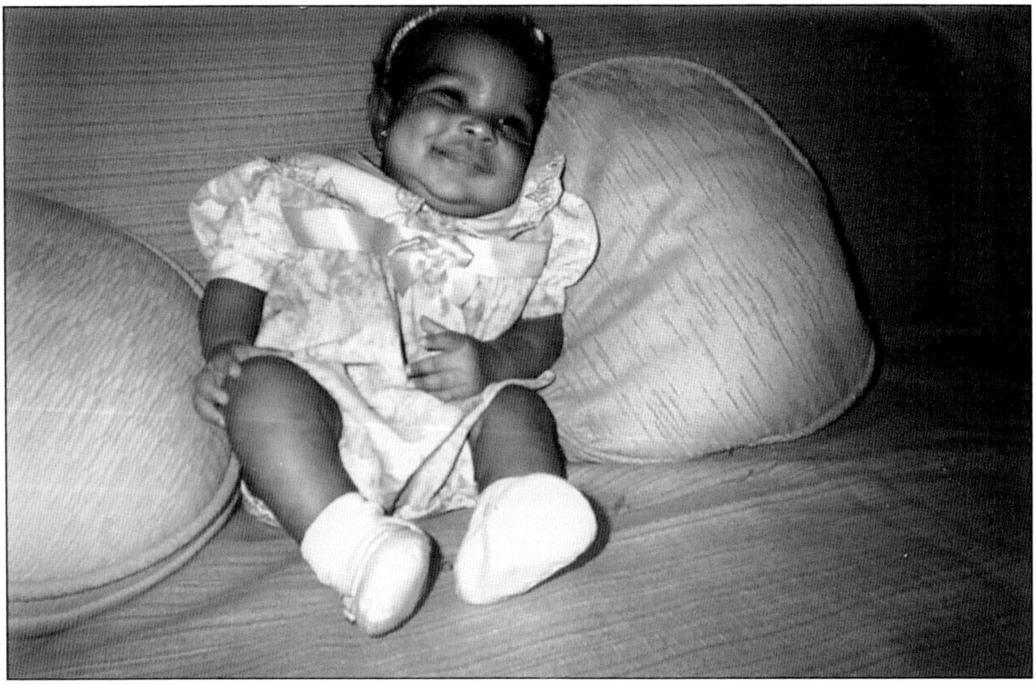

The photo above shows little cousin, Brianna Cole, resting comfortably with a cute smile.